Here's what the readers of this

"Dusty, you are amazing! This wonderful and extremely wel_ explanations and meanings for each card including reversed cards. All areas ha. _ you every step of the way on how to make sensible and meaningful readings, understand how each card relates or influences other cards, and finally create a connection pertaining to the person or situation in question.

"Dusty White defines the basic spreads and most popular ones, the card positions; how to relate these spreads with anything so memorization is not really too much of an issue here. He emphasizes constant bonding with your cards and the reason for it. The information has clarity, congruence, conciseness, fluidity, organization, and sense of humor. It is very encouraging, inspiring, and makes Tarot learning fun for me! Using this book consistently in my practice readings has allowed me to give more accurate readings. Most importantly, as a novice in Tarot, I am gaining invaluable experiences including the opportunity to help other people, which was my primary goal. I feel strongly that I will be able to gain significant progress through the use of your book, website, and professional advices. The work that you did in putting together this book is a reflection of your years of experience, love, and dedication to your students and readers. I am extremely happy with the knowledge that I have gained from it and I am absolutely recommending this to anyone who seriously wants to learn Tarot, or anyone who likes to read books of various interests, or anyone with an open mind.

"Truly awesome! Thank you so much for your love of writing, it is priceless!"

— Bobby D.

"As a professional psychic of 20 years I am smart enough to know to keep up with my study of the tarot, but never have I found such a fresh and intuitive workbook that has so greatly broadened my view and my connection with my cards. This extremely user friendly, and fun if I might add, guide will take even the novice reader to a professional level gently in a relatively short amount of time. I whole heartedly agree with the techniques found in these pages and preferably refer it to my own students as the guide to becoming great at the craft of tarot reading."

— Stina Garbis

"I have purchased approximately 25 tarot books this year but after 24 hours with your book I would have to say NOTHING compares....you have soooo much knowledge between the front and back covers and you really know your stuff.....I am very happy I accidentally/incidentally fell over this on one of my Amazon Cruises. Thanks."

— Arlene Phillips

"Your book has allowed me to start reading for others! That use to scare me! But your way of approach is fun and non-intimidating! Read on! can't wait for your next, and your deck!!! Thank you Dusty (because your book has made my other ones dusty)."

— Marco Zarate

"This is a book for those who want to learn to read the tarot, not just repeat standard meanings. Dusty White has written a wonderful book with exercises that will have you reading the tarot with your own voice, in a much shorter time than you can imagine. Get this book, a Rider-Waite deck (or your favorite), and a pen. Give it thirty days...you will find yourself amazed that you can read the tarot, not just recite meanings. Reading the tarot with your intuition can be taught, and Dusty White has written the book that can teach you."

— Craig R.

"Although it can be sometimes intimidating for me to interpret my own readings, I've noticed some of the simplest techniques to be VERY accurate. i.e. Three card-spreads, yes/no questions. I use it for fun and have actually become scared to ask certain questions because the results are eerily accurate. This book has made it very easy for me to learn basic spreads and increases my fascination with tarot every time I open it."

— *A. Singh*

"Your book, *The Easiest Way to Learn the Tarot – EVER!!* has fast become a personal favorite of mine; it's an instant classic and one of the most recommended books I have ever had the pleasure of sharing with my friends, family members, students, peers and teachers alike. It's a phenomenal piece of work and a worthy addition to any library, a Tarot reader's or not! I say this because I've found so much in your offering that is applicable outside of the realms and direct practice of interpreting the Tarot that I've now begun to implement in my daily life and regular metaphysical & spiritual practice as well.

"My greatest thanks and heartfelt appreciation for what I consider to be one of the most important books ever written about how to actually READ TAROT CARDS and work effectively with the lush details and rich symbolism inherent within this incredible tool, and this, in a manner that anyone can comprehend and put to practical "real-world" use immediately is definitely in order.

"Thank you so much, truly."

— *Jerome Finley*

"This is THE BOOK that I have been searching for without the general definitions and memorizing card techniques that have always left me mental blocked in a reading. I have been reading the cards on and off for several years, but still got stuck on certain card combinations that didn't seem to make any sense when put together. Your book and its visual cues techniques, give me the strategy that I feel I need to master the cards.

"Dusty, I thank you so much for your hard work and effort in writing and preparing your book. I salute you for a job extremely well done! . . . I need to do many readings on myself for sure as I am a filmmaker and really need insight into my craft and where I should go. Everyone tells me to read myself and see the best path to go on, but I always love to read other people and enjoy the joy in helping them."

— *Len Rosen*

"Dusty White has created the perfect text-book for a tarot course whether in a class-room setting or for self-study. I have been a professional tarot card reader for over two decades: I wish *The Easiest Way to Learn the Tarot – EVER!!* had existed when I was first learning and that is the highest praise I can offer. Furthermore, even now, as an extremely experienced and well-read *tarotista*, I still received many new insights, perspectives, and information from White's wonderful book. This is a book to keep close at hand – it serves as a reference and a guide through the tarot as much as an instructional manual. I expect to return to my copy repeatedly.

"*The Easiest Way to Learn the Tarot – EVER!!* is exceptionally well-organized, lucid, practical and extremely comprehensive but also tolerant: White appreciates that there are many varied and disparate ways to read tarot and presents readers with a wide selection. A particularly nice aspect of this book is that it may be used with any tarot deck although White recommends that beginners use a Waite-Smith or Waite-Smith derived deck – I concur – and explains precisely why. The book contains suggested exercises and workbook pages. Each card is discussed in depth as are a variety of spreads. This book is highly recommended for beginners and adepts alike. My only suggestion: perhaps Dusty White would like to expand this series by adding similar volumes focused on astrology and runes."

—Judika Illes
Author of *The Encyclopedia of 5000 Spells, The Encyclopedia of Spirits, The Weiser Field Guide to Witches,* and *Pure Magic: A Complete Course in Spellcasting.*

The Easiest Way to Learn the Tarot—EVER!!

By

DUSTY WHITE

Edited by

BRENDA JUDY

— *A House of White Textbook* —

_____
Student name

_____
Start date

_____
Instructor*

*If you don't have a teacher please sign up for our
<u>free audio and video lessons</u> at EasyTarotLessons.com

House of White, Montrose 91020
©2009, 2015 by Dusty White
Printed in the United States of America

All rights reserved. No part of this publication may be reproduced or transmitted in any form or by any means, electronic or mechanical, including photocopying, recording, or by any information storage and retrieval system, without the prior written permission from the publisher or the author, except where permitted by law. Contact the publisher for information on foreign rights.

ISBN: 978-1-41969288-8

Library of Congress Cataloging-in-Publishing Data
Library of Congress Control Number: 2009902275

Book Design by Dusty White
Cover Design by Dusty White, Thanabodi, and Ryan Capogreco
Edited by Brenda Judy

Illustrations, including House of White logo and author skull & bones logo, by Dusty White
Tarot Card images are from "Pamela A" deck circa 1910 in possession of author. Further reproduction without permission is prohibited. (Write for permission: me@dustywhite.net)
Clipart used on page 71 appears under paid license through iclipart.com

∞ This paper meets the requirements of ANSI/NISO Z39.48-1992 (Permanence of Paper).

www.DustyWhite.net — Author's website
www.HouseofWhite.net — Corporate website and Tarot foundation
www.EasyTarotLessons.com — Free easy tarot lessons to all knowledge seekers
www.AdvancedTarotSecrets.com — Free advanced tarot secrets to all professionals
www.EasyAstrologyLessons.com — The only place to start learning astrology on the web. From here you can go anywhere.

THIS BOOK IS DEDICATED TO

My most favorite student—EVER!!

Christina Garbis

ALSO BY DUSTY WHITE

The Easiest Way to Learn the Tarot—EVER!!

The Easiest Way to Learn Astrology—EVER!! (2015)

Aphrodite's Book of Secrets (Spring 2016)

Sign up for our FREE tarot lessons

delivered to you by email to help you master what you learn in this book at:

EasyTarotLessons.com

Contents

Preface . . . . *ix*
Acknowledgements . . . . *xi*
Formal introduction . . . . *xiii*

Section One
GETTING STARTED

What you need to get started 1
Recommended Decks for Beginners 3
Tarot Journals 5
What the cards mean 5
Upside-down Tarot cards 6
Tarot cards and the directions 7
Five great ways to start an argument 8
Easy Study Guides (Part 1) 9

Section Two
THE FASTEST WAY TO GET TO KNOW YOUR CARDS . . .

The fastest way to get to know your cards 11
"First 30 days" checklists 12
What did I do today? 13
Introduction to the basic exercises 14

First things first: Easy one-card exercise (do this often)

Exercise One: Face value 15
Exercise "1A":   Looking beyond "face value" *(practice with a friend)* 18

Easy two-card exercises

Exercise Two: "Me and You" 19
Exercise Three: "Exactly what do you two have in common anyway?" 22
Exercise Four: From here to there 23

Easy three-card exercises

Exercise Five: There and back again 24
Exercise Six: Birds of a feather 26

Blended meanings

Exercise Seven:	Hey! What does THIS card mean? *(Aspecting cards)*	27
	The process of "opening up a card"	30
Exercise Eight:	One plus one equals *what?*	34
Exercise Nine:	One plus one plus one equals *what?*	35

Mildly advanced exercises to drive you crazy

Exercise Ten:	The never-ending story	36
Exercise Eleven	Something to look at	40
	Extra credit exercises	41
	Extra credit exercises *(two-card practice spreads)*	42
	Extra credit exercises *(three-card practice spreads)*	53
	Okay, let's review	64
	Really Advanced Exercises	65

Section Three
SPREADS AND STUFF

Introduction to *spreads* 69
The hardest *spread*—EVER!! 71

Basic spreads you will use often

One-card *spreads* 72
Two-card *spreads* 73
Three-card *spreads* 74
Multiple-card *spreads* 75
Quick and easy *"Yes or No" spreads* 76
Aces-up 76
"Up or Down Vote" 77
"Gyaaa! How long will this take?!!" 78
This or That 79
The Celtic Cross ("Old Faithful") 80

Mildly advanced spreads

Astrological and time *spreads* 85
Generic Astrological *spread* 86
The Roundabout *spread* 87
Time spreads: Twelve-hour or "one-day" forecast 93
Time spreads: A basic one-year forecast 94

Additional ways of learning your Tarot cards—quickly and easily

Fun Things You Can do to Your Tarot Deck! 95
Quick and easy "Cheat Sheets" 99

Section Four
THE "MINOR" ARCANA

Introduction to the "minor" Arcana 115
A sneak peek at the royal family 116
The House of *Wands* 117
The suit of *Wands WITH* worksheets 118

A sneak peek at the royal family 146
The House of *Cups* 147
The suit of *Cups WITH* worksheets 148

A sneak peek at the royal family 176
The House of *Swords* 177
The suit of *Swords WITH* worksheets 178

A sneak peek at the royal family 206
The House of *Coins* 207
The suit of *Coins WITH* worksheets 208

Section Five
THE "MAJOR" ARCANA

Introduction to the "major" Arcana 237
The "major" Arcana *WITH* worksheets 238

Section Six
"OKAY, SO WHAT DO I DO NOW?..."

"Okay, so what do I do now?" 283
Easy Study Guides (part 2) 285

Appendices

Appendix A: Troubleshooting *(what to do when . . .)* 289
Appendix B: A Tarot F.A.Q. 291
Appendix C: A brief history of the Tarot 299
Appendix D: How to be a hit at parties 302
Appendix E: Fun party games 303
Appendix F: "Secret societies" and mystery schools you may want to join 304
Appendix G: What to do next 307

Glossary 309
Index 321
Personal note space 325

Preface

The purpose of this book is to enable anyone interested in learning the Tarot to quickly and easily understand the concepts involved without unnecessary dogma, and to be able to bond with any well-designed deck for the purposes of meditation, magic, or divination. It is our experience that too many books rely on preaching a set meaning to each card that the student must adhere to before they can fully appreciate the complexities and meaningful interactions of each card with its neighbors. All of that nonsense ends here. This workbook can be used with or without the aid of a teacher, as the bulk of the instruction lies in the mastery of a set of basic exercises to be practiced at the convenience of the student. These exercises allow the student to work with their cards to explore meanings and interpretations in real-life scenarios they will encounter when they read for other people.

Each card meaning will always be subjective to the *reader,* and to the situation at hand, and is, in turn, affected by other cards that aspect it. There is no one set meaning to any particular card that applies in exactly the same way each and every time that card appears. Life is far too complex for a set of 78 cards to provide pat answers to any possible situation one might encounter. This is why *spreads* are so popular in using the Tarot. Tarot *spreads* assign set meanings to various card positions, allowing the resultant card landing in that "reserved spot" to clarify the interpretation (what to expect in that area of existence). But a true understanding of the Tarot, and how the cards affect one another, magnifies the impact and understanding of each *spread* cast. This understanding comes from actual hands-on practice with Tarot cards more than it will ever come from a study of outdated views on science and society laid down in the distant past.

If it is possible for you as the student of the Tarot to work with a qualified instructor, we strongly advise that you do. There is no substitute for the in-person interplay of teacher/student, and the process is usually a lot more fun in a small class environment. However, if you cannot find a qualified teacher who uses this book to guide you along, we encourage you to become a member of our *free* online community at **EasyTarotLessons.com** and join in our ongoing discussions on the Tarot.

Please share your thoughts about this book! Please review it on Amazon or BarnesandNoble.com, write the author, and come to our Tarot forums and let us know what you think.

Acknowledgments

This is not important to read, but it is important to say, so please bear with us: How do you thank someone for a lifetime of learning—that one aspect of awareness that allows you complete freedom from any past insolvency, the gift that gives you wings to fly as high as you dare, and the ability to forge deeply into the great unknown(s) and discover what no one has seen before?

Extra special thanks to our teachers, to whom we are personally indebted far beyond our own abilities to give back to society at large.

"Formal introduction to the Tarot"

The Tarot is a collection of visual symbols designed specifically to relate meaning and mystery. The images come from a time and way of life that is long since past in societal evolution. These images reflect certain timeless human values in a setting of primitive, even barbaric, political structures. Even so, it remains a highly useful "study guide" for personal advancement along metaphysical lines and a truly nifty tool for predicting future events. Simply put: The Tarot is fun, it is a bit spooky until you "learn it," and it is highly misunderstood by the general public due to the mystery surrounding it. There are various levels of understanding the Tarot, from being able to give simple *readings,* to delving into the psychological aspects of development layered into modern decks, and even working with the cards in advanced magical techniques to effect positive changes in your life. This last part we will cover in our *Advanced Tarot Secrets* course.

The Tarot, as a divination system, has evolved over the centuries as a never-ending parade of extremely talented artists have put their own touches on an old favorite, enhancing their preferred meanings and completely eliminating others. Cards that remain a vital force of the Tarot have seen their meanings blatantly changed by pop-metaphysical "experts," which in itself is as valid as it is sacrilegious, flying in the face of traditionalism that the Tarot embraces as a source of its inherent mysterious nature. The Tarot has changed over time, but that does not make it any less effective. Students and teachers can argue endlessly on the "origins" of the Tarot or which level of symbolism is more integral to the "hidden meanings" of the Tarot. That is all fine in theory, but the sum total of all of the Tarot lessons, articles, books, courses, seminars, debates, (and arguments) is simply the two most important questions of all time:

What does it mean?

How does it work?

The answer to these questions shall comprise the basis of this workbook. We will do our best to inform the initiate and the adept. Our opinions of the Tarot are personal and based on years of meticulous study and no small amount of practice. *As such, we welcome dissenting views.*

The Tarot is one of life's great mysteries, but it is simply a deck of cards with 78 pictures of some of the esoteric morals and daily experiences of life broken down into two sections: The 56 cards of the "minor" Arcana, which looks quite suspiciously like a "normal" deck of playing cards (except that it has one extra face card per suit), and the "major" Arcana, which are the 22 spooky cards we usually see in horror movies. Of course, even though there are 22 cards in the "major" Arcana, isn't it funny how movie directors almost certainly make sure we see "Death" or "The Tower" (two very destructive looking cards), or "The Lovers." These three cards are very dramatic to look at and they look great on a TV, but they are simply pictures of things happening to people, just like the other 75 cards. It really is no wonder that most people are a bit spooked by the Tarot. Television and movie directors love to use these cards as visual props to scare or intrigue us, and we, in turn, love to be scared and intrigued.

The reality is that there are 78 cards in the Tarot, divided into two "camps" and the whole "major" and "minor" thing has come to be thought of as the "major leagues" and the "minor leagues" (like baseball) where one camp or "Arcana" is somehow better, or more important, than the other. *This is completely absurd of course.* It is like saying that breathing is more important than eating, or sleep. We need to do all three on a pretty regular basis or none of us will be around very long.

So we have a deck of cards, and we can play various games with them (just like a "regular" deck of cards) or we can tell fortunes with them (also just like a "regular" deck of cards), or we can use them as magical tools, meditate on their significance, hang them on the wall, even amaze our friends by doing magic tricks with them. The first thing to do is to become friends with your personal deck, just like a poker player or gin rummy player becomes acquainted with a "regular" deck of cards. The Tarot is only as mysterious as you want it to be, although the pictures make it a lot more fun to look at than a plain old "regular" deck of cards.

The easiest way to understand the Tarot is to learn the basics first and start practicing. The exercises provided in this course will help you build a thorough understanding and good working relationship with your deck in no time at all. You will learn to look *into* the card instead of looking *at* it, eliciting meaning through your impressions of what you see. **Any generic written definition of a card's meaning is at best secondary to your "hunch," or psychic impression at the moment you are giving a *reading*.** Never forget that. Card meanings are given as indications of direction, not as absolutes. In "real life" circumstances, things are rarely "black and white," because there are always variables and outside influences to every situation that need to be considered. In the same way, every card in a *spread* affects other cards, and is, in turn, affected by at least one other card. This nudging of meaning guides you to the answers your are looking for. Your psychic insight will "fill in the gaps" between each card that comes up in a *spread*.

Don't worry about the layers of esoteric stuff people like to pile on top of each card right now. It's a lot easier all around if you wait until after you are comfortable with your preferred deck before you start adding complexities. If you study the Tarot for any length of time, you will find all kinds of conflicting information, some of which you will not like or agree with at all. This is because every "expert" has their own opinion on this deck of 78 cards. Like anything else in life worth arguing over, these debates can get quite heated. All that matters right now is that you learn the basic traditional meanings and simultaneously learn to listen to what the cards are telling you. We have done our best to make this all fun and easy for you.

Use this book as a guide to help you understand what your cards are saying to you. Explore your sensory abilities by practicing the exercises in this book with the help of your Tarot cards. Your cards will work together to provide visual stimulus to guide you to the answers you seek, but the real magic is always within you. From the moment you pick up your deck, question in mind, through shuffling and laying the cards down in a *spread,* you are exercising your psychic abilities. Your cards are merely a tool, like a brush and canvas are to an artist. Ultimately, you are the one painting the picture of each *reading* you give. Like any other acquired skill, you will improve over time as you train psychic muscles you didn't even know you had.

Learn the exercises in this book and then go practice them. Feel free to read through our interpretations of each card in Sections Four and Five whenever you have a question about a card's meaning. Our interpretations of each card have come from centuries of research and practice by metaphysical scholars. But never take any one person's word on the Tarot as inviolate or unquestionable. A true understanding of the Tarot comes from your ability to enhance your own psychic abilities, not from a memorization of rote instruction.

If you need more information, please come back to the book. At any time, you can also visit us online at ***www.EasyTarotLessons.com*** and ask any questions or share your ideas with us.

Section One

GETTING STARTED

This is what you need right now to have fun learning the Tarot, quickly and easily:

- ☞ This book.

- ☞ A deck of Tarot cards (preferably one of the ones we recommend below).

- ☞ A notepad or journal and a pen to keep track of your Tarot *spreads*.
  (This is completely optional—alternatively, you can write in this book.)

Before we get you started doing the actual exercises, we would like to cover some basic groundwork over the next few pages. Here we will cover some basics, such as what decks are the best for beginners, why you might want to keep a *Tarot Journal*, and other helpful information to get you started successfully listening to your Tarot cards quickly and easily.

We also have an easy 30–day guide to help you get started right away and track your progress. The 60– and 90–day guides are at the end of the book, along with a history of the Tarot, should you be curious about that. Additionally, we have included a section of frequently asked questions (FAQs) at the end of the book. If you ever get stuck, frustrated, or feel like you want to quit, please visit us online immediately at ***www.EasyTarotLessons.com*** and we will see what we can do to help you get back to having fun learning the Tarot.

Most of your understanding of the Tarot will come from actually playing with your Tarot cards, not from reading words in any book. *Use this book as a guide* to help you understand what your cards are saying to you. **Learn the exercises and then go practice them.** If you need more information, please come back to the book. At any time, you can also visit us online and ask any questions or share your ideas with us.

Recommended Decks for Beginners

Learning the Tarot can be a daunting task, but it is a lot easier if you choose the right deck to learn with. "Starter decks" are ones that have the basic symbolism of the Tarot in bold, clear imagery. They are usually not as pretty as some of the artsy or experimental decks, but they are easy to learn and are consistently easy to interpret. Some professional readers use these "starter decks" throughout their careers, so they are not in any way inferior to any other deck—**they are just easier to use**. These decks remain true to the basic symbolism of the "modern Tarot," all but established by *Pamela Coleman (P.C.) Smith* when *Arthur Edward Waite* had her draw up the artwork for his "public" deck. There are hundreds of published variations on a central theme, with thousands more private decks people have designed for their own personal use. **Ultimately there are only two kinds of divination symbolism systems in the Tarot:** those that work for you, *and those that do not*. In this book we have recommended decks that remain close to the Rider-Waite deck due to the universality of acceptance of the symbolism and meaning used in that deck, and the ease of spot-identification of meaning. Obviously, it does no good to stare blankly at the *7 of Clubs* from a "regular deck of playing cards" and have to figure out mentally what that means while you are trying to engage your intuitive senses to discern meaning from the card's placement.

Any of the "Waite" decks by U.S. Games are recommended for study and practice. This includes the *Rider-Waite* deck, the *Universal Waite* deck (which is the same deck only with "enhanced" artwork), or if you are into interestingly colored decks you might like the *Albano-Waite Tarot,* which retains the exact artwork but uses colors that are quite "vibrant." The *Golden Rider Tarot* is yet another incarnation of P.C. Smith's art seen through the eyes of another, and the *Radiant Rider-Waite Tarot* is a "high-definition" edition you may like. The symbolism and imagery in all of these decks is the same. Only the colors and level of detail have been changed.

The *Hanson-Roberts* deck—This deck is somewhat of a stylistic departure from the P.C. Smith envisioning, and it is more "up close and personal," even to the point of being "in-your-face" at times, as the scenes tend to be extreme close-ups of the general action seen in the Waite symbology. All in all, however, it is *an excellent deck* and a popular one as well. Once you get into the artistic style this deck presents, it will be hard to break away to other, more "traditional" layouts.

The *Morgan-Greer Tarot* is another highly popular deck that draws from the P.C. Smith symbolism, but is even more close-up than the *Hanson-Roberts*. This really is a hit or miss deck; you will either fall in love with it and its borderless designs or you will simply pass it by in search of something more to your interpretive preferences.

The *Halloween Tarot* is one of the few, rare exceptions to the *(general)* rule that any modern Tarot deck will usually sacrifice a bit of traditional interpretation or divinatory detail for artistic license. This deck follows the *Rider-Waite* decks faithfully. Without prejudice, this is simply one of the best Tarot decks ever. Kipling West is a genius. She has managed to capture the *essence* of the Tarot and interpreted her artwork to fit the original meanings in a fun, approachable, and surprisingly detailed style. This is an excellent "second deck" as, while it is possible to learn directly from this deck, it lacks much of the traditional symbolism needed by students to perfect their understanding of Tarot symbolism. This deck is very highly recommended, but most especially if you like Halloween.

Decks such as the *Antichi Tarocchi Bolognesi,* the *Lombardy,* or any of the *Marseilles* variations are, of course, "historically older" and, therefore, *fundamentally* "more correct" (if you are into the whole Fundamentalist movement thing), but in reality they leave a lot to be desired. They are fun to own and show off at parties; but when you need a quick-and-dirty *reading* on the local gossip, you will more than likely find yourself grabbing one of the *Waite* decks.

We strongly recommend avoiding such decks as the *Quick and Easy Tarot,* as they make it too easy to skip the process of actually learning your craft and rely on other people's interpretation of the cards. The problem with this is when your client asks for more information, you simply have none to give because your cards do not speak to you—they shout generic meanings at you. Don't be tempted by the promises of a substitute for proper study and practice.

By contrast, decks like the *Salvatore Dali* deck with its unique designs are pretty to look at but nigh-impossible to get a reliable *reading* from when you need it most. The *Gummy Bear Tarot* is another carefully produced, highly colorful deck that is a *lot* of fun, but due to the extremely limited symbolism, we recommend it as an art collectible or a tool to help children understand the basics of the Tarot rather than using it for in-depth *readings*. Remember that the first job of any Tarot deck is to provide you with answers to questions. You need to like the artwork, but you also need to understand what the cards are telling you in great detail. Save the "fun and silly" Tarot decks for fun and silly games, and have a preferred deck for serious *readings*. Ultimately the choice is yours as to what decks you will like and use. But as you have many years to develop your skills, we recommend you start with any of the recommended decks and build your psychic muscles a bit before venturing too far into the forest of Tarot decks, as there are literally hundreds to choose from. Always remember that accuracy and ease of *reading* trump all other aspects when choosing a Tarot deck to work with. Otherwise, it is just a pretty deck of cards.

Where to buy your first deck

Fortunately, Tarot cards have exploded in popularity over the past few decades, making them quite easy to find. In the past, you might have found an occasional deck in a bookstore or a metaphysical shop, but today you can get them on Amazon, at any decent bookstore, and even in some of the super-retailer mega-stores. If money is a serious issue at the moment and you happen across a used deck at a garage sale for one or two dollars, you can start with a used deck, but you want to *carefully* wipe each card clean individually with a damp cloth, and dry it *immediately* and *thoroughly*. Then let the whole deck sit overnight in a nice, clean pile of salt to remove any psychic residue that previous influences may have left behind. Used cards are "pre-broken in," making them easier to shuffle, but they must be cleaned and *cleansed* before you start practicing with them. When you can, be sure to get a new deck and enjoy the experience of cards slipping all over the place.

What do I keep my cards in?

Some *readers* swear by the old *silk scarf* superstition. The Tarot has been around for a few centuries, and silk has been around a lot longer than that, earning a reputation as a highly magical fabric. Silk originated in China *several millennia* ago. It is created by tiny worms that love to munch on mulberry trees that spin cocoons of one long continuous thread. Silk was discovered in China and was one of history's great secrets. NO ONE was allowed to export silk worms or reveal the secret of how silk (as a fabric) came to be. It is reported that it was a crime punishable by death. After several thousands of years (mid-6th century CE) a few monks brought eggs to Europe, but even then the worms did not thrive and prosper, as they really liked mulberry leaves, which Europe was sadly lacking in at the time. To this day, *most silk* still comes from Asia. The cocoons have to be boiled (and they do so like to float), carefully unravelled, and spun into thread. This makes silk one of the most high maintenance of natural fabrics, and the most mysterious, sought after, and "magical." The fact that it is a bodily excretion of delicate worms who are just trying to build a little house to protect themselves while they transform into moths lends itself to the legend that silk is a protective material, like eggshell chalk.

If you have a silk scarf that you like, this is a very pretty way to keep your cards, but then you will need something else to put your silk scarf in, and you have to make sure that your scarf is wrapped correctly so that the cards don't fall out when you pick them up suddenly (this advice comes from years of silk scarf mishaps). A decorative wooden box is another popular option (and specifically designed "Tarot boxes" are usually big enough to accommodate your silk scarf as well). Other *readers* simply keep the original box (after discarding the mini booklet that comes with their deck) and add tape to hold the box together over the years as necessary. It's all very personal. At the risk of offending any traditionalists, it's really much ado about nothing. Just keep your cards safe and clean.

Tarot Journals

A *Tarot Journal* is simply a notepad or book that you keep track of your Tarot *spreads* in, and any impressions or notes you want to save for later review. It is your "Tarot diary." Some people swear by the idea of a journal to jot down *every* reading and *every* revelation they receive, and this is good—because *it works for them*. Other, highly skilled *readers* ignore this completely. You may start a *Tarot Journal* of your own only to stop writing it in altogether, and that is fine as well. The dilemma is the personal importance you assign to tracking every minute detail of your Tarot progress **versus spending more time writing than *reading*** (your cards). This is a decision only you can make for yourself.

If you decide that you want to try your hand at a *Tarot Journal,* simply grab a notepad, three-ring binder, or a bound book of blank pages (any generic journal will do) and scribble out any *spreads* you *cast* that seem interesting enough to note. Just remember to actually make the time to go back and look at them later. You may find that you are having too much fun *casting* new *spreads* to spend a lot of time reading up on old *spreads* you *threw* months ago. We neither recommend nor discourage you in keeping a *Tarot Journal*. Just make sure that if you do keep a *Tarot Journal,* **it does not interfere with your actual hands-on time spent playing with your cards.**

What the cards mean

One of the most important things to know and spend some time thinking about when first deciphering the Tarot is that the Tarot was devised under a culture of Feudalism. **Everyone had their fixed place in society.** Kings and queens, dukes, knights, and peasants all existed in their own worlds of experience. A cobbler, farmer, or blacksmith could not begin to fathom the world his or her emperor lived in. The very notion of endless days without manual labor, and dirt from it that got under your skin and never truly went away, was as foreign as any invading army.

The "common man" spent his days from sunup to sundown working his trade for his family and community. The luxuries of court were completely unknown and unimagined to most peasants, lest they rebel or go insane at the injustice of it all. This very schism of society naturally found its way into the Tarot and continues to this day. Looking at the cards, we are looking back in history, where ownership of land and animals or standing armies meant power of life and death over others as far as one's eye could see. These cards record history and its societal beliefs in picture form, and the stories they tell reveal humanity, often in a very dark light. This is why we have an overclass of cards (the "major" Arcana) as well as a permanent underclass (the "minor" Arcana—which include the court, or ruling cards of the underclass). For beyond the command of the kings and queens of every country were the gods themselves, the very forces of nature. The Tarot is at once both polytheistic and monotheistic, being born of that time of Christian domination of Europe, but when old beliefs still held tightly among the majority of its citizens. *"God" above all* was the mantra, but peasants and nobles alike still hung horseshoes above their doors, warded off vampires with garlic, and left honey cakes out for the fey.

Poverty, abuse of all kinds, death, and disease were far more commonplace than we can begin to imagine today, and generally thought of as evil spirits, thus necessitating good luck charms and various protections to keep them at bay. The Tarot reveals these beliefs in images, but so many beliefs of the Middle Ages and even the Renaissance are so laughable today that it is hard to fathom people taking them seriously.

Because the Tarot is so steeped in these beliefs and opinions of how the world functioned, it remains a mystery to most people—inaccessible through its saturation with the mindset of times long abandoned. So when we look at the images of the Tarot, most especially those of the oldest surviving decks, we see concepts that appear almost fairy tale-like, and often alien to common sense. We have to look at their symbolism rather than seeing cards as concrete ideals of nature and science. Ultimately, we realize that the world is hardly flat, but the creators of the Tarot did not. Thus, we must translate a vision of the world around us that has long since been displaced into our own "modern" views (for certainly future humanity will laugh at us as well) and apply the inherent wisdom left behind in the cards to our own existence to create healthier and happier lives "here and now."

In the end, it all comes down to this: "historical meaning" versus what the cards say to you overall, and what they say "right now." Who is "right"? *Why, you are, of course!* You learn to listen to your intuition which will tell you whether the scholarly interpretation is applicable or not. The Tarot is notoriously capricious at times. Practice makes you an expert. Knowing the "traditional meaning" is as essential as knowing how to read cards at face value, and knowing when to trust your instincts, even in the face of obstacles or "obvious" meanings.

Upside-down Tarot cards

("Reversals" and what to do with them)

When you are dealing out your cards (*"casting a spread"*) for a *reading* and a card comes out "turned around," so that it is pointing down instead of up (like the rest of the cards), you have two basic choices; turn it around so that it matches all of the other cards, or *read it reversed*. Either choice is perfectly acceptable. Some Tarot *readers* spend their entire career not *reading* cards *reversed*. The whole point of a *reversed* card is simply that of giving you more information to work with. The meaning of a *reversed* card is usually pretty straightforward. It means the opposite, or "less of" what the card would normally mean. Okay, so there is the general guide. Now for the sake of your sanity when *reading* for clients, keep in mind that every card is ALWAYS affected by the other cards in your *readings*. If you are too rigid with your interpretations of each card, you limit yourself to 78 meanings, or 156 (if our math is correct) meanings when you include *reversals*.

So, let's have an example: The *Ace of Swords* comes to mind, and it is an excellent card as it is very cardinal and uncluttered with subtle innuendo. If the *Ace of Swords* comes up at the end of the *reading*, you might say "You win!" The *Ace of Swords* (upright) is a card of victory: victory through struggle, victory over your enemies, domination of others, or someone coming to help you. This is where other cards comes in. They can explain "how" and "where" you will win. If the *Ace of Swords* comes up in a *reading reversed,* it could mean "you lose."

But how? Does it mean that your plans will not turn out how you like? That could be losing; but just like the *Sword of Damocles,* it could be something you dodge, versus say the *Ten of Swords,* which is more of a "hitting every step of the stairs on the way down" *unhappy ending*. Sometimes the cards are not as plain as the pictures on them. This is where "the mystery of the Tarot" and all of that spooky stuff comes in. The future is not exactly easy to decipher, which is why we recommend lots of practice. *Reading* cards *reversed* simply allows you more information, but it is still up to you to figure out how the cards all fit together and how they match up to physical reality. Only time and practice *reading* (and seeing results) will fully teach you the ins and outs, but at the beginning (when you are first learning all of this) it may be easier to simply turn the cards "upright" while practicing your exercises until you have a solid grasp of the Tarot. If *reading cards reversed* is making your head spin, or even slowing you down in any way, try *reading* your cards only "upright" for 60 days and then see where you are.

Tarot cards and the directions

This is a touchy subject *for so many reasons.* If you would like to avoid the whole of it and simply subscribe to the notion that the four suits of the Tarot point to any particular direction because you read something somewhere, or someone told you this or that, then please by all means do so. In *most* of your *readings,* the suit will hardly be an indicator of direction. As to magical work, your particular school (Wicca, Druidic, Kabbalistic, et al.) will demand that you follow their traditions.

We believe differently. For simplicity (at least in this book) the *elemental* correspondence of the Tarot suits are given as follows: *Wands=Fire, Cups=Water, Swords=Air, Coins=Earth.* This is the common general consensus and there are very few arguments on this, so that is what we will use here. It is worth noting that the suits of *Swords* and *Wands* can be swapped *elementally,* but we won't worry about that in this book—as it would only enrage too many people who have invested their belief in the Tarot with far too many layers of meaning anyway. We have assigned each card its own direction based on the astrological correspondence of its unique energy. You will see these on each "minor" Arcana card detail page. You can use or ignore these meanings as you wish. But . . . if the Tarot suits are assigned to *elements,* then the simple question is what the direction of those *elements* are. Here are the most basic associations available and they will serve you well should you choose to use them.

Suit	Direction	Season	Element
Wands:	East	Spring	Fire
Cups:	North	Summer	Water
Swords:	West	Fall	Air
Coins:	South	Winter	Earth

We will look at the "minor" Arcana first because they "make sense." They fit together nicely in *everyday society.* The "major" cards are a humble-jumble to most people, so we will leave them until later, even though they are more exotic and mysterious. It is important not to overlook the importance of the "minor" Arcana. The term *"minor Arcana"* is actually a misnomer. It gives the impression that these 56 cards are somehow less important or less powerful than the 22 "majors."

The "minor" Arcana serves to clarify the actual details needed for interpretations, while the "major" Arcana serves as a set of symbols of *elements of* existence or society. They all have psychological correspondences, but they are impossibly vague for daily use without the "minors" to help *clarify* them. The four suits of "minor" Arcana are called *Wands, Cups, Swords,* and *Pentacles* in the *Rider-Waite* deck, which we will be using to illustrate the Tarot in this book, as the *"Waite"* decks are some of the very best "beginning decks" that can also serve you well into decades of practice. Most modern Tarot decks draw from the symbolism set forth in the *Rider-Waite* deck.

The names of the various suits change from deck to deck with no loss of credibility. "Uncle Al" (Crowley) uses the term *Disks* in his *Thoth* deck. In this book we will use the term *Coins* as that is what the suit represents: coins (wealth, earthly energies, and possessions). Other suits may use the terms "coins," "staves," "acorns," "chalices," and so on. What matters is that you build a familiarity with the deck that appeals to you. After that, everyone else can call the suits of their deck whatever they like as it won't affect the quality and accuracy of *your readings.* That being said, we have included a quick breakdown of what each suit "traditionally implies" at the beginning of each suit (found later in this book). Take all of this with a grain of salt. If it helps you give better *readings,* use it. If not, toss it aside until you decide differently. Remember at all times that what is most important is that *you know what your cards mean* and that they work consistently *for you.* This comes mostly from practice, but scholarly knowledge is of inestimable value to both the beginner and the "expert."

Five great ways to start an argument

One of the most interesting aspects of the Tarot is the highly democratic nature of it all. Everyone has an equal voice in what any one card means, both to themselves and to the world. We all get to choose what we think the cards mean, and over time we develop our own intimate understandings of each card based on both study *and* our experiences. But we also have the power of our individual belief adding to the "collective wisdom" of the Tarot every time we give a *reading* or have a discussion about the Tarot. We may not notice the power of our persuasion when our client runs into a friend three days after we gave them a *reading* and says something to the effect of ". . . and then in my *reading* Saturday *The Tower* came up and that means my jerk boss is going to get fired!"

Each time you give a *reading* or have a debate (or heated argument) about what this card means versus that card, you are contributing to a discussion that has spanned *centuries*. Your personal opinion is as valid as anyone else's as long as (a) you have studied the scholarly information and, therefore, are quoting someone else, or (b) *you actually used your cards* and are reporting your own personal findings.

As an example: One expert may write in the book that *The Lovers* represents the astrological sign of Gemini. Being a professional astrologer and Tarot *reader* for several decades with tens of thousands of clients, I may respond (after I finally stop rolling around on the floor in violent fits of hysterical laughter) that "in my humble opinion" I have found that *The Lovers* is more properly indicative of the qualities of Venus (the planet) or Aphrodite (the Goddess) and relates directly to the *feminine* sign of Taurus (*Earth:* when *The Lovers* indicates sensual obsessions, such as food, chocolate, sex, perfumes, jewelry, etc.) or the *masculine* sign of Libra (*Air:* when relating to the arts, romance, marriage, contracts, fashion, and so on). In the interest of us all getting along nicely, so that we can collectively share our interest in the Tarot and not haggle over trivialities of *our personal beliefs,* it would be prudent of me to refrain from shouting at said author that, "You, sir, are a poo-poo head!" They may be quoting Levi, or simply reciting what *their* teacher taught them. **If it works for you in "real life," it is valid.**

The true test of the Tarot as a divination tool is whether it works with you to provide reliable answers in a clear fashion that is easily decipherable and highly repeatable. Can you rely on it consistently? Do you feel comfortable (as you gain experience through practice) giving advice based on what you see? We can all argue over what each and any card means until we are hoarse from shouting, but what matters more than what any (living or) long-dead "authority" says about the cards *is what the cards say to you.* Listen to your teachers and to the advice from the past, and see (over time) how these work for you. Take what you learn as a starting point, not an ending one. Developing this attitude toward learning metaphysics will save you years of frustration and lackluster results.

Using the Tarot as a magical tool or psychological aid (this is more heavily covered in our advanced courses) *requires* you to have an implicit understanding and trust of the symbols you are working with. You can't pull out your deck of cards and a random book of Tarot meanings and expect to conjure up a better life for yourself, or work the *laws of attraction and repulsion* based on a generic interpretation laid out on paper for the masses. Your situation in life is unique to you, even though it contains commonalities and similarities with millions of other people. **Most of the process of magic or miracles is intent and clarity of purpose and motivation.** Tarot cards make a great visual stimulus that can work with your subconscious to magnetically affect the world around you—but unless and until you have an understanding of, and a bond with, the cards you are using—you are simply playing with pretty pictures that are about as effective as generalized visualization boards. So, please leave the arguing to the novices and acolytes, and you invest your time more fruitfully by actually playing with your cards and keeping an open mind when discussing the Tarot with others.

Easy Study Guides

Learning the Tarot should be fun. Don't push yourself too hard or try to master every nuance of the Tarot too quickly or you will drive yourself crazy. The basic meanings of each card are easy enough to learn (which is why they have pictures instead of numbers and "pips" like *poker cards* do). But over the coming years you will gradually begin to see all sorts of interesting meanings and messages from your Tarot cards, different uses for them, and even symbolism you missed before. **The only important symbolism in the Tarot is the symbolism that you see "right now."** That is one of the most well-kept secrets of the Tarot, so we might as well give you your *grand-master adept* hat now.

You see, the various layers of symbolism that have been added to *any* of the hundreds of Tarot decks (currently available on the market) over the years are only "activated" when you interact with them. This is Mystery School 101, and you might as well know it now: **Hide your secrets in plain sight and watch your students "realize them" as their education progresses.** We can point to a symbol and explain it to you; but until you are ready to "see" it *and you have the need,* it will just be a meaningless squiggle with no more power over you than a picture of a flower. "What you *see* is what you *get.*" This holds true for visualization-based magical work and it holds true for the Tarot. You only need to know enough to understand what you are seeing in *a reading*. The more you study and practice, however, the more you will see, and the more clearly you will be able to explain to your clients what they face and how to make the best of it all. So don't worry about what you can't see just yet, and have fun exploring the world around you with a new set of eyes. With that in mind, take the "study guides" we have provided as simply that: guides, not gospel. You will learn at your own pace no matter what anyone tells you, so you might as well have fun with it along the way. Just don't give up. You can do this. It's easy! Remember, there is always someone close by to help you if you get stuck: at *www.EasyTarotLessons.com*

Your first 30 days

Make sure to read through the entire book at least once during your first 30 days. This is above and beyond any "exercise and practice time" you spend bonding with your cards. This includes reading our interpretations of each card, but feel free to *skim over any part that is too confusing at the moment*. We want you to get a feel for the cards and see where your learning is progressing, but we do not want you to get overwhelmed with your new toy and all of its subtleties.

Start with the exercises: Do the exercises in order (don't jump to exercise 11 before doing exercise 4), even if you have *read* cards before. The exercises are laid out in the order to build your skills in the actual *readings* you will be doing later, especially the *multi-card spreads*. If you can grab a friend (especially if they have their own deck and a copy of this book as well), work with them as much as possible, but make time to do *all* of the exercises on your own as well. This "me time" is essential to developing *your own* highly personal opinions of the cards. Practicing with your friends or other students is extremely helpful and makes the learning process more fun, but it also has the effect of making the Tarot a *third party object* rather than a voice you are communicating with, and through. Your deck will eventually become an extension of your voice as well as your ears, so it is *imperative* that you develop a bond with your cards early on to make your learning process easy and fun.

Once you are comfortable with each exercise, try *casting* simple *spreads* several times during the day or throughout the week (depending on how often you can slip out your cards for a "quickie") just for fun. Ask your deck meaningful questions on extremely simple or even trivial matters, like whether you should have a salad or a sandwich for lunch, or how many hours before your boss sneaks out to play golf on company time. Have fun getting practice speaking with your cards without the pressure of "life or death" *readings* and people hanging on your every word. The actual answers right now are less important than the overall feel you are getting for your cards. Sometimes you will be cornered by a friend or a coworker who "has to know" if their boyfriend *really loves them,* or if they will get a raise, have kids, or if their wife is having an affair. Laugh politely at the thought of suddenly becoming *"the all-seeing Zolar"* when you feel pressured by people, who are close to you, begging for a *reading.* Explain to them that you can *toss out* a few cards "just for fun" but that you are still learning, and so you don't want them to take anything they see too seriously. Also, if you are at work, make sure you are on your lunch break lest jealous coworkers try to get you in trouble with the boss. Basically, have fun and keep your cards as close by as you can so you can "play with them for a moment" whenever you see an opportunity to ask them a fun question.

Try to get some serious *alone time* with your Tarot cards every day. *We recommend at least 5-15 minutes every day,* and when you can, spend 30 minutes doing your exercises or *casting* simple *spreads.* This is in addition to time you spend with your friends or fellow students. This means that your deck will have to be fairly accessible. Otherwise, it will become a chore, and reading the Tarot should never become a chore. At some point in your first 30 days, preferably after you have spent a few weeks doing the exercises and you have *thrown* several *one-, two-,* and *three-card spreads* ("just for fun"), try *casting* either the *Celtic Cross* or the *Roundabout spreads.* Pick a mildly serious question, one that faces you right now. Sit quietly shuffling the cards and think carefully on the answers you are looking for. *Cast* the *spread* and be sure to write out the *card positions* in a *Tarot Journal,* or leave the cards out for a while and come back and look at them a few more times over the next few days. Take the *reading* with a grain of salt for now. Just "watch and see" while you go about your daily actions as you would without the advice of the Tarot. You want to start to see *spreads* play out in your "real life" over time so you can develop a better instinct for timing and the subtleties of meaning.

If you ever see something "scary," *don't panic.* You might have not bothered to shuffle thoroughly, or you may have been daydreaming about something else, or you might be in a bad mood. Never be afraid to pick up a *spread* and shuffle the deck to *re-cast* it. If the meaning comes out the same, even with different cards, then you should make a note of the advice (and the cards of *both readings*) and visit us online if you need help. Someone in the forums will certainly have an opinion (as people are never at a loss for opinions). By the way: If all of the cards come out *reversed,* just turn the deck around. It sounds basic, but it really does work.

So your first 30 days should see you practicing as often as you can (at least 5-15 minutes a day, and more on some days of the week), doing exercises 1 through 11, and *casting* simple *spreads* for trivial matters "just for fun." Never underestimate the value of "just for fun," as it gives you the experience of actual practice and the ability to experiment leisurely, but it removes the pressure of performing for an audience or the "need to be right." Once again: When you feel fairly comfortable with exercises 1 through 11 (and you have done them all *at least* 20 or 30 times over the course of a few weeks) and you have *cast* several *one-, two-,* and *three-card spreads,* try your hand at the *Celtic Cross* and the *Roundabout spreads.* You can, of course, try them out earlier, but the whole point of having you do all of the exercises and simple *spreads* first is to help you build an intimate understanding of *the relationship* cards play with each other in multi-card *spreads.* If you *cast* a *Celtic Cross spread* now and then again *after* you have spent the next few weeks doing the exercises (1-11, not the really crazy "advanced" ones we torture you with), you will see much more a few weeks from now because you will understand how the cards interact with each other and change the meanings of their friends (kind of like our friends influence us, even when we don't want them to).

Most of all, you should be having fun asking silly and serious questions, but not putting *too much* stock in the answer you get just yet, and you should be doing this while dodging pressure from your friends and complete strangers to predict their future: ***"Pleeeease, no . . . really anything you see will be fine, I promise!!"*** (Expect to hear a lot of this over the next few years.)

Section Two

THE FASTEST WAY TO GET TO KNOW YOUR CARDS . . .

The exercises in this section have been used throughout the years to help initiates become adepts by removing the process *rote memorization* of generic meanings, and replacing it with actual *hands-on intuitive interpretation* of the cards, just as if you were actually giving a *reading* to a client or ferreting out information on a particular mystery you are confronted with. **These exercises will feel awkward and strange at first.** Please do NOT give up and look for written explanations of the card meanings during your exercise time. Instead, put yourself in the picture. You could be one of the people involved in the action (e.g., you may be the bully in the *5 of Swords*, or you may be one of the unhappy people walking away from him), or you might be standing just off to the side of the picture watching the people in the card interact. Some of those people may be your friends, and others you may dislike completely.

Don't try to see the card you are staring at as an omen of something that is going to happen. Get inside it and walk around. Ask the people, "Hey! Just what do you think you are doing here, anyway?" Ask the people walking in the snow outside of the church in the *5 of Coins* why they are not inside where it is warm. Poke "Mr. Magician" and ask him whether he *really* knows his stuff, or if he is just posing for a portrait. If you were walking down the road and a giant hand suddenly popped out of a nearby cloud and offered you a large gold coin the size of a small house (as happens in the *Ace of Coins*), what would you do? Do this any time you are looking at a card during an exercise or a *reading* and you can't find a clear meaning.

The exercises in this book are designed to train your psychic muscles as well as pattern recognition, spatial thought processes, and are of key importance to mastering the ability to manifest from visual stimulus ("Laws of Attraction and Repulsion"). The point is not simply to be able to tell someone what you see in their future, *but to help them* (and yourself) *control their future* by being able to use the images on the cards to actually conjure up something pleasant. These exercises have not been put forth to the general public before now, but we have faith in your ability to grasp them, and sharpen your talents quickly by using them on your own.

Due to the processes involved in self-study of metaphysics, magic, and philosophy, some answers must be discovered by the student, and cannot be spoon-fed. Thus, it is up to you to practice each exercise until you master it and can execute it on command any time, anywhere. You can work on these exercises in any order you like, but we strongly recommend that you become at a minimum "somewhat proficient" with them in the order they are presented. Once you are capable of performing each of the exercises herein, you can do them in any order you like to keep from getting bored. As always, if you get lost, stuck, or frustrated at any time, you can visit us online at *EasyTarotLessons.com* and get help. You are also welcome to share your thoughts and advice with others as you advance in skill and esoteric wisdom.

"First 30 days" checklists

We added these to help you better measure when you are ready to move on to something more advanced. Simply check each box below when you feel you have reached that stage. Please do each exercise at least twice—don't skip ahead by checking the most advanced box the first or second time you do the exercise or you are defeating the whole point of practicing. <u>Read the entire book once through</u> (highlight any sections you like, and feel free to scribble in the margins as needed). Try to spend at least 5 minutes every day *actually playing with your cards*. Stop in at *EasyTarotLessons.com* at any time if you get stuck.

Exercise   *<u>Current skill</u> (or practice) <u>level</u>*

Exercise	You want me to do <u>what</u>?	I am trying!! (leave me alone)	I'm getting this...	I think I've got this	I sooo got this!
Exercise 1 — Face value	☐ ☐	☐ ☐	☐ ☐	☐ ☐	☐ ☐
Exercise 1a — Looking beyond "face value"	☐ ☐	☐ ☐	☐ ☐	☐ ☐	☐ ☐
Exercise 2 — "Me and you"	☐ ☐	☐ ☐	☐ ☐	☐ ☐	☐ ☐
Exercise 3 — ...what do you two have in common..."	☐ ☐	☐ ☐	☐ ☐	☐ ☐	☐ ☐
Exercise 4 — From here to there	☐ ☐	☐ ☐	☐ ☐	☐ ☐	☐ ☐
Exercise 5 — There and back again	☐ ☐	☐ ☐	☐ ☐	☐ ☐	☐ ☐
Exercise 6 — Birds of a feather	☐ ☐	☐ ☐	☐ ☐	☐ ☐	☐ ☐
Exercise 7 — Hey! What does THIS card mean?	☐ ☐	☐ ☐	☐ ☐	☐ ☐	☐ ☐
The process of "Opening up a card"	☐ ☐	☐ ☐	☐ ☐	☐ ☐	☐ ☐
Exercise 8 — One plus one equals what?	☐ ☐	☐ ☐	☐ ☐	☐ ☐	☐ ☐
Exercise 9 — One plus one <u>plus one</u> equals what?	☐ ☐	☐ ☐	☐ ☐	☐ ☐	☐ ☐
Exercise 10 — The never-ending story	☐ ☐	☐ ☐	☐ ☐	☐ ☐	☐ ☐
Exercise 11 — Something to look at	☐ ☐	☐ ☐	☐ ☐	☐ ☐	☐ ☐
<u>Extra Credit Exercises</u> & Really Advanced Exercises...	☐ ☐	☐ ☐	☐ ☐	☐ ☐	☐ ☐
<u>Basic spreads</u> — One-, Two-, and Three-card spreads	☐ ☐	☐ ☐	☐ ☐	☐ ☐	☐ ☐
<u>Mildly advanced spreads</u> — Celtic Cross, Roundabout, or Time spreads	☐ ☐	☐ ☐	☐ ☐	☐ ☐	☐ ☐

What did I do today?

You can use or ignore the chart below. It is simply a place where you can keep track of how much time you spent playing with your cards, and any interesting accomplishment you made that day.

Today is: . . . and I learned/did this:

Day 1: _____
Day 2: _____
Day 3: _____
Day 4: _____
Day 5: _____
Day 6: _____
Day 7: _____
Day 8: _____
Day 9: _____
Day 10: _____
Day 11: _____
Day 12: _____
Day 13: _____
Day 14: _____
Day 15: _____
Day 16: _____
Day 17: _____
Day 18: _____
Day 19: _____
Day 20: _____
Day 21: _____
Day 22: _____
Day 23: _____
Day 24: _____
Day 25: _____
Day 26: _____
Day 27: _____
Day 28: _____
Day 29: _____
Day 30: _____

Introduction to the basic exercises

Full "descriptions and traditional meanings" of the cards are in Sections Four and Five. If you get the urge to look up a particular card, you will notice that there are shaded tabs to make finding your exact card quick and easy. However, the whole purpose of this book is to teach you how to quickly and easily learn and master the Tarot, *becoming friends with the cards in your deck,* without having to become dependent on a book for answers. *Any* book can tell you what that particular author believes the Tarot cards mean. This is important knowledge to have, and reading books on the Tarot by several authors will certainly help expand your understanding of the cards. But . . . *Only you* can decide what *your* cards mean when you are face-to-face with a friend, a client, or some random stranger who saw your cards and simply begged you to do a *reading* until you finally caved in (this happens a lot more than you can imagine).

When you find yourself faced with worried eyes from across the table, asking you, **"Is that bad? It looks bad! What does it mean?"** we won't be there holding your hand (sorry). Neither will any of the authors whose books you have read. It will be up to you, *and you alone,* to relax, politely *"shh"* your audience, and listen to what the cards are telling you *at that moment.* Your scholarly knowledge of the cards will be invaluable at times like these (so please don't skip the part where you read up on what the cards "traditionally mean"), but far more important will be the inner voice or subtle nudge that tells you that *this card over here is exactly what it looks like in the picture, while this other card is the reversed traditional meaning, but cards three, four, and seven all combine to point to . . ."* So, the first thing we will do is have you set aside "traditional meanings" for now, and start getting acquainted with your cards. These exercises will help you greatly strengthen your psychic muscles, and enhance your perception abilities. They will also teach you *how to spot and work with patterns* to build a solid foundation of knowledge in each *reading* before you start handing out advice.

In the following exercises we will ask you to separate out the "major" Arcana cards of your deck (the 22 cards with the captions at the bottom such as *"The Fool," "Strength,"* and *"The World,"* etc.) and simply set them aside for now. **We will be working exclusively with the remaining 56 cards** (the "minor"Arcana) **at the beginning.** This will greatly simplify the learning process for you as the "minor" Arcana cards are far more expressive and "accessible." We will call this 56-card deck (the "minor" Arcana) your **"study deck."** That is the term you will see throughout this workbook.

Later, after you are quite comfortable with the exercises and you can quickly and easily spot patterns and develop story lines with the "minor" Arcana, we would like you to add the remaining 22 "major" Arcana cards to your deck and repeat your study of these exercises. Once you thoroughly grasp the concepts that are involved, learning the "major" Arcana will be easier than you can imagine now. When we add the "major" Arcana back in, the whole deck will be called your **"practice deck."**

Finally, the term we will use to describe any deck you *read* with for yourself or clients (paying or not) will be your **"working deck."** Your *working deck(s)* will be your "go-to" Tarot decks, the ones you rely on when you are serious about getting results. This differentiates them from any other decks that you play games with (at parties) or have around because they are pretty. Over time you will probably buy a few Tarot decks you like, and you may find that some are pretty to look at but don't *read* very well and others that are not as aesthetically pleasing give you solid answers. If you are fortunate, you will hopefully find "just the right deck" that is pretty—and—works the best for you. Just remember though, your *working decks* (pretty or not) are your bread and butter. They help you change lives. Your artsy and party decks are for fun.

Exercise One
FACE VALUE

This is an easy exercise, but it is also the most important part of your journey along the path which is the Tarot, so please do this one often, even long after you have "mastered" the meanings and hidden wisdom of the Tarot. Regardless of what you read anywhere, *including in the pages of this book, the most important meaning you can discern from the Tarot is the one that resonates within you.* Nothing else matters. *That* is why Tarot cards have images on them. Visual symbols provide an immediate stimulation of your subconscious mind that written descriptions cannot achieve.

You are impacted and affected by what you see, so rather than allowing your knowledge of the Tarot to become little more than a knee-jerk reaction to the writings of some long-dead "authority" of mysticism, we want you to *see with your own eyes first*. This skill is vastly underrated by too many people, but it is the fundamental talent of the grand master *(shh! Don't tell anyone we told you that—you aren't supposed to learn that until year 7 of mystery school)*. What makes a "master" just that is their ability to combine traditional scholarly knowledge with ageless wisdom (which we can all use some of), and their finely attuned instinct to know what the best course of action is at the moment. This is true of any profession, and most especially true in the esoteric sciences. So the easiest and most direct path is to start training you to trust and sharpen your instincts from the very beginning, rather than try to force you to learn a set of rules and dogma in a sterile environment. Look at it this way: Long before you learned *vowels* and *consonants*, you knew what an apple was, or what flavor of ice cream you liked the best. Labels are identifiers; they are not the object itself. That being said, let's start with the objects. We will begin with the so-called "minor" Arcana.

Dig out your cards, and if they are not in order, please take a moment to put them so. **Make five piles:** One for each suit, *or house,* and one pile for the "major" Arcana, which you can simply toss haphazardly in no particular order. They are not important right now. Sort out each of your suits Ace through 10 and then Page, Knight, Queen, and finally King.

Now pick up the suit of *Wands*. If you are using a different deck than the one we use to illustrate this book, your deck may use any of the following terms: *"Rods, Staves, Clubs, Sticks,* etc." Once you have the right suit in your hand, please proceed.

Starting with the *Ace of Wands,* look at it and ask your mind what it sees. If you were standing in that picture, how would it affect you? You can describe the image to yourself ("I see a hand holding a stick—so what?"), or you can focus on any symbols you happen to be familiar with. The image may be static, or in this case, the falling leaves may indicate that the stick is being shaken, as in the term "shaking the tree." It's all very personal and highly individual. All that matters is that you look at the card and see what it says to you.

If any particular card makes an impression on you beyond what is in the picture, that is good as well. For example, if the *Ace of Wands* says to you, *"God's got his thumpin' stick!"* that is just as valid as any interpretation you will ever read in a book, for it is your mind processing the visual stimulus to create a sense of meaning and order from the card. This is the purpose of the Tarot in *any case*.

So, on to the next card. Take a look at the *2 of Wands*. That's the one with the man standing between two sticks, holding a globe. What does that say to you? What does it look like he is doing? Why would he possibly do that anyway? If you were standing next to him, what would you ask him? What is he looking at anyway? Is he planning something big? Can you tell who he might be in society (a merchant, a guard, a king, a thief . . .) by the way he is dressed and what he is doing?

Go through the rest of the suit of *Wands,* examining each card casually for as long as you like. Generally we recommend no more than 2-3 minutes per card your first few times through. You can even "spot" *read* them, forcing yourself to look at them for only 10-15 seconds before flipping them over and asking yourself what you just saw, and what it means to you *at face value.* Remember, your opinion is as valid as any "expert's" you will ever meet. Other people can *enhance* your understanding of what you experience, but no one can *dictate* what you see and feel. When you feel comfortable, go through the rest of the suits, looking at each and asking each card who it is and what it does. Start with the *Cups,* then the *Swords,* and finally the *Coins* (or *Pentacles*). Don't push yourself too hard, but try to do this at least once a day over the next few weeks.

A quick note on "Pentacles." No matter what your deck calls them, see them as gold coins, not as religious or magical symbols. The seditious act of changing coins into pentacles in the circles of the suit of Coins was a whim of an artist long ago that detracts from the meaning of the suit, which is "money." Instead they look like wooden pagan symbols painted yellow, which makes interpretation needlessly confusing and counterintuitive. Adding "stars" to the suit of Coins has served no purpose except to confuse and intimidate the public, and of course to enrage conservative Christian sects in the twentieth century (which is always fun). When you create the art for your own personal deck one day, you can add pink fuzzy bunnies if you like to your coins with no ill effects. In any case, please proceed with your glances at each individual card of the "minor" Arcana, suit by suit, asking yourself what surface impressions you get from each card.

Okay I did that . . . now what?

Hopefully now you have gone through each of the suits, *1* through *10* and glanced at the royal family of each suit. You should see the subtle themes of each suit starting to form, and the differences between the royal families. Now pick a suit and lay out all fourteen cards of that suit. If you have the space available, toss the royal family down in order (*Page, Knight, Queen, King*) and make either two horizontal rows of five cards each, or one long row of ten cards with the rest just below the court cards. In either case, put them in order from *Ace* to *10.* Leave the "major" Arcana off to the side for right now. Do any patterns jump out at you? Do you see any themes? It's okay at this moment if you can, or if you can't. At this point we are just glancing at the cards *as a group* and seeing if anything jumps out. If not, pile them back up in order and set them aside and do the same with the rest of the suits. If you would like an example of what we mean, please see the shaded box below. Our example theme below is *entirely optional,* and should not impede *your* personal conclusions.

Throughout this book we will consistently admonish you *not to accept* other people's interpretation of the Tarot cards as your own unless you agree with their perceptions, and even then we *strongly* encourage you to remember that meanings change from *reading* to *reading.* Listen to your teachers but hold random opinions you hear or read in polite contempt until you have had an opportunity to verify them for yourself. The very worst thing you can do to yourself is to accept any teaching as sacred and sacrosanct, above questioning. The sooner you learn this and adapt to the liquid nature of the Tarot, the easier (and more accurate) your *readings* will be. Modern "traditional meanings" are nothing more than a confusing amalgamation of centuries of opinion and interference by countless "experts," *much of which is highly contradictory.* Keep studying, keep practicing. Perhaps one day in the near future you will rewrite the "true meaning" of the Tarot and we will all have to listen to you as "*the preeminent authority.*"

> *Here is one possible theme or pattern one might see in the suit of Wands (Rider-Waite deck): perhaps the ease of life (we see in the 4) leads to competition and strife (in the 5), and the victor claims his dominance (in the 6), until he is challenged (in the 7). Some cards will flow together, while others* do not. *Also, each suit has its theme: for example, the suit of Wands is more physically aggressive than the suit of Coins.*

Exercise One visual examples

Here are a few visual examples with some thoughts on what the cards might be saying at first blush. These are intended only as an aid to those who are having difficulty with this exercise. Please do not allow these examples to cloud or distort *your own* unique perceptions.

This guy looks like he is trying to hold onto his money and show off how wealthy he is at the same time.

This card looks pretty happy. Family, nice house with lots of land, even a rainbow. Looks like they got what they want.

What a jerk! It's bad enough to bully people, but to stand and gloat over them as well won't make you any friends.

And here are three cards in sequence . . .
(make up your own interpretations if you like)

So much fighting here! Notice that everyone has their own take on things.

Well, looks like this guy won. Now he is the king of the hill for a time.

Well, that didn't last very long. It seems now that everyone wants to take him on.

Exercise "1A"

LOOKING BEYOND "FACE VALUE"

(Please get out your study deck.) This is a good exercise to practice with a friend or two, or in a class. There are no "right" or "wrong" answers to the questions posed here, merely the value of each observation in a particular *reading*. The goal of this exercise is to quickly spot the "face" value of each card, and then to quickly spot additional implications suggested. Take no more than five seconds per person. If you see something, give yourself a gold star. If not, simply flip the card and proceed to the next. In a classroom setting it is usually best to ask for students to volunteer answers due to the escalating difficulty with each additional meaning applied. If you happen to be alone at the moment and want to stretch your perceptive abilities, then simply give yourself a few seconds to "look beyond the most obvious," but limit yourself to what comes to mind quickly. There is absolutely *no value* at this time in adding stress to your studies. Below are a few visual examples.

(Person one:)
Okay, first impression: Our friend here has "had enough" and now he is leaving. He has set everything in order and he doesn't even stop to say goodbye.

(Person two:)
Yes, but look! It's night! He's probably skipping town.

(Person three:)
I thought he was going hiking actually. See? He has a jacket, and boots, and a walking stick

(Person one:)
I dunno . . . It looks like a thief to me.

(Person two:)
I got nothing. (grr . . .)

(Person three:)
But look at those guys in the background on the left. They look like the camp belongs to them. It seems that someone is goofing around instead of doing their job. They probably should have had a guard dog rather than the lazy bum they hired to watch their swords.

(Person one:)
This is emptiness of the soul. It is an allegory of having wealth without a deeper connection to what is most important in life: health, love, and a connection to nature.

(Person two:)
I thought they were just homeless.

(Person three:)
Ow. I got this card once. Two days later, my jerk landlord kicked me out of the house!

(Person four:)
No, can't you see? This is the abject failure of religion to attend to the needs of the poor, the injured, and the downtrodden. These are the very people religion claims to help when the church asks you to fork over your wallet! This is the basis of everything that is wrong with society, when compassion is just a marketing tool for greed and a lust for unquestionable power—

(Person one:)
Okay, I think my beloved activist girlfriend has had a wee bit too much caffeine today.

(Person two:)
I want a Pop-Tart . . .

Exercise Two
"Me and you"

First, take the "major" Arcana and toss them aside. We won't be using them for a while. Place them back in the box, or bag, silk wrap, or whatever protective container or wrapping you keep your cards in. We will get to them later on. *(e.g., Please get out your study deck again.)*

This exercise builds on what you just learned. This is the first time we will ask you to *shuffle your deck*. It is important to shuffle them thoroughly and completely for this exercise. Speaking of shuffling your Tarot cards, unless you have a very small deck, they will more than likely be difficult and even annoying to shuffle, *especially* when they are "brand new," stiff, and *very* slippery. If your cards fly in all directions, don't take it personally—it happens to all of us. Just try not to let them get dirty or damaged while you are figuring out your preferred method of shuffling. *So let's talk about shuffling:*

Unless you have very large hands, the Tarot cards of your deck will be all but impossible (at first anyway) to shuffle "lengthwise," like most people shuffle a "regular deck of cards" (the 52-card playing deck). The Tarot has 78 cards *and* they are much larger *and each card is also thicker*. After cutting them into two piles, some *readers* like to shuffle them sideways (holding them by their sides, instead of their ends), while other *readers* have success with the "Las Vegas" method of bending up the corners rather than the sides or the ends. This method leaves the cards sitting on the table so all you have to do is to pick up the corners, not the whole deck. Another perfectly acceptable method if you *read* cards *reversed* (as long as your table or surface area is clean) is to simply *spread* the cards in a massive mish-mash pile, and keep circulating them gently under, and over, and through each other until they are successfully randomized to cut or shuffle.

Cutting can be done from one hand to another, and can be used as a form of shuffling, or you can cut the cards into three piles, or let your clients cut them. The important thing to remember is that these are *your cards* and thus they are subject to *your rules*. If you don't want anyone touching them, that is just fine. On the other hand, if you want to use them as party favors, or play games with them, that is fine as well. Just try not to damage them, as they are an important *tool*. The other thing to remember is that the cards must be thoroughly randomized *while you are considering the question at hand, or you will simply get a bunch of random cards to try to interpret. Listen to your inner voice when it comes to telling you when to stop shuffling.* Over time you will develop habits that work for you. Allow others to share their methods, but don't allow anyone to convince you that they hold some deep and mighty secret of how to handle *your* Tarot cards that no one else knows. Use what works for you.

Once you have your cards shuffled . . .

Draw the top card from your deck and place it in front of you, slightly to the right, and say to yourself (or a friend if you have one handy to help you with this exercise), *"This is what happens to you,"* and place the second card in front of you, slightly to the left and say, *"This is what happens to me."* Now look at each of those cards in turn. Quickly ask yourself what each one means *individually* at face value. What is the very first thing that pops into your mind? Spend no more than three or four seconds analyzing each card. Just go with what you see on the card "right now." Explain it in three short sentences or less (less is better here) to your friend if you have one nearby. Otherwise, quietly phrase it to yourself. *Don't just feel it.* Physically say it in words as if you were *reading* a story out loud to someone. Now flip another two cards in the same fashion and do the same with them as well. Work your way through your stack of cards, "good" or "bad." Whatever happens to you or your friend (in the cards), it is all hypothetical, so you are both safe from harm. Otherwise, it would be a very busy day for you both.

The first point of this exercise is to develop your spot analysis and *compare and contrast* abilities with each card in your deck, no matter what order it comes in relation to any other card. It is far too easy to get lost in *one particular card* when *reading* the Tarot, especially one of the major cards, *and most especially* when that card is *Death*, or *The Hanged Man*. Repeat after me, kiddies: No one card is more important than another. Every card you draw has its place *and is an important part of your reading*, just as every breath you draw is necessary to life. You can't simply *skip* a breath. Sooner or later you will have to take it. Don't get in the habit of favoring one card over another in a *reading*.

The second point of this exercise is to remove any apprehension you have about drawing *any card* of your deck. Leave all of that drama to cheesy horror movies. When you draw *The Devil*, you may be describing an evil boss, an evil landlord, a cheesy movie role you are hoping to get because it pays well, or even a new flavor of Ben and Jerry's ice cream. ("El Diablo! With habaneros, jalapeños, chocolate fudge, and 'extra-dark' chocolate!" Hey!—We thought of it first!) Our examples are below. As these are all hypothetical, we are not concerned with what impressions we come up with. Neither should you. This is practice. You will learn a lot by doing this on a regular basis, and it will make your *readings* infinitely better. Try to avoid coming up with the same exact meaning every time you flip a certain card. Have fun creating variations and looking for unique ways of seeing each card. *That is what practice is for.* It is the only time when you are completely in control of your world.

This is what happens to me

This is what happens to you

My cheap boss refuses to give me a raise. I don't like him anyway.

You have so much money you have to stop and think on where to invest it.

This is what happens to me

This is what happens to you

I got dumped? Why do I get all the BAD cards?

Oh sure, that's probably my ex you are going out with I'll bet.

This is what happens to me

This is what happens to you

I win the lottery! Woo hoo! In your face "*ex*-boss!"

Your mother-in-law comes to live with you. She drives you crazy. (Hee hee! I won the lottery!)

This is what happens to me

This is what happens to you

Hey! Look at me! My boss shows up with HIS boss and I end up getting the raise!

Meanwhile you get a job in the mailroom.

This is what happens to me

This is what happens to you

Everyone ends up fighting at my birthday party.

You get married and have kids and a happy life. Why do YOU get all the good cards?

Exercise Two visual examples

This really is a fun exercise between good friends who share a love for the Tarot. Just for fun, we decided to record one of our own practice sessions. Here is what happened:
(We have included the commentary and reactions that went along with our little game.)

This happens to me

This happens to you

This happens to me

This happens to you

This happens to me

This happens to you

Oooh!
Hot date!
Don't wait up!

Uh oh . . . you died. So sorry. Game over. But what about my hot date?!!

(Nancy) Hey! No fair! We just started! I want a hot date! Let's trade cards!

(Dusty) You know that's not how the game of life is played! Now be quiet! You're dead now and I happen to have a date!

. . .You know, since you're dead and all, you wouldn't mind if I borrowed your new car for the night.

(Nancy) But!

(Dusty) Shh! Dead people don't talk! I wanna see how my date turns out!

(Nancy) Dead people can so too talk! Haven't you been paying ANY attention to horror movies lately?

(Dusty) Oh sure, if you are a zombie!

(Nancy) Zombies can't talk.

(Dusty) That's it! You're a zombie! Now shh!

Oh my god! We couldn't get in the club?

(Nancy) Ha ha! You should have called ahead and made reservations! Remind me not to go on a date with you!

(Dusty) Shh ghostie!

Hey! How'd you get so rich?

(Nancy) I save my money, unlike some people I know.

(Dusty) Well as you can see, I'm poor. Can I borrow some money? I want to buy that club and then I can get in any time I like!

(Nancy) Um . . . let's see . . . If I'm dead, how exactly do I give you a loan?

(Dusty) Fine. You didn't "die," it was a silly Halloween costume you wore to scare everyone. Now can I have some money to buy that club so I can get in any time?

(Nancy) Yaaay! I'm rich! First you have to kiss my ring peasant.

Oh great! I'm in jail now. It's your fault. If you would never have died in the first place, my date would have gone a lot better. Now what am I going to do?

(Nancy) Never mind that! Look at the card I got!

(Nancy) Ooh, look! Everyone loves me now that I am rich! Let's see . . . I think I will move to Malibu, and then I want a horse ranch, and a jet, and . . .

(Dusty) I don't like this game any more. Let's play something else . . . something fun.

(Nancy) Shh! You're in jail! "You have the right to remain silent!" Ha ha ha! I will come visit you when I run out of money to spend.

Now about that jet, I'm thinking something blue . . .

The point of this exercise is to have fun trading situations with a friend (or a fellow student). The message of the cards is not that something is happening, but that something is happening *to someone*. By taking turns witnessing events from an objective point of view *(this happens to you)* and a subjective one *(Hey! This is happening to me!)*, you build up an understanding of the effects of actions and circumstances revealed by the cards rather than seeing them in a sterile "theoretical" environment. *Readings* become more real when they happen to you, or to someone you care about. This *personalization of meaning* and the resultant consideration of the consequences (albeit playfully) will give your future *readings* a far more profound depth of clarity and compassion that your clients will truly appreciate.

Exercise Three

"EXACTLY WHAT DO YOU TWO HAVE IN COMMON ANYWAY?"

Please get out your *study deck*. Shuffle your deck thoroughly. Take the top two cards from your deck and place them on the table in front of you, or select two cards randomly from the deck. Don't put a lot of effort into this, because you will be doing a lot of this, and there is no sense in complicating the parts of this exercise that are supportive rather than instructive. Just grab two random cards.

Once you have done that, look at *card one*, and tie it to *card two*. They are still two individual cards, but do they have anything in common that jumps out at you? Please keep this part simple. If you see a connection, great! If not, simply flip two more cards. Spend no more than three or four seconds glancing at each pair of cards. In any case, you will have probably already spotted some similarities in *exercise two*. Later you will combine this exercise with others, so don't add a lot of stress to your life right now trying to get everything "perfect."

Below are some visual examples to help you understand the process. Please note that any examples we show you are simply that: examples. You can use them as your own if you like them, but do not allow our interpretation to limit your own ideas as to how cards can relate to each other. Later on we will go into *blending* card energies. Right now we are just looking for connections and similarities between any two cards you happen to come across.

Hmm . . . "Okay class, here we see the correct way to carry a heavy load, and the wrong way. This is essential to a healthy back."

To us, these two cards looks like two people exchanging gifts, although it could also be a doctor handing a man a glass of medicine, and in the second picture someone is buying a gift basket of flowers. The commonality could be people buying things, or maybe a hospital.

This presents a few interesting options for interpretation. On the left we have the "master" and on the right we have the "apprentice." Or perhaps it is that on the left we have people interrupting your work to complain or ask questions, but on the right you get to work happily without people nagging you. Or perhaps it is creating your art in public versus privately in your studio.

You know . . . neither one of them look very happy right now. Perhaps we should do this later.

Exercise Four
FROM HERE TO THERE

Shuffle your *study deck* thoroughly. Take the top two cards from your deck and place them on the table in front of you, or select two cards randomly from the deck. Don't put a lot of effort into this, because you will be doing a lot of this, and there is no sense in complicating the parts of this exercise that are supportive rather than instructive. Just grab two random cards.

Once you have done that, look at *card one,* and tie it to *card two.* How would you get from *card one* to *card two? If* you are having any trouble finding a connection between these two cards within a few seconds, simply flip two new cards on top of these two and forget these cards completely. This is another exercise we would like you to keep doing over the years. It is quick, easy, and keeps you sharp. You will also find over time that *this is the basis of* powerful magic. Examples below:

Here we have a "love triangle" (3 of Swords) leading to (the 9 of Swords) someone sleeping alone in bed and being very unhappy about it. Perhaps someone cheated on their spouse, and this led to much unhappiness.

Uh oh . . . It looks like everyone was having a good time at the party, drinking and dancing (3 of Cups), and then someone had too much to drink and one thing leads to another and a fight breaks out (5 of Wands).

Hey! Look at this! It looks like our friend "Michelangelo" (the apprentice in the 8 of Coins) worked his tail off and got a commission (3 of Coins) to do the Sistine Chapel. (If only we were so lucky . . .) This is a classic example of progressing from one card (or situation) to another. If the cards were 3, then 8 (instead of the 8 then the 3 above) it could be being fired from a great job and back to breaking rocks at the quarry. Oh well . . .

"So, like, there I was dude, and all these guys were like totally ready to pound on me, but I was like 'C'mon cowards! I'll fight you all!' **But then** *like, the cops showed up and chased them away. It's too bad. I would have beat them all to a pulp you know."*

Exercise Five

THERE AND BACK AGAIN*

This is a revisiting of *exercise four*. The purpose of having you extend the previous exercises from *two* cards to *three*, is to prepare you for full *readings* where you will have to tie the energy and meaning of *many cards together*, blending, coordinating, prioritizing, sorting, and spotting all sorts of patterns from all points of the *spread*. Working with three cards will help you expand your awareness simultaneously to four, five, even ten cards all impacting each other *without* having to actually practice regularly with cards of these multiples. Once you are comfortable working with *three* cards, you will have the skill set to enhance and expand card meanings as needed in your *readings*.

With three cards we now introduce the problem of *order*. Going from one card to another is easy enough, but three cards calls into question whether to *read* left to right (Western), right to left (Eastern), or is the center card "flanked" by two *supporting* cards? Which card is *dominant*?

This is something you will have to decide for yourself when you practice, as well as when you *"cast spreads"* (do *readings*). This is the part of the Tarot where *you make the rules,* and it applies to students as well as "masters." You have to know in advance *how you read your cards.* If you prefer to *read* right to left, then by all means *read* right to left, or upside-down or however you like. Just don't go into a *reading not knowing* how you want to lay your cards down, and refrain from changing the rules in the middle of a *reading*. Very rarely, *and this will happen later, when you are very skilled with the Tarot,* you will see cards that need to be *read* obliquely, or even "re-placed," but don't you dare start worrying about that until you have been *reading* cards for several years. It is better to scoop up the entire *spread* and start fresh than it is to try to guess why the cards "aren't making sense."

So . . . grab your "minor" Arcana and flip three cards over, one at a time, so *you* know the order they appeared in. Then *read* them "left to right" chronologically (this happens, and then *this other thing* happens, *and then* this last thing happens). Without flipping new cards, reread them, this time "right to left" chronologically (this happens, and then *this other thing* happens, *and then* this last thing happens). Then flip three new cards.

We will worry about "aspecting," "supporting," and "dominant" cards in a bit.

Please keep in mind that in our practice exercises these three cards will appear together, where in your actual *readings*, "aspecting cards" (which we will deal with next) will appear in chronological order (past, present, future), they will appear in linear order (card 2, card 3, card 4 . . . no matter what each card "position" means in the *spread* you are *casting*), and in no order at all, but will point to, affect, and even change the meaning of other cards. But for now let's keep things nice and simple.

Visual examples appear on the next page.

* Why yes, we *are* huge Tolkien fans.

Exercise Five visual examples

Here are a few examples based on what we might see. Take these *only as examples*. First we identify each card (1), then we see if we can see an easy connection or similarity (2), then we see if we can make a *three-card story* about them. For this example we are *reading* "left to right" only. Here we go. Wish us luck!

(1) A mausoleum, a miser, someone who is completely closed off.
(2) They are all 4's (completely by accident, we promise). They are all sitting or resting (especially the dead guy). No one is doing anything. There's our connection.
(3) "So your rich uncle died (sorry) and you went to his funeral, but you were cut out of the will, and that made you very unhappy."

Another tough one . . . (1) A message, a date, not happy with the result of your labors.
[oh, this is going to be too easy]
(2) Commonalities: we can't see any—but . . .
(3) [P. Wands] You call up a girl and ask her out on a date. She says yes. [2 Cups] You two go out and you buy her a drink (probably at a bar—how original and "romantic"). [7 Coins] The date doesn't go very well. You two don't hit it off at all.

Our advice: Next time be more creative. Plan ahead and make it an interesting date. You might do better for your efforts.

(1) A raise, your wife, emotional distress.
(2) Nothing at the moment.
(3) "You get the promotion at work you have been fighting for, and that comes with a bump in pay. But your boss makes you work late to justify the extra money he is 'giving you,' which puts a strain on your relationship. Your wife misses you, and while she is happy for you, she wishes you two had more time together."

> We hope you can see how we reached our conclusions in the examples above. The meanings we assigned each card came from a combination of "traditional interpretations," as well as our personal impressions of each card—at the moment we flipped them.
>
> (These were not "staged" examples.)

This book comes with free lessons. If you are not taking them you are making all of this a LOT harder on yourself.

Exercise Six

BIRDS OF A FEATHER

This is simply a three-card version of *exercise three*. Adding a third (or even fourth) card often makes it easier to spot commonalities among the cards in question, but it can also skew your initial feelings on the cards you are interpreting. For this exercise, we would like you to view all cards as equal in importance, and simply look to find any similarities or a "common thread." Same rules apply: Toss the "major" Arcana aside for now and shuffle your *study deck*, flipping all three cards at once. Spend no more than ten seconds scanning any set you flip. State out loud what you see. Our examples are below:

Commonalities . . . They all have colors . . . Who flipped these stupid cards anyway?

They are all <u>results</u> cards. Notice how everything pictured above is a result of previous action. (Wow, that was <u>hard</u>!) If these came up in a "3-card spread" we would say first that the answer is <u>strongly</u> affected by the past.

A river runs through two cards, two are cups; two "could" involve mourning. We are just looking for commonalities here. Leave the interpretations for the following exercises. No stress, right?

Hmmm . . . more colors . . . that's a start isn't it? (grr . . .)

Okay, we're stumped. Rather than sit here all day and try to salvage our egos (and our reputations) we are going to simply give up and move on. Not all cards will share easy-to-find commonalities. This in itself is a lesson in knowing when to let go and move on to more pressing areas of the reading you are giving (or shuffle more thoroughly next time while <u>focusing</u> on the question at hand).

Okay, so two 5's here and a Queen . . . Sky color means nothing as there is no "weather" in the Tarot to speak of. Sure, a few cards have a cloud here or there, or a few drops of rain, but for the most part, weather symbolism was overlooked by the "experts" who added the kabbalah, numerology, astrology, color meanings, and chakras. (You could draw your own weather in if you like, though.

But they all "happen outdoors" (if you discount the fact that ALL of the court cards are outdoors). And notice that every one of the people in these cards are intent on something. <u>None are inactive</u>. They are all going somewhere, or engaged in something. Also, there are no shadows in any of these cards. Perhaps they are all vampires. Something to think about . . .

Exercise Seven
HEY! WHAT DOES THIS CARD MEAN?

Aspecting cards

So far we have concentrated on each card having a meaning of its own, only toying gently with the idea of card relationships, and mostly in a linear form (going *from this to that*). We're not ready to *blend* card energies just yet, but we do want to look at how a card can be *aspected* by another, or a card can be *clarified,* or *defined* by another, a term we call "opening up a card" to unlock its meaning. We will start with visual examples this time, as the concept and the process are both simple and easy to understand. You will use these a lot in your readings, most often without even thinking much about them.

Here we have the *9 of Swords* that has come up in a *reading*. Our client has asked about her love life, and this card has come up in the past. It says she has been very unhappy. We want to know *why,* so we look to other cards already in the *spread*. Off to the side, in a spot of the *spread* that we interpret as "things that are affecting you" we see the *Knight of Wands*. Now we see that the *reason for* our client's misery is an ex-boyfriend, and in this case, the *Knight* looks to be galavanting around "waving his wand at anyone who passes."

This is by far *not a* "traditional interpretation" of the *upstanding and heroic nature of the Knight of Wands,* but this interpretation is what our instinct tells us, and the essence of the Tarot is that the cards are merely visual symbols with no more magical power than a wine grape. True, they are standardized symbols, loaded with undercurrents of inference and subtle meaning you may choose to use or ignore at your convenience, but the real power is always in you, not the tool you use to assist you. This is true of an artist and a mechanic, and it is true of you. A better wrench won't make you a better *mechanic.* Either you develop your talent, or you do not; but the quality of your tools can only *enhance* your abilities—they do not do the work for you. This means that sometimes the cards will speak to you "at face value," and at other times they will read "by the book," while still other times they will point you in a direction for you to find the answer in alternative ways (like asking the client—whether any of us likes it or not, clients sometimes lie, stretch the truth, tell only *their* side of the story, or conveniently omit certain rather important facts).

This is why we emphasize that practice is more important than book study. *Both are essential* to learning this wonderful skill, but your own interpretations will begin to reach amazing accuracy as you hone your instincts and learn to trust your judgment as you weigh "what you have been taught" with what *feels* right deep inside you. It's kind of like a hamburger. Without the bun, it's really not much of a hamburger, and there's no way to call two slices of plain bread a "hamburger." **Study *and* practice.**

So back to our example . . . In this case, the *9 of Swords* is *aspected* by, or *clarified* by, the *Knight of Wands* from a supportive position. We have a suspicion that this joker was making it pretty obvious to everyone (including our client) that he was out to "play," and he validated his ego by showing off what a "man" he was by running around with other women, causing our client a lot of suffering. Now we have two options: We can verify this directly by stating what we see and asking our client if this is the case, or we can *open the 9 of Swords up* for further clarification. Let's *open her up*, just to see what happens. (We are assuming for the sake of argument that the *9 of Swords* is a woman. The timeless debate rages on . . .)

We are going to draw three cards from the deck to explain the meaning of the *9 of Swords*. To do this we want to make sure that we draw the right three cards, not just three cards at random that make no sense at all. So we are going to shuffle the cards (since we have already *cast* the *spread*) and while we are shuffling we are going to focus our own question of what the *9 of Swords* entails.

The three cards we draw from our deck will each individually point to the *9 of Swords,* just like the caption under a photo in a newspaper explains to the *reader* exactly what they are seeing in the picture. Here's what we get:

Here we have our *9 of Swords*. We want to know a bit more about it. We want to know *why* our client was upset, and *what happened* to make her unhappy. This is what we will focus on while we are shuffling the rest of our cards (the ones not already laid out in the *spread*).

While we are shuffling this card jumped out at us.

When you are shuffling and a certain card seems to leap out on its own, set it aside and give it careful consideration. Occasionally it is simply an accident, but most often the card will point to an answer to whatever you were considering while you were shuffling. If you can see a connection, you have a *priority message* on the matter at hand. If you happen to see no connection at all, *note the card and ignore it for the time being.* It is far worse to spend time and energy superstitiously hunting down omens than it is to miss a clue here or there occasionally.

In this particular case, the *6 of Cups* flipped out of the deck and landed face up on the *spread* while we were shuffling. It didn't slide, or fall out. It actually catapulted a few inches into the air and fluttered down on to the cards we had already laid out. The *6 of Cups* "traditionally" refers to a gift, or a reunion among old friends. In the picture a boy is giving a girl a cup filled with flowers.

To us, this new twist looks *a little too much* like the "ex" is slipping *his* "ex" (previous to our client) a little of his fertility, or nature's bounty. We may be completely off base here, but this is what *we* see. As this happens to support our existing theories, we will place this card below the *9 of Swords* and ask for two more cards to further extrapolate the meaning of our client's previous emotional despair. We continue shuffling and draw two cards off the top of the deck when we feel the moment is right.

Here's what comes up next:

dissatisfied with what you have created.

feeling trapped

So putting it all together, here is what it looks like in our *spread*. We have the *9 of Swords* that we asked about, and the *6 of Cups* flew out, so we will put that one in the center, since it seems to have a priority, and then we have the *7 of Coins*, and finally the *8 of Swords*. Please note that we have not shown any other cards of the original *spread* only because they do not affect this exercise.

Here's our take on it. Yours may be different. Our client was miserable because her boyfriend (now "ex") was romantically involved with an "ex" of *his*. He was unsatisfied with *their* relationship, or he felt certain things left undone in his *past* relationship. Either way, he felt *trapped*, and decided to validate his ego by showing off how free he was in public (back to the *Knight of Wands*), and by reuniting with *his* ex-girlfriend. Now we have a wealth of information that makes the reasons for our client's unhappiness abundantly clear. This allows us to see what baggage she is dragging along behind her into any new relationship. This, in turn, helps us give her better *advice*.

The process of "opening up a card"

Now that you have an understanding of the basic process, here's the exercise we would like you to do. **Draw a card from the deck of your choosing.** Once again we are still leaving the "major" Arcana off to the side to make this easier to grasp and retain. The process is the same with the "major" Arcana as it is with the "minor" Arcana, but the "majors" are so over-hyped and static that at this point their inclusion would only serve to make the learning process more complicated, so please bear with us.

Once you have a card that you like, simply place it before you. Look at that card and decide to yourself what it could imply. Focus on that particular meaning and start shuffling your deck, while asking what your interpretation of that card *means*. How could that be expanded, or what is hiding behind that card? <u>All you are looking to do is</u> to draw three cards that individually relate to the card you chose. We will do a few examples with you, just to make sure that you have this concept down. Be sure to do this exercise occasionally until you have complete confidence in your abilities.

As a side note: When "opening up a card," there are various methods professional *readers* subscribe to. <u>*Do what works for you*</u>. Here are a few popular variations.

1: Draw *one* card. This is a *"clarification card."*

2: Draw three cards off of the deck without shuffling.

3: Draw three cards off of the deck after shuffling until you are content.

4: Draw three cards while shuffling, one at a time.

5: Take the card *out of the original spread* and *cast* a whole new *spread* based on that card alone, to see what that card means.

6: _____
_____
_____

7: _____
_____
_____

8: _____
_____
_____

Our examples appear on the following pages.

"Opening up a card" visual examples

In this example our initial card is the *5 of Cups* (another joyous card). We want to know why *anyone* could possibly be unhappy. So we drew a few cards to see what would come up. *Here's what we got:*

The *4 of Wands* generally indicates the stability of plans realized. People are dancing and having a good time at a feast in an estate. Seems like a happy enough card . . . No luck here so far.

Next we drew the *9 of Wands*. This guy looks pretty weary, like he has been on guard duty too long. Still not a lot of help, but at least it fits in with *"Mr. I'm unhappy because three of my cups are knocked over, even though there are two left."* (Not that we see any reason to be *happy* just because 40% of anything you value was saved from destruction. You <u>definitely</u> could be *happy* if 100% of your "stuff" was saved from destruction.) But the point so far is that the *9 of Wands* and the *5 of Cups* seem to go well together, since misery loves company.

Then we drew the *2 of Coins*. He is juggling his finances (or playing with his money, which is no way to treat it). We know from personal experience how "juggling your finances" can be *very* stressful. It's hard to think clearly or plan out your life and passions when you are constantly under the pressure of not having enough money to get by.

So there we have it. Three cards, two "kind of" help, but that happy home just doesn't fit. So we stare at the cards for a bit and suddenly it hits us. *Of course* it fits! This guy is unhappy (3 down, 2 up means he has something good that is also a stone around his neck). He bought his "happy home" *(4 of Wands)* during a time when *loan interest rates* were low. But he bought "too much house" for himself (this is actually a common mistake) and now the interest rates on his adjustable mortgage have gone *up*. Suddenly his house payments (the amount he has to pay the bank every month) have gone through the roof *(please pardon the pun)* and he is scrambling to keep up. He is constantly worried about this *(9 of Wands)*, and feels lethargic from all of the stress. No wonder he's unhappy!

But don't think <u>you</u> are getting off that easy . . .

Oh no, my friend . . . Now it is your turn to look at the cards above and decide why "Mr. Grumpy-face" *(5 of Cups)* is unhappy. You have three *opening cards* to clarify his disillusionment with his fate. The answer lies between the *4 of Wands,* the *9 of Wands,* and the *2 of Coins.* We may not have the right answer at all. So, without causing yourself too much stress, please draw your cards out and look at them as we have laid them out above. What do <u>you</u> get from the *clarification cards?* What possible answers look right to you? If nothing comes to you right this moment, please remember to come back to it later, or set the cards out and glance at them from time to time until you have an answer you like.

Your solution to this puzzle: _____

_____

_____

_____

Another example

Our client has come to us to ask about her new boss. She likes working for the company, but this guy just rubs her the wrong way. She wants to know if "he hates her" because he is extremely impatient, commanding, pushy, rude, and sometimes downright *mean*.

Instead of *tossing out a spread,* we first see what we can find out about this man by using our intuitive connection with our cards. *Here's what we get:*

After asking our client to clarify her question and her problem, we get a better picture of her boss. The *King of Coins* really seems to sum him up. So we use that card to represent him. We pick the *King of Coins* and say to ourselves, *"This is her boss. This card signifies the man she is asking about."* Once we have that image firmly in place mentally, we ask about him: **who he is,** *what is his personal motivation* in the workplace, especially in respect to our client? Then we draw our three cards.

The *Knight of Swords* indicates a hyper-aggressive nature, while the *6 of Wands* shows us someone who is used to getting his way and being praised for it (this guy probably has a whole crew of sycophants or "yes" men). The *Ace of Swords* shows victory. This might be a good indication, *but we didn't ask how she should deal with her boss, or what was going to happen.* In our question we asked *only* about the man she works for. When you compare the smugness of the *King of Coins* with the rest of the cards it looks to us like this guy has an "aggressive leadership style" (he's a real jerk), and he finds that intimidation works for him. Looks like someone read that old book *Winning Through Intimidation* and took it as gospel. He constantly reinforces his beliefs with books and seminars on "aggressive leadership" or the opinion of other executives who support that notion (and validate his position on the matter). The *Knight* shows us his inner aggression. The *6* shows us everyone backing down from confrontation— even joining in his parade of dominance to keep their jobs, and the *Ace* shows us that it works for him. No one is willing to stand up to him (or maybe he fires anyone who does). So we make our client a nice cup of cocoa and tell her, *"It's not you honey—it's him,"* because it really is after all.

Okay, so now it's your turn again . . .

How does your opinion differ from ours? Where did we go wrong? Assuming her boss *is* the *King of Coins,* what do the *clarification cards* reveal about him? What do you see? If you find our wisdom infinite and unquestionable (or if you just happen to be too lazy at the moment to stress yourself over finding alternate meanings, and that is just as well), please feel free to draw out the *King of Coins* from your own deck and repeat what we did above (shuffle and ask about "her boss") and draw three *clarification cards* to *"open him up"* and get your own answers about this man. Either way, please do spend time on this exercise. This practice will help you immeasurably in the times (and *readings*) to come.

Your solution to this puzzle: _____

_____

_____

_____

One more example

A gentleman in an expensive suit comes in to see us. He says up front that, *"he doesn't believe in all of this voodoo and superstition,"* but that he wants a *reading* anyway. We politely reply that we don't really believe in Santa, but that we still like getting presents every year, so since we both seem to operate from a stance of suspended disbelief, we would be happy to do a *reading* for him *"just for fun."*

We ask him what he wants to know about. At first he is evasive and assuming, expecting us to know why he is here. Before tossing him out on the street for wasting our time, we take a deep, cleansing breath, smile, and we explain very carefully (as if to a child) that if we are to give him a valid answer, we must know what his question is. Five minutes later he reveals that he has a business plan and he wants us to tell him how wonderful it is, how clever he is for coming up with it, and how it will make him millions of dollars. Of course, he doesn't say this as directly and forthright as that, but we know what he wants to hear, **so we tell him:**

"Sir, it looks like your plan (we have selected the *2 of Wands* above to represent his plan and *act of planning*) will be facing some challenges (*7 of Wands*) when you announce it to the world (*Page of Wands*). Perhaps there is more competition than you realize, or someone may claim that *they* had the idea first and force litigation on the matter. It looks to us like money will be very tight (*4 of Coins*). Perhaps this plan needs to be worked over a bit, or reviewed by one of your peers. I see resistance to getting funded (this is our personal take on all three cards together as an *end result*)."

The gentleman stands up, calls us charlatans, says he refuses to pay (we are only a few minutes in so far, so that is really not an issue, although he doesn't have to be so abusive about it). Before he can storm out, we casually ask him if he has shown his plan to anyone yet, and what their opinion of it is. He snarls and says that his "no-good boss said it was *weak*," and that his wife laughed at his idea. "Imagine that! That insolent harpy actually *laughed* at the very idea!" he protests before tossing five dollars on the table and stomps out. We don't know whether to laugh or feel sorry for the poor guy.

Oh you had to know this was coming . . .

So, wise and enlightened oracle of the East (of somewhere, after all *everywhere* is east of some place or another). What do your sources tell you? *(And no cheating by using a Magic 8-Ball!™)* Take your time considering this man's dilemma: He has a plan and he wants you to reassure him that he will "show them." *He will show them all!* How do you handle clients who expect you to know everything? "You're the psychic—you should know why I am here!" The first time you hear that you may shriek with laughter, but the twenty-seventh time you may have a baseball bat ready for the occasion (we do not recommend violence when dealing with psychically abusive *querents—that is "those who come for a reading"*). How would you *help* a querent (paying or "friend"—as a psychic you will find that you have a lot of "friends" who believe you should *read* for them at no charge—try to at least get a $5 coffee and some decent chocolate out of the deal if you can) when they see things only as they want them to be—and they believe that the entire world is *wrong*? How would you turn lemons into lemonade?

There are no answers to fill in here, only thoughts to consider before these things happen to you. Ask your teacher (if you are fortunate enough to have one) about various situations. Spend some time thinking about *how you want to be seen* as a *reader*. What is the image you want to project?

Have questions about clients? We have a course that will help you master every aspect of tarot as a paying job.

Exercise Eight

ONE PLUS ONE EQUALS WHAT?

Blending two card meanings into a new "central meaning"

This exercise is easy to grasp, but it will be difficult to figure out at times. That's okay. It happens to *all* of us. Anyone who says different is selling you something. Ultimately, however, this is one of the most important skills you will develop in reading the Tarot (*or palms, or astrology, or manifesting any of your desires through affirmations, visualization, and the "Laws of Attraction and Repulsion,"* for that matter*). Fortunately, you have been well prepared for this in the previous exercises, so you should get the hang of this so easily you will be amazed.

We will be blending the meanings of two cards to create a third meaning, *a new meaning*, one that is applicable to your situation. The exercise itself is easy enough (*be sure to remove any "major" Arcana cards first*): simply shuffle your deck thoroughly and draw two cards from the top, and identify their basic meaning. Then compare and contrast them, looking for similarities, differences, and combinations. Ask yourself how they fit. Ask *your* guides (faeries, angels, friendly alien entities, et al.) how they fit. Add the two cards together, subtract one from the other, or even multiply one *by* the other. Once you have a meaning you like, forget about them and flip two more cards. Work your way through the deck. Below are our examples.

So there you are working on your boss's new project and, of course, he brings along a "consultant" who decides that all of your work is "not to standard" (the consultant has to earn his fee, so he decides that his input is needed). Now you look incompetent in front of your boss, and you have to do all of your work all over again.

Okay, that's our take on this. What do you think?
(please fill in your answers below)

You marry a wealthy woman. (or) You are a wealthy, independent woman who gives generously to charity often. (or) You own a winery and you are hosting a chic wine tasting before snooty judges. (Sorry, we are having too much fun. Okay, it's your turn now.)

That's our take on this. What do you think?
(please fill in your answers below)

_____   _____

_____   _____

_____   _____

* Technically, the PROPER term is psychic magnetism, and the whole attraction/repulsion thing is a subset of that. See *Aphrodite's Book of Secrets* to understand the actual processes involved, or enroll in a *real* mystery school if you are interested in learning how to re/create your own destiny, and get everything you want from your life.

Exercise Nine

ONE PLUS ONE *PLUS ONE* EQUALS WHAT?

Blending multiple card meanings into a new "central meaning"

Same thing as *exercise eight,* only using three cards instead of two. <u>Additionally</u>, we have provided several pages of practice exercises (just after the next few pages) to help you sharpen your skills, even if you don't have your deck with you at the moment.

These three cards come up in a reading. Combine all three cards into one <u>new</u> meaning. This new meaning can be a cause, an effect or "end-result," a situation, a person, or anything you can realistically expect to encounter in daily life.

Hmm... decisions, decisions... someone is giving out money, and is that a party going on? Okay, we're stumped. Got any ideas? There are two Cups (cards) so that lends weight, or prominence, or priority to the suit of Cups.

Well, you have a <u>choice</u>: *Money or happiness?*

This sounds like a job question—"Job I like, or job that pays well?"—or—"I got a Christmas bonus!" (The 6 of Coins.) "I'm going to celebrate! What should I <u>buy</u>?"

Here is an excellent example of *"reading* cold." Occasionally you will want (or have) to *read* for a distant situation, one where you have very limited facts and you are trying to reconstruct events, or do some detective work. This exercise, as onerous as it is, teaches you how to "read cold" so that you can build a picture of events that have transpired, or events that <u>will</u> transpire in any situation where you just don't have the facts you need. For example, if you wanted to *cast a spread* for some event in the ancient past, to try to glean the details from a sketchy account, or if you wanted to predict an election in the future when you have no idea who will be running. Each of these examples are <u>very</u> advanced Tarot work, but the skills you are building now will make them much easier.

Okay, that's our take on this. What do you think?

_____

_____

_____

_____

Exercise Ten

THE NEVER-ENDING STORY

This is more of a party game; but if you are comfortable with all of the previous exercises, you can do this one alone, <u>anytime, anywhere</u>. It is *excellent* practice and will make your *readings* infinitely easier (and better, as well). But be forewarned: sometimes you will be able to happily breeze through this, and other times it will tax your nerves and your imagination to the point of frustration. At those times, it is probably better to go do something else. But please do your best to master this game *(it works best as a 3-4 person game if you have creative, fast-thinking friends)*. It is more than worth the frustration it will sometimes put you through. Mastering this will make you a <u>very</u> good *reader* by anyone's standards.

Okay, here we go. The object of this easy game is simply to *not* be the person who gets stumped, or cannot *continue* the story. Shuffle your deck thoroughly. You can use the "major" Arcana in this game, but at first we would like you to continue using just the "minor" Arcana until you are thoroughly comfortable with them.

Pick any card to start; or if you are feeling especially brave, just take the first card from the deck and flip it over. That is the beginning of your *story*. If you are playing alone, you can hold your deck. If playing with friends (who you trust to touch your cards), it is best to leave the deck on the table, and have everyone just flip the top card. It's a good idea to use an old deck, obviously. Alternately, you can hold the deck and flip the cards for people, but that may hamper the game's spontaneity. Use your best judgment. Here is an example game.

(This is the first card flipped)  (story) *"So, a man was sitting under a tree one day, looking at his cups when a hand popped out of a cloud and said 'drink me' . . ."*

(you can use a funny voice if it makes your game more fun)

(flip a new card)  (story) *". . . And the man says 'I'm not going to drink that! It's poison and it will make me die!!'"*

(and then . . .)

(flip a new card)  (story) *". . . So he <u>jumped</u> up onto his horse and shouted 'I am going to get a Diet Pepsi!'"*

(. . . and suddenly one of our narrators leaps off of the couch and runs to the kitchen so she will be back in time for her next turn) *(flip a new card)*  (story) "... *And the nice lady brought back one for her best friend too!*"

(technically this borders on extortion and is not an official part of the game; but if you can tie in the card meaning to a free Diet Pepsi in the course of the game, then more power to you)

(flip a new card)  (story) "... *And when he got back there was a party going on, with food and dancing.*"

(and then ...)

(flip a new card)  (story) "... *But he forgot to bring along his invitation, and he had to go home and get it.*"

(and then ...)

(flip a new card)  (story) "... *And when he gets home his mom says, 'Oh, I'm glad you're home dear. Since we're all out of that soda you are always drinking, I want you to pick some grapes and make me some of that delicious wine I like so much.*'"

(and then ...)

(flip a new card)  (story) "... *And he was very unhappy, because all he could think about were the girls dancing at the party. Now he would never meet any of them.*"

(and then ...)

EXERCISES

(flip a new card)

(story) "... *And so he quietly tiptoed out of the house to go back to the party, and he took his juggling swords along to impress the girls he was hoping to meet there.*"

(and then ...)

(flip a new card)

(story) "... *But when he got back to the party everyone had already gone home. All that was left were empty cups of Diet Pepsi. So he decided to go find some fun somewhere else.*"

(and then ...)

(flip a new card)

(story) "... *And his father showed up and said (in an authoritative voice), 'Son! Your mother wanted you to make her some wine. You are a disgrace, young man. Now get me a Diet Pepsi or you will be grounded forever!'*"

(and then ...)

(flip a new card)

(story) "... *And so he was grounded for a very long time, because he didn't even like Diet Pepsi. But he saved up a lot of money since he couldn't spend it on anything.*"

(and then ...)

(flip a new card)

(story) "... *And one day he jumped back on his horse and said, 'That's it! I'm leaving forever! I am going to dress like a circus clown and be a rock star!'*"

(and then ...)

(flip a new card)　　(story) "...And then he met the woman of his dreams, and she said, 'Drink this!' and this time he did!"

(and then...)

(flip a new card)　　(story) "...And he got signed by a big record company who liked his band 'Circus Clown Rockstars' and they gave him a HUGE advance.!"

(and then...)

(flip a new card)　　(story) "...But the cup that the girl of his dreams gave him was filled with poison, and he died. <u>The end</u>!!"

(no—and then...)

Well, that wasn't a very happy ending. Sometimes the cards just go like that. It wasn't the best story, anyway; but it should serve to show you the importance of being able to string cards together and see how individual cards can mean anything that is "correct" to the *reading*, whether it is the "traditional meaning," or something at "face value," or even something that you noticed about the card but you just know that it's appropriate <u>for this particular reading</u>.

We hope that you will play the never-ending story on at least a semi-regular basis while you are learning the Tarot. It is an easy way to get practice and the story is never the same twice. Each time you go through your deck you will come up with new variations of meanings, and with each variation you will understand your deck a little better. The cards will start to *talk to you*. Over time you will learn new things about individual cards you missed earlier and will never read in any book. *These things you learn are <u>just as valid</u> as anything set down by Crowley, Levi, Mathers, Agrippa, White, Case, or Regardie.*

All of our students and community members get to play our various tarot games. You should join us!

As an example, one of our students once vehemently argued with us that the man in the *7 of Swords* was "dancing." As much as that idea shocked us, we stopped and thought about it, and found that there really are no images of a man dancing in the Tarot, so why not? (Well, there is that guy in the *2 of Coins* but he seems preoccupied, so this might be two styles of dancing.)

Another example is found in either the *9 of Coins* or the *10 of Coins*. In both of these images we see animal lovers. The woman has a connection with birds, and the old man in the *10* has a strong affection for his dogs. These ancillary tidbits of information will usually not have much meaning in most *readings*, and suddenly you will come across a *reading* where this is *all that matters* about that particular card. This is why you want to allow your cards to *talk* to you, rather than simply memorizing 78 versions of what someone else decided that *your cards* should mean "each and every time you *read* them, without fail." Nothing can replace book knowledge, and your scholarly studies are of paramount importance, but please develop *your intuitive understanding* of your deck as well.

Exercise Eleven

SOMETHING TO LOOK AT

This is not so much of an exercise as it is homework designed to drive you crazy. Take one of your older decks and tape it up to the wall like a multiplication table. It will take up a good three to four feet across, and two to three feet down, unless you have one of the "tiny" decks. Tape it up where you can see it often, but somewhere you can leave it taped up for a long time. We recommend starting from *Ace* and going across all of the way to *King* (although you can mount them vertically if you like, as well) starting with the suit of *Wands,* then *Cups, Swords,* and finally *Coins*. Tuck the "major" Arcana afterwards in two rows of eleven cards each, or as you like.

The point of this exercise is to be able to see the natural progression of the suits (*Ace* through *10*) and compare the various suits. This allows you to study the Tarot at your convenience, glancing at all of the *3's* for example, or the *7's* . . . Take time often to look for the similarities of the numbers in the various suits, as well as the blatant inconsistencies. Don't just believe a book that tells you that, "each *8* is exactly the same and is a representation of the element the suit embodies," or any such nonsense. Take a look at your cards for yourself and see what comes to you.

The point of taping up a deck is to remove the pressure on you to cram all of this information into your head at once. Your life with the Tarot should become as intuitive and natural as eating or breathing. At times you will hunger for your cards, and at other times you will glance at them only in passing. This is how you truly and deeply learn to become comfortable and immersed in your understanding of the cards and their symbology. This will also start to subconsciously encourage you to one day perhaps doodle out your own images, ones that you can bond with more closely.

In any case, ideas will come to you easily and often when you have your Tarot deck mounted for spot analysis. You will also have 78 extremely useful images handy for your visualization needs. The Tarot makes a great meditation aid, whether you need to manifest some positive change in your life, or you are seeking some deeper wisdom. We have created a set of "Cheat Sheets" in *Section Three* that are written versions you can glance over if you like.

Extra credit exercises

The following exercises are entirely optional. They are designed to help you thoroughly master the Tarot and give you ideas on how to structure *your own* exercises for your ongoing study throughout the years, and those of your students whom you will someday teach in kind.

Each of the exercises over the next few pages starts with the standard evaluation of a card or a set of cards that have come up in a *reading*, popped out of the deck in response to a question, or are being used to *open up* another card for further clarification. We generally discourage *"one-card readings"* except in personal practice or matters of complete triviality. Nonetheless, the value of being able to *spot analyze* any card that announces itself is worth the effort of intense study. Similarly the ability to work comfortably with two and three card groups that aspect each other in a *reading*, whether they are *"surrounding cards"* or if they are spread out all over the *reading* but seem to "work together" to create secondary and tertiary meanings, is one that will mark you as a true adept rather than a casual performer.

We have endeavored to make the *process* of learning the Tarot as easy as possible, but to make it completely effortless would be to rob you of actual knowledge and prowess that only dedicated, attentive practice can bring. We hope that you will continue your study of and practice with the Tarot for many years to come, and share your findings with others in time.

Of course, we strongly encourage you to create your own personal Tarot exercises to keep yourself sharp as your skill develops. Maintaining a *Tarot Journal* is a good way to record your ideas, your progress, *and any experiments you find entertaining*. In the meantime, we hope that you enjoy the practice exercises we have laid out before you.

If you have your *study deck* with you, please draw out the corresponding cards so that you can see the level of detail of your cards. If you do not have your deck with you, it is still possible to gain much benefit from these exercises by using the images provided on the following pages. Fill in what you are sure of at the moment. Anything else you can always come back and work on later.

Extra credit exercises
(two-card practice spreads)

Please draw the cards from your deck that correspond to the images below. Then simply fill in the blanks. Remember that your answers are just as valid as anything you read anywhere, as long *as they work for you.*

These two cards came up in a spread. What do they say to you? What do you see? You can direct these cards to any situation that you feel they apply.

What are the meanings of each card (at this particular moment, *according to you*)?

_____.

What do these two cards have in common? *(if anything)*

_____.

How would *card one* get to *card two*? What is happening here?

_____   _____
     This happens   *(and then)*   *this other thing happens.*

If *card one* (the one on the left) were the <u>primary</u> <u>card</u>, how would *card two* <u>aspect</u> *card one*? How would it "shape" or clarify *card one*?

_____

_____.

If *card two* (the one on the right) were the <u>primary</u> <u>card</u>, how would *card one* <u>aspect</u> *card two*? How would it "shape" or clarify *card two*?

_____

_____.

If you *blended* these two cards into one meaning, what would the *new meaning* be?

_____

_____.

Any other thoughts or opinions you would like to add? *Perhaps something we may have missed?*

_____

_____.

These two cards came up in a spread. What do they say to you? What do you see? You can direct these cards to any situation that you feel they apply.

What are the meanings of each card (at this particular moment, *according to you*)?

_____.

What do these two cards have in common? *(if anything)*

_____.

How would *card one* get to *card two*? What is happening here?

_____   _____
           This happens   *(and then)*   *this other thing happens.*

If *card one* (the one on the left) were the <u>primary</u> <u>card</u>, how would *card two* <u>aspect</u> *card one*? How would it "shape" or clarify *card one*?

_____

_____.

If *card two* (the one on the right) were the <u>primary</u> <u>card</u>, how would *card one* <u>aspect</u> *card two*? How would it "shape" or clarify *card two*?

_____

_____.

If you *blended* these two cards into one meaning, what would the *new meaning* be?

_____

_____.

---

① Any other thoughts or opinions you would like to add? *Perhaps something we may have missed?*

_____

_____.

If your teacher has assigned you additional work, please fill in your answer here:

②
_____

_____

_____

_____.

EXERCISES

These two cards came up in a spread. What do they say to you? What do you see? You can direct these cards to any situation that you feel they apply.

What are the meanings of each card (at this particular moment, *according to you*)?

_____.

What do these two cards have in common? *(if anything)*

_____.

How would *card one* get to *card two*? What is happening here?

_____   _____   _____
          This happens   *(and then)*   *this other thing happens.*

If *card one* (the one on the left) were the <u>primary</u> <u>card</u>, how would *card two* <u>aspect</u> *card one*? How would it "shape" or clarify card one?

_____

_____.

If *card two* (the one on the right) were the <u>primary</u> <u>card</u>, how would *card one* <u>aspect</u> *card two*? How would it "shape" or clarify card two?

_____

_____.

If you *blended* these two cards into one meaning, what would the *new meaning* be?

_____

_____.

Any other thoughts or opinions you would like to add? *Perhaps something we may have missed?*

_____

_____.

       If your teacher has assigned you additional work, please fill in your answer here:

_____

_____

_____

_____.

(1)

(2)

These two cards came up in a spread. What do they say to you? What do you see? You can direct these cards to any situation that you feel they apply.

What are the meanings of each card (at this particular moment, *according to you*)?
_____.

What do these two cards have in common? *(if anything)*
_____.

How would *card one* get to *card two*? What is happening here?

_____   _____
  This happens   (and then)   this other thing happens.

If *card one* (the one on the left) were the <u>primary</u> <u>card</u>, how would *card two* <u>aspect</u> *card one*? How would it "shape" or clarify *card one*?

_____

_____.

If *card two* (the one on the right) were the <u>primary</u> <u>card</u>, how would *card one* <u>aspect</u> *card two*? How would it "shape" or clarify *card two*?

_____

_____.

If you *blended* these two cards into one meaning, what would the *new meaning* be?

_____

_____.

Any other thoughts or opinions you would like to add? *Perhaps something we may have missed?*

①
_____

_____.

If your teacher has assigned you additional work, please fill in your answer here:

②
_____

_____

_____.

EXERCISES

These two cards came up in a spread. What do they say to you? What do <u>you</u> see? You can direct these cards to any situation that you feel they apply.

What are the meanings of each card (at this particular moment, *according to you*)?

_____.

What do these two cards have in common? *(if anything)*

_____.

How would *card one* get to *card two*? What is happening here?

_____   _____   _____
       This happens   *(and then)*   *this other thing happens.*

If *card one* (the one on the left) were the <u>primary card</u>, how would *card two* <u>aspect</u> *card one*? How would it "shape" or clarify *card one*?

_____

_____.

If *card two* (the one on the right) were the <u>primary card</u>, how would *card one* <u>aspect</u> *card two*? How would it "shape" or clarify *card two*?

_____

_____.

If you *blended* these two cards into one meaning, what would the *new meaning* be?

_____

_____.

Any other thoughts or opinions you would like to add? *Perhaps something we may have missed?*

_____

_____.

        If your teacher has assigned you additional work, please fill in your answer here:

_____

_____

_____.

① ②

These two cards came up in a spread. What do they say to you? What do you see? You can direct these cards to any situation that you feel they apply.

What are the meanings of each card (at this particular moment, *according to you*)?
_____.

What do these two cards have in common? *(if anything)*
_____.

How would *card one* get to *card two*? What is happening here?

_____   _____
    This happens   (and then)   this other thing happens.

If *card one* (the one on the left) were the <u>primary</u> <u>card</u>, how would *card two* <u>aspect</u> *card one*? How would it "shape" or clarify *card one*?

_____
_____.

If *card two* (the one on the right) were the <u>primary</u> <u>card</u>, how would *card one* <u>aspect</u> *card two*? How would it "shape" or clarify *card two*?

_____
_____.

If you *blended* these two cards into one meaning, what would the *new meaning* be?

_____
_____.

(1) Any other thoughts or opinions you would like to add? *Perhaps something we may have missed?*
_____
_____.

If your teacher has assigned you additional work, please fill in your answer here:

(2)
_____
_____
_____
_____.

These two cards came up in a spread. What do they say to you? What do <u>you</u> see? You can direct these cards to any situation that you feel they apply.

What are the meanings of each card (at this particular moment, *according to you*)?

_____.

What do these two cards have in common? *(if anything)*

_____.

How would *card one* get to *card two*? What is happening here?

_____   _____
     This happens   (and then)   this other thing happens.

If *card one* (the one on the left) were the <u>primary</u> <u>card</u>, how would *card two* <u>aspect</u> *card one*? How would it "shape" or clarify *card one*?

_____

_____.

If *card two* (the one on the right) were the <u>primary</u> <u>card</u>, how would *card one* <u>aspect</u> *card two*? How would it "shape" or clarify *card two*?

_____

_____.

If you *blended* these two cards into one meaning, what would the *new meaning* be?

_____

_____.

Any other thoughts or opinions you would like to add? *Perhaps something we may have missed?*

_____

_____.

If your teacher has assigned you additional work, please fill in your answer here:

_____

_____

_____

_____.

These two cards came up in a spread. What do they say to you? What do you see? You can direct these cards to any situation that you feel they apply.

What are the meanings of each card (at this particular moment, *according to you*)?

_____.

What do these two cards have in common? *(if anything)*

_____.

How would *card one* get to *card two*? What is happening here?

_____   _____   _____
         This happens   (and then)   this other thing happens.

If *card one* (the one on the left) were the <u>primary</u> <u>card</u>, how would *card two* <u>aspect</u> *card one*? How would it "shape" or clarify *card one*?

_____

_____.

If *card two* (the one on the right) were the <u>primary</u> <u>card</u>, how would *card one* <u>aspect</u> *card two*? How would it "shape" or clarify *card two*?

_____

_____.

If you *blended* these two cards into one meaning, what would the *new meaning* be?

_____

_____.

Any other thoughts or opinions you would like to add? *Perhaps something we may have missed?*

①
_____

_____.

If your teacher has assigned you additional work, please fill in your answer here:

②
_____

_____

_____

_____.

EXERCISES

These two cards came up in a spread. What do they say to you? What do you see? You can direct these cards to any situation that you feel they apply.

What are the meanings of each card (at this particular moment, *according to you*)?

_____.

What do these two cards have in common? *(if anything)*

_____.

How would *card one* get to *card two*? What is happening here?

_____   _____
   This happens   *(and then)*   *this other thing happens.*

If *card one* (the one on the left) were the <u>primary</u> <u>card</u>, how would *card two* <u>aspect</u> *card one*? How would it "shape" or clarify *card one*?

_____

_____.

If *card two* (the one on the right) were the <u>primary</u> <u>card</u>, how would *card one* <u>aspect</u> *card two*? How would it "shape" or clarify *card two*?

_____

_____.

If you *blended* these two cards into one meaning, what would the *new meaning* be?

_____

_____.

Any other thoughts or opinions you would like to add? *Perhaps something we may have missed?*

_____

_____.   ①

If your teacher has assigned you additional work, please fill in your answer here:

_____

_____

_____   ②

_____.

50

These two cards came up in a spread. What do they say to you? What do you see? You can direct these cards to any situation that you feel they apply.

What are the meanings of each card (at this particular moment, *according to you*)?

_____.

What do these two cards have in common? *(if anything)*

_____.

How would *card one* get to *card two*? What is happening here?

_____   _____   _____
       This happens   *(and then)*   *this other thing happens.*

If *card one* (the one on the left) were the <u>primary card</u>, how would *card two* <u>aspect</u> *card one*? How would it "shape" or clarify *card one*?

_____

_____.

If *card two* (the one on the right) were the <u>primary card</u>, how would *card one* <u>aspect</u> *card two*? How would it "shape" or clarify *card two*?

_____

_____.

If you *blended* these two cards into one meaning, what would the *new meaning* be?

_____

_____.

**① ** Any other thoughts or opinions you would like to add? *Perhaps something we may have missed?*

_____

_____.

If your teacher has assigned you additional work, please fill in your answer here:

**② ** _____

_____

_____

_____.

These two cards came up in a spread. What do they say to you? What do you see? You can direct these cards to any situation that you feel they apply.

What are the meanings of each card (at this particular moment, *according to you*)?
_____.

What do these two cards have in common? *(if anything)*
_____.

How would *card one* get to *card two*? What is happening here?

_____ _____ _____
          This happens   (and then)   this other thing happens.

If *card one* (the one on the left) were the <u>primary</u> <u>card</u>, how would *card two* <u>aspect</u> *card one*? How would it "shape" or clarify *card one*?

_____

_____.

If *card two* (the one on the right) were the <u>primary</u> <u>card</u>, how would *card one* <u>aspect</u> *card two*? How would it "shape" or clarify *card two*?

_____

_____.

If you *blended* these two cards into one meaning, what would the *new meaning* be?

_____

_____.

Any other thoughts or opinions you would like to add? *Perhaps something we may have missed?*

_____

_____.

      If your teacher has assigned you additional work, please fill in your answer here:

_____

_____

_____

_____.

① ②

Extra credit exercises
(three-card practice spreads)

Please draw the cards from your deck that correspond to the images below. Then simply fill in the blanks. Remember that <u>your answers</u> are just as valid as anything you read anywhere, as long *as they work for you.*

These three cards came up in a spread. What do they say to you? What do <u>you</u> see? You can direct these cards to any situation that you feel they apply.

What are the meanings of each card (at this particular moment, *according to you*)?
_____.

What do these three cards have in common? *(if anything)*
_____.

How would *card one* get to *card three*? What is happening here?

_____ _____ _____ _____ _____
    This happens   *(and then)*   *this other thing happens* *(and then)* *this other thing happens.*

If *card one* (the one on the left) were the <u>primary</u> <u>card</u>, how would *cards two* and *three* <u>aspect</u> *card one*? How would they "shape" or clarify card one?
_____
_____.

If *card two* or *three* were the <u>primary</u> <u>card</u>, how would the other cards <u>aspect</u> that card? How would they "shape" or clarify it?
_____
_____.

If you *blended* these three cards into one meaning, what would the *new meaning* be?
_____
_____.

Any other thoughts or opinions you would like to add? *Perhaps something we may have missed?*
_____
_____.

EXERCISES

These three cards came up in a spread. What do they say to you? What do you see? You can direct these cards to any situation that you feel they apply.

What are the meanings of each card (at this particular moment, *according to you*)?

_____.

What do these three cards have in common? *(if anything)*

_____.

How would *card one* get to *card three*? What is happening here?

_____ _____ _____
     This happens   *(and then)*   *this other thing happens*   *(and then)*   *this other thing happens.*

If *card one* (the one on the left) were the <u>primary</u> <u>card</u>, how would *cards two* and *three* <u>aspect</u> *card one*? How would they "shape" or clarify card one?

_____

_____.

If *card two* or *three* were the <u>primary</u> <u>card</u>, how would the other cards <u>aspect</u> that card? How would they "shape" or clarify it?

_____

_____.

If you *blended* these three cards into one meaning, what would the *new meaning* be?

_____

_____.

Any other thoughts or opinions you would like to add? *Perhaps something we may have missed?*

_____

_____.

①

If your teacher has assigned you additional work, please fill in your answer here:

_____

_____

_____

_____.

②

These three cards came up in a spread. What do they say to you? What do you see? You can direct these cards to any situation that you feel they apply.

What are the meanings of each card (at this particular moment, *according to you*)?
_____.

What do these three cards have in common? *(if anything)*
_____.

How would *card one* get to *card three*? What is happening here?

_____   _____   _____
This happens   *(and then)*   *this other thing happens*   *(and then)*   *this other thing happens.*

If *card one* (the one on the left) were the primary card, how would *cards two* and *three* aspect *card one*? How would they "shape" or clarify *card one*?

_____
_____.

If *card two* or *three* were the primary card, how would the other cards aspect that card? How would they "shape" or clarify it?

_____
_____.

If *you* blended these three cards into one meaning, what would the *new meaning* be?

_____
_____.

**① **Any other thoughts or opinions you would like to add? *Perhaps something we may have missed?*
_____
_____.

If your teacher has assigned you additional work, please fill in your answer here:

**② **
_____
_____
_____.

These three cards came up in a spread. What do they say to you? What do you see? You can direct these cards to any situation that you feel they apply.

What are the meanings of each card (at this particular moment, *according to you*)?

_____.

What do these three cards have in common? *(if anything)*

_____.

How would *card one* get to *card three*? What is happening here?

_____   _____   _____
 This happens (and then) this other thing happens (and then) this other thing happens.

If *card one* (the one on the left) were the primary card, how would *cards two* and *three* aspect *card one*? How would they "shape" or clarify card one?

_____

_____.

If *card two* or *three* were the primary card, how would the other cards aspect that card? How would they "shape" or clarify it?

_____

_____.

If you *blended* these three cards into one meaning, what would the *new meaning* be?

_____

_____.

Any other thoughts or opinions you would like to add? *Perhaps something we may have missed?*

_____

_____.

①

If your teacher has assigned you additional work, please fill in your answer here:

_____

_____

_____.

②

These three cards came up in a spread. What do they say to you? What do you see? You can direct these cards to any situation that you feel they apply.

What are the meanings of each card (at this particular moment, *according to you*)?
_____.

What do these three cards have in common? *(if anything)*
_____.

How would *card one* get to *card three*? What is happening here?

_____   _____   _____
    This happens   *(and then)*   *this other thing happens*   *(and then)*   *this other thing happens.*

If *card one* (the one on the left) were the <u>primary</u> <u>card</u>, how would *cards two* a*nd three* <u>aspect</u> *card one*? How would they "shape" or clarify *card one*?

_____
_____.

If *card two* or *three* were the <u>primary</u> <u>card</u>, how would the other cards <u>aspect</u> that card? How would they "shape" or clarify it?

_____
_____.

If you *blended* these three cards into one meaning, what would the *new meaning* be?

_____
_____.

① Any other thoughts or opinions you would like to add? *Perhaps something we may have missed?*
_____
_____.

If your teacher has assigned you additional work, please fill in your answer here:

② _____
_____
_____
_____.

EXERCISES

These three cards came up in a spread. What do they say to you? What do you see? You can direct these cards to any situation that you feel they apply.

What are the meanings of each card (at this particular moment, *according to you*)?

_____.

What do these three cards have in common? *(if anything)*

_____.

How would *card one* get to *card three*? What is happening here?

| _____ | _____ | _____ |
| This happens (and then) | this other thing happens (and then) | this other thing happens. |

If *card one* (the one on the left) were the primary card, how would *cards two* and *three* aspect *card one*? How would they "shape" or clarify card one?

_____
_____.

If *card two* or *three* were the primary card, how would the other cards aspect that card? How would they "shape" or clarify it?

_____
_____.

If you *blended* these three cards into one meaning, what would the *new meaning* be?

_____
_____.

Any other thoughts or opinions you would like to add? *Perhaps something we may have missed?*

_____
_____.

①

If your teacher has assigned you additional work, please fill in your answer here:

_____
_____
_____
_____

②

These three cards came up in a spread. What do they say to you? What do you see? You can direct these cards to any situation that you feel they apply.

What are the meanings of each card (at this particular moment, *according to you*)?
_____.

What do these three cards have in common? *(if anything)*
_____.

How would *card one* get to *card three*? What is happening here?

_____   _____   _____
 This happens   (and then)   this other thing happens   (and then)   this other thing happens.

If *card one* (the one on the left) were the <u>primary</u> <u>card</u>, how would *cards two* a*nd three* <u>aspect</u> *card one*? How would they "shape" or clarify *card one*?

_____
_____.

If *card two* or *three* were the <u>primary</u> <u>card</u>, how would the other cards <u>aspect</u> that card? How would they "shape" or clarify it?

_____
_____.

If you *blended* these three cards into one meaning, what would the *new meaning* be?

_____
_____.

1
Any other thoughts or opinions you would like to add? *Perhaps something we may have missed?*
_____
_____.

If your teacher has assigned you additional work, please fill in your answer here:

2
_____
_____
_____
_____.

EXERCISES

These three cards came up in a spread. What do they say to you? What do you see? You can direct these cards to any situation that you feel they apply.

What are the meanings of each card (at this particular moment, *according to you*)?

_____.

What do these three cards have in common? *(if anything)*

_____.

How would *card one* get to *card three*? What is happening here?

_____   _____   _____
   This happens   *(and then)*   *this other thing happens*   *(and then)*   *this other thing happens.*

If *card one* (the one on the left) were the primary card, how would *cards two* and *three* aspect *card one*? How would they "shape" or clarify *card one*?

_____
_____.

If *card two* or *three* were the primary card, how would the other cards aspect that card? How would they "shape" or clarify it?

_____
_____.

If you *blended* these three cards into one meaning, what would the *new meaning* be?

_____
_____.

Any other thoughts or opinions you would like to add? *Perhaps something we may have missed?*

_____
_____.

①

If your teacher has assigned you additional work, please fill in your answer here:

_____
_____
_____
_____.

②

These three cards came up in a spread. What do they say to you? What do you see? You can direct these cards to any situation that you feel they apply.

What are the meanings of each card (at this particular moment, *according to you*)?
_____.

What do these three cards have in common? *(if anything)*
_____.

How would *card one* get to *card three*? What is happening here?

_____   _____   _____
This happens   (and then)   *this other thing happens*   (and then)   *this other thing happens.*

If *card one* (the one on the left) were the primary card, how would *cards two* and *three* aspect *card one*? How would they "shape" or clarify *card one*?
_____
_____.

If *card two* or *three* were the primary card, how would the other cards aspect that card? How would they "shape" or clarify it?
_____
_____.

If you *blended* these three cards into one meaning, what would the *new meaning* be?
_____
_____.

1 Any other thoughts or opinions you would like to add? *Perhaps something we may have missed?*
_____
_____.

If your teacher has assigned you additional work, please fill in your answer here:

2
_____
_____
_____
_____.

EXERCISES

These three cards came up in a spread. What do they say to you? What do you see? You can direct these cards to any situation that you feel they apply.

What are the meanings of each card (at this particular moment, *according to you*)?

_____.

What do these three cards have in common? *(if anything)*

_____.

How would *card one* get to *card three*? What is happening here?

| _____ | _____ | _____ | _____ |
| This happens | (and then) | this other thing happens | (and then) this other thing happens. |

If *card one* (the one on the left) were the <u>primary</u> <u>card</u>, how would *cards two* and *three* <u>aspect</u> *card one*? How would they "shape" or clarify card one?

_____

_____.

If *card two* or *three* were the <u>primary</u> <u>card</u>, how would the other cards <u>aspect</u> that card? How would they "shape" or clarify it?

_____

_____.

If you *blended* these three cards into one meaning, what would the *new meaning* be?

_____

_____.

Any other thoughts or opinions you would like to add? *Perhaps something we may have missed?*

_____

_____.

①

If your teacher has assigned you additional work, please fill in your answer here:

_____

_____

_____

_____.

②

These three cards came up in a spread. What do they say to you? What do <u>you</u> see? You can direct these cards to any situation that you feel they apply.

What are the meanings of each card (at this particular moment, *according to you*)?
_____.

What do these three cards have in common? *(if anything)*
_____.

How would *card one* get to *card three*? What is happening here?

_____ _____ _____
 This happens *(and then)* *this other thing happens* *(and then)* *this other thing happens.*

If *card one* (the one on the left) were the <u>primary card</u>, how would *cards two* and *three* <u>aspect</u> *card one*? How would they "shape" or clarify *card one*?

_____
_____.

If *card two* or *three* were the <u>primary card</u>, how would the other cards <u>aspect</u> that card? How would they "shape" or clarify it?

_____
_____.

If you *blended* these three cards into one meaning, what would the *new meaning* be?

_____
_____.

1 Any other thoughts or opinions you would like to add? *Perhaps something we may have missed?*
_____.

If your teacher has assigned you additional work, please fill in your answer here:

2
_____
_____
_____.

Okay, let's review:

Before you continue, you should have practiced each of the previous exercises, and developed an initial understanding of your *study deck*. Even if you had to cheat a bit (by looking up "our" meanings in the back of the book—and that's okay too), **you should be able to pull any card from your *study deck* and be able to say,** "When this card comes up in a *reading* it makes me think of _____." It is always okay to look up the meaning of any card *whenever you want,* but we don't want you to become reliant on any book to tell you what this or that card means. Ultimately your understanding of your deck will be the deciding factor on how good you are and how much fun you have *reading* the Tarot. **Great Tarot readers know how to listen to their inner voices,** and know when the "traditional meaning" applies, and when it *does not*. The fastest and easiest way to develop your inner voice is to start seeing what the cards say to you from the very beginning, and use the "traditional meanings" as guides rather than hard, fast rules. Otherwise, you will just end up like that lady in the *8 of Swords*.

So, we would like you to keep practicing the exercises. These will turn you into a *very good* Tarot *reader* very fast, but now that you have a rudimentary feel for your "minor" Arcana, we want you to add your "major" Arcana to your *study deck* to make it your *practice deck* (which is the same deck you will be *reading* for your friends and clients eventually). The only difference is that when you see a "major" Arcana card, it may seem a bit stilted, authoritative, static, or even overwhelmingly vague at first in comparison to your familiar "minor" Arcana. Don't hesitate to look in the back of the book and review what we have to say on any particular card whenever you get stuck or desire some "extra information" or *verification* of what you already know or feel.

Now that your deck is complete again, do all of the exercises in this book again, and use your *practice deck* for all kinds of *readings* and exercises. Try out new ideas and fun ways of shuffling and *spreading* your cards. This is "you" time, and it does not belong to your friends or your clients. You have to answer to no one (but yourself). This is when you get to experiment and play, and no one can (or will) judge you. Most of all, this is where you develop a deep working relationship with your cards (off stage) so that when you do go "on stage" and give a *reading* to a friend or a stranger, you will be confident and relaxed, knowing how your cards "talk to you" even if your "clients" don't want to hear the actual truth that the cards want to impart. Sometimes people will come to you and expect you to tell them exactly what they already believe. By practicing regularly with the exercises we have laid out for you, and trying out various *spreads* (to see which ones you like the best), you are preparing yourself for *any* occasion.

The next set of exercises is meant to help you sharpen your skills thoroughly by looking at events from a completely new perspective. If you can (at some point) successfully complete the following exercises you will be on your way to developing the ability to *read* events from the distant past and even the future with great accuracy. If you have any questions that you simply cannot find answers to in this book or through your teacher, you are always welcome to hop online to our forums and ask anyone there for advice or suggestions.

Really Advanced Exercises . . .

For no other reason than the pleasant fact that we were born with shriveled up coal-black raisins for hearts, we have designed this next set of exercises for those of you who enjoy a little pain occasionally. We advise anyone with a low tolerance for mental stress to please simply pass these few pages by as if they do not exist. *(This part will not be on the final exam—unless you attend <u>our</u> mystery school.)*

The following exercises will require the use of your personal Tarot deck WITH all of the "major" Arcana cards included *(choose any particular deck that you are comfortable with)*. These exercises contain no images to reference, no samples, or examples. If you choose to test your skill with any of the following, we are assuming that you have completed the previous exercises and have a solid grasp of Tarot fundamentals as well as a personal relationship with your favorite deck(s). Feel free to redesign any of these exercises for your own <u>personal</u> use, and *do let us know* if you end up conjuring up your own sadistic Tarot brain-teasers (as long as they are truly fair and equitable for student training). That being said, we hope you enjoy the following:

1: Pick any *three cards* from your *practice deck* to illustrate getting a raise from your boss.

    1a: Change *one card* above to turn your boss into a tyrant.

    1b: Change any *one card* above (1a) to make the raise insubstantial or irrelevant in its ridiculous *smallness*.

    1c: Change any *one card* above (1a or 1b) to make that raise a promotion.

2: Pick any *three cards* from your *practice deck* to reflect meeting a new love interest, someone who might be a potential spouse one day.

    2a: Change *one card* above to turn that into a date.

    2b: Change any *one card* above (2a) to make that same situation a *bad* date.

    2c: Change any *one card* above (2a or 2b) to make that same situation *a complete disaster*.

    2d: Change any *one card* above to make that *justified*.

3: Pick any *one card* from your *practice deck* to indicate a bartender.

    3a: Add *one card* to give him (or her) a job in an expensive night club, a place with a high amount of energy.

    3b: Now fire him. Use *one card* to make it clear that all three cards show him being fired from his high-paying job.

    3c: Now add a *fourth card* as a follow-up or an "*and then . . .*" card showing him moving.

    3d: Change that fourth card into a follow-up or an "*and then . . .*" card showing him <u>getting a new job</u>.

    3e: Change the fourth card into a follow-up or an "*and then . . .*" card showing him <u>buying a car</u>.

    3f: *Change <u>that</u> fourth card and add a fifth card* as well, as a *follow-up pair* showing him <u>getting a job on a cruise ship</u>.

3g: *Remove* the fifth card, *change* the fourth card
as a follow-up or an *"and then . . ."* card
showing him <u>going to vocational school</u>.

3h: Change that fourth card *again* as a follow-up or an
"and then . . ." card showing him <u>becoming a priest</u>.

4: Pick any *two cards* from your *practice deck* to designate a student artist.

    4a: Add *one card* above to give the artist her first art opening.

    4b: Add *one card* above (4a) to make the art opening a
huge success for the artist *(lots of people come to see her art,
maybe some artwork sells that night)*.

    4c: Add *another card* above (4b) to turn the art opening
into an event where she gets a huge commission
to do art, or she gets signed to a fancy New York agency.

5: Pick any *four cards* from your *practice deck* to suggest a healthy, happy relationship between a man and a wife.

    5a: Change *one card* above to turn that into an unhappy one.

    5b: Change *one card* above to turn that into an abusive one.

    5c: Add *one card* above (5b) to get help and protection.

    5d: Add *one card* above (5c) to finally resolve the situation.

6: Pick any *one card* from your *practice deck* to indicate a lawyer or a judge.

    6a: Add *one card* to make him go on a picnic.

    6b: Add *another card* to <u>make it rain</u> on his picnic.

    6c: Add *another card* to give him a pet (at the rainy picnic).

    6d: Now add *one card* that changes the entire meaning
of the *spread* and indicates something entirely different,
but something that you can justify and clearly defend
its meaning.

7: Pick any *two cards* from your *practice deck* to denote a single mother.

    7a: Add *one card* above to give her a boyfriend.

    7b: Add *another card* to make him a *good* boyfriend.

    7c: Add *another card* to make him propose.

    7d: Now give her a job she *loves*. Do this by removing
two cards, and replacing them with *three* of your
choosing, but none of the ones you removed.

    7e: Now add *two cards:* one representing *her past*
(that she is running away from, something unpleasant),
and the other card shows us *what she is afraid of*.

    7f: Now add *two more cards:* one representing
her hopes and dreams (she hopes to own a huge house
in the country one day), and the other card shows us
her secret allies that will help her reach her goals.

7g: *Open up* her "secret allies" card using *three new cards* to show us who or what are her "secret allies" and how they can and will help her reach her goals.

8: Pick any *eight cards* to show a wealthy house in turmoil. The house patriarch has died, leaving a widow (protagonist) who is being manipulated or courted by an evil man (villain), while her various children (support characters) senselessly squabble over their expected inheritance, while money is slipping away.

8a: Add *one card* above to indicate the villain's motives.

8b: Add *two or three cards* to "solve" all of her (current) problems.

8c: Take the widow's card, make it the *significator* in a *new reading* and give her a new life based on what you now know. Use any *spread* you like, but include her "past" and her concerns.

9: Using as few cards as possible, please accomplish all of the following:

9a: Pick a card to represent "the Devil."

9b: Now fire him for doing a lousy job.

9c: Make him wash dishes at a roadside diner.

9d: Now make him sell his soul to the *King of Coins*.

9e: Show us what he got for his efforts.

9f: Make him fight an angel and lose.

9g: Have *Death* laugh at him (include "minor" Arcana to complete this effect).

9h: Now remove all of the cards except for *Death*. Using him as a *significator card* in a new *reading*, have him go to the mall to buy a smoothie, but he doesn't have enough money so he has to beg for change. But then he *gets* money, enjoys his beverage and is very happy. Do this in a linear format.

10: Pick any *two cards* from your *practice deck* to denote a college professor. Then, using as few cards as possible, please accomplish the following:

10a: Have him quit his job and become a mechanic in a completely new country.

10b: Now have his daughter call him up and ask him for money for some reason *(spread three cards beneath her to show her reasons for wanting or needing money)*.

10c: Have him meet the Pope, and they become fishing buddies.

10d: Lastly, using *five more cards,* give him a long and healthy life with many interesting adventures.

The above exercises varied from the mundane (experiences you will encounter on any given day of doing *readings* for your clients) to the bizarre, *which you will also encounter* if you give enough *readings* over your lifetime. Most professional psychics easily give upwards of ten or even twenty thousand *readings* over their careers. Very few give more than that as the propensity for "psychic burnout" escalates after hearing enough people's problems. Take your time and have fun *reading*. Perfect your skills over time; and when it stops being fun, *stop doing it*.

Section Three

SPREADS AND STUFF

When you want to have a question answered using the Tarot, you will almost always be doing "spreads" (versus merely drawing a single card for an answer). A *spread* is an organized way of plopping down a certain number of cards to fit the needs of your question. A "traditional spread" is one that has been accepted by a large number of people. This does not make it any better than any *spread* you may design on your own, but it does make it more universal and easier to compare notes on. The number of cards you use in your *spread* is entirely a personal choice; but to start with, it is best to try out some *traditional spreads* so that if you have any questions, you can relate your concerns to someone who might help. It is far easier to get help posting a note in a forum, or asking your teacher, *"The Knight of Swords came up in my 'Hopes and Dreams' spot of the Celtic Cross for my love life . . ."* than it is asking something like, *"Hi, um . . . I designed my own spread and the Knight of Swords came up . . ."*

The nuts and bolts of designing your own *spreads* are extremely simple actually. *Use what works.* This means that you should practice a <u>lot</u> before you start inventing anything too crazy. Many of the *traditional spreads* will serve you well, and they can always be used, even after you have been *reading* cards for a few decades.

Before we get into any *multi-card spreads* that use several cards, we are going to cover some basic *mini-spreads*. These *one-, two-,* and *three-card spreads* are viable in their own right, but they will also help you in your *multi-card spreads* by showing you how cards interact with each other. They will also help you when you need to draw *clarification cards* in a larger *spread*. All of the following methods examined are valid and will produce solid answers for <u>you</u> if you are truly in tune with your cards. However, the true test that only time and practice will impart is knowing exactly what *spread* to *toss* for any given question. When in doubt, remember *Ockham's razor,* or *"the Law of Parsimony,"* meaning here that you shouldn't complicate a *reading* by using a lot of cards simply because your deck hands you 78 to choose from. Use *spreads* <u>you are comfortable with</u>, and if using a *three-card spread* will give you enough knowledge to decide whether the question warrants a *twenty-eight-card spread,* then by all means do so.

SPREADS

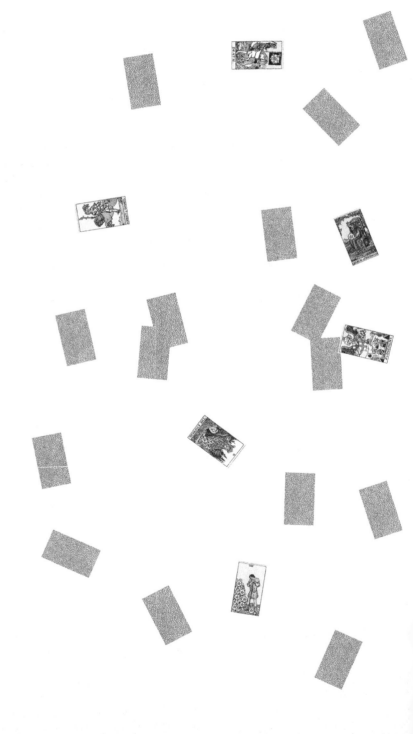

The hardest spread—*EVER!!*

You may never use the method we are about to relate, *not because this spread doesn't work,* but because it requires so much time and patience (not to mention *space*) that it just isn't very popular, nor economical, in any way, when you measure the amount of effort to result. But it is a fun *spread to cast,* and it does represent the very least effort you can put into *casting a spread* (as you draw no cards at all), and *the most effort* you will ever have to endure in successfully interpreting one. Here's how it works: Spend three days meditating on your question (it should be a very large question, obviously), carefully shuffling your cards as you consider the various aspects involved when you are awake; and when you are asleep, sleep with your cards under your pillow. Clear out a space, focus your question firmly in your mind, and toss your entire Tarot deck into the air.

That's it!

That's all there is to it. Now . . . <u>read *'em*</u>! Of course, this is where the hell (er . . . "fun!" *Sorry!*) begins. You will need to note each card's placement (front, right, left, behind you), its relative distance from you and to other cards, whether it is face up or face down, whether it is buried or buries another card, whether that card is reversed or not, and what that card is and its effect on the *reading,* as well as what cards touch it and are near it. We only mention this *spread* here as it is the very least amount of effort you can do (just toss 'em into the air!), and it is also part of the final exam in certain secret mystery schools, and if you ever plan on attending one, you should probably get some practice in now . . .

SPREADS

One-card Spreads

"Pick a card, any card..."

One-card spreads are not very glamorous, but they are <u>infinitely</u> <u>helpful</u> in almost any situation. Here are some of the ways you will probably find yourself using them over the next few years:

1: The first, and most economical, is a simple choice. This works best for matters of little or no consequence, and when you want to get in some Tarot practice but you are "out and about." Think of your question and draw a card from the deck at random. *This method has a few caveats you should know in advance.* First, you should <u>focus</u> on your <u>question</u>. It does no good—and infinite harm—if you get in the habit of drawing cards for answers without seriously (if even briefly) considering the question.

Proceeding without first developing a <u>bond</u> with your cards, you become nothing more than a *random card generator,* and you can expect no more reliable answers than a computer program might hand you. You don't have to meditate for hours on end before drawing a card, but take a moment and see and feel your question as clearly as you can, or the results you get over time will convince you that you have no talent, and that would be a shame.

So you think of your question and draw a card. Now what? Let's step back a moment (again) and state something of vital importance. Tarot has *rules*. In any *spread* you must know the basic rules of the *spread,* meaning that when you place a card in a certain "slot," you *already know* what that "slot" means. It would be impossible to give consistently accurate *readings* if you simply threw cards down and assigned meanings to their locations as you went *(at least until you have developed your intuitive abilities to near god-like status).* But let's leave the fairy tales for another time. When a card comes up, you need to know how you will *feel* and react if it comes up *reversed,* or if it is a *Sword* rather than a *Coin,* or a man rather than a woman, a family, or a crowd.

By knowing these "rules" ahead of time, you take a lot of pressure off of yourself. *"Oh, It's the Knight of Swords reversed. I am probably being too cautious,"* is far more productive and fun than *"Oh, it's a Knight, but he's upside down. Does that mean someone is angry at me?"*

Here are a few things to consider before tossing any cards out, *in any situation.* These are things only you can decide for yourself eventually, although you might as well know now that there is no shortage of people who will gladly make it their duty in life to tell you how *you should* handle each of these. Rather than take an authoritarian approach, we will simply make suggestions based on centuries of advice we have learned and found that works. Use what you like, discard the rest.

What to do when a card...

a) *is reversed.* Some "experts" give a "traditional meaning" *(we have 78 of those at the end of this book if you like),* while other "experts" will tell you to simply rotate the card back to its upright position "as the cards are quite capable of expressing themselves if *you* are skilled enough to properly interpret their intent." We favor *reading a reversed* card <u>as just that</u>. Its meaning is limited, skewed, reversed, or altered in some way as to change its "normal" state.

b) *flips out of the deck.* Sometimes you will be focused on a question and (this usually happens mid-shuffle) a card flips, jumps, or sails out of the deck and onto the table, or even across the room towards your cat. The "universe" is telling you something, but what is it? Should that card be taken as a priority? What if it doesn't make any sense when you look at it? What if it falls out of the deck *face down?* Personally, we go with it, examining the card; and if we can't make sense of it right away, we set it aside and proceed with the *reading*, keeping an eye on it in case it fits in as we know more. After all, accidents *do occasionally happen,* and there is no sense looking too hard for omens when working divination, or you will drive yourself crazy.

c) *obviously makes no sense at all.* Okay, so you were asking your deck whether you should have macaroni and cheese for lunch or spaghetti, and *The Tower* pops out. Does this card mean you will accidentally knock the pot off of the stove spilling pasta on the floor? Should you ignore that card and pull a different one? Knowing ahead of time what you will do *"no matter what"* before you start any *reading* and building positive habits (with few and rare exceptions) will create a set of basic guidelines that make your *readings* more reliable and less confusing. In fact, if you start out doing this early on, it will make the Tarot *infinitely easier* to learn. Don't worry about "what could be." Worry about *what is—right now,* and deal with the rest of it as it comes. This will save you endless amounts of time and hassle. Once you know what your basic personal guidelines are whenever you draw a card "at random" from the deck, the next question is simply one of *what the card means.* You have your question in mind, and you have an answer. Obviously you will have to have a certain set of rules in place to handle simple "yes or no" questions.

2: Next, we have the situation where you are nagged by someone *who sees you* with Tarot cards and assumes that you have the time, skill, and desire to stop whatever it is that you are doing and give them deep, profound, and highly personal advice that will make their life easier and more fun. You can't really blame anyone who sees you with a deck of Tarot cards for coming up to you and asking. Tarot cards are a real conversation starter. But if you *are* engaged in something, or you just don't feel like doing a full-on *reading* at the moment, you can pull a card for them and explain it. This is a very polite way of brushing someone off but still giving them something free, and (hopefully) helpful.

3: In this particular situation *you are in the middle of a reading,* and your friend or client is talking (and talking . . .), and you simply think of one particular point of their dilemma and casually draw a card while they continue. Some professional *readers* do this all of the time. They encourage their clients to explain their concerns, and they draw cards at various points, looking for verification, lies, advice, and whatnot. All in all, this is a highly effective method once you are comfortable with your deck. You may already have your *spread* cast, or you may be politely listening to them when you do this.

Two-card Spreads

Two-card *spreads* are usually drawn as *a pair,* where both cards contribute to one central meaning (rather than two meanings, as in "*this* will happen, and then *that* will happen next"). Of course, like every "pair" one finds in life, these will function less like "a pair of Aces" in poker, where both *Aces* are of equal value. In life it all too often seems that when two or more people get together to do something, one person works harder than the other(s). Tarot cards are no different. Your *two-card spread* will often have one card leaning on, or even defining, the other. The trick is to be attuned enough to see if one of the cards is pulling the lion's share of the meaning, or they seem to balance nicely.

As an example: Your boss assigns you a workload on Wednesday that looks more like a small mountain than a "short stack of paperwork I am certain you can whip out by Friday afternoon, but it *must* be done *before next Monday.*" You are working furiously at your task, but Thursday follows Wednesday (as it usually does) and it seems that either evil shoemaker elves are adding fresh sheets of paperwork to your load every evening after you leave work or the stack has found a way to replicate itself. Either way, it is starting to look like your weekend is going to be spent *at the office* instead of *at the beach.* So you decide to playfully ask your Tarot deck for advice. You decide to draw two cards to see what that response is before wasting any more time worrying about *work.*

You draw the *Knight of Wands* and the *8 of Coins*. ("Get busy time!") Wow, thrilling. On the bright side, if you bought a UV bulb from the hardware store, you could at least get a tan while plowing through all of that paperwork. As long as you have your answer you might as well make plans. With the boss going fishing this weekend he will be nowhere in sight, so perhaps you can convince your best friend to keep you company and have some pizza delivered so the weekend is not a total waste.

In this particular case, the *8 of Coins* bore the brunt of the meaning *(work, work, work!)* while the *Knight of Wands* indicated a need to draw up and charge right in (after doing what you can to seek some support—the *Knight of Wands* prefers to rally the troops if possible, whereas the *Knight of Swords* just charges in and "asks questions later").

True to his nature, however, the *Knight of Wands* comes through with a surprise visit by a coworker who secretly has a crush on you (like that matters as long as he helps!) and he spends Saturday afternoon with you and your best friend finishing off the never-ending pile of paperwork, playing music, making funny cartoons of the boss, and salvaging your Sunday for the beach.

Two-card spreads are useful and quick. They clarify information more than a *one-card spread* can, but they can occasionally be difficult to decipher if you haven't concentrated properly, or shuffled your deck at all, and you get "random" cards. As noted, one card will usually—but not always—be the focus. Time and persistent proper practice will reveal *all*.

Three-card Spreads

Three-card spreads are a mainstay of Tarot *readings*, and you will probably "draw three cards" more often than just about anything else. *Three-card spreads* are extremely useful and very flexible as well, but they can bring even more confusion when you are first starting out. The important thing to remember in the beginning is not to fuss over the order the cards come out in—not if you are drawing them as *three*. For example, the basic mechanics are that you could draw three cards off of the top of the deck, draw three cards (all together) from the middle of the deck, draw one card at a time from various parts of the deck—or draw one card, and then draw "two more." All of this over-analytical gibberish simply means this: No matter *how* you choose to draw your cards, *draw them as three* (mental focus), or you are simply drawing a *one-card spread* followed by a *two-card spread*. Decide beforehand how you will draw them. This is something you need to develop into a habit, rather than anything you need to worry about. Once in a while you will change how you draw your cards, or circumstances will throw cards at you. That is fine. Exceptions are just that: *exceptions to the rule*. For your own reliability (and sanity), simply develop a style that you like and stick with it.

What you can do with three cards . . .

Three cards can be blended, they can indicate several forces independently or working together, or they can have one primary card supported by two others. You can assign meanings (in advance) to the first, second, and third card to show up. This is a very popular method among many *readers* (*past, present future; you, your spouse, what's in between you; physical, mental, emotional; linear (time) spreads—as in* "this will happen and then this other thing, and then this will be the result; and so on, ad nauseum).

Here's what you need to know "right now." Practice drawing three cards in response to serious questions to get the feel of the process. Look for patterns in the cards (two or three of the same suit or number, several face cards or "majors," cards with similar meanings such as the *8 of Cups* and the *6 of Swords* showing up in the same *three-card spread*). Your ability to spot these patterns, combined or similar meanings, and various ways cards *aspect, support, augment,* or *clarify* each other will quickly develop your skill *in all of the readings* you do.

Three-card spreads are also great for *opening up* cards. *Opening up a card* is simply drawing three cards to explain one that is giving you trouble, or is ominous enough for you to want more information on that particular card without having to *tear down* the entire massive *spread* you have laid out just to do a new *spread* on that card.

Practice doing *one-card spreads* and then *opening up* that card. This will give you quick, easy, and fast answers that help you address several issues, even hypothetical ones you create simply to develop your bond with your deck. Do this as often as possible as this one exercise will develop your skills fast, and you can do it anywhere, at any time, and you can grab the four cards and "pack everything up" with no hassle, should you suddenly need to be somewhere (or if you get bored).

Multiple-card Spreads

There are more *multiple-card spreads* than you really should ever bother to try out. Anyone can invent their own *spread*, and the popularity of the web has brought most of them online. **Master your one-, two-, and three-card spreads first** while you develop your skills at combining, comparing, contrasting (etc.) cards, because those same skills apply to every *spread* you will ever do. Please also remember that the more cards you *pull*, the more time you will spend answering one question. You can always *pull* one, two, or three cards and get a valid answer for a question. But if you get in the habit of casting *forty-two-card spreads* on a regular basis, you will be spending hours on each *spread*, and that is time we hope you will be getting paid for.

That being said, there are a few basic *spreads* you will want to know. We have provided a few easy and reliable *"yes or no" spreads,* an easy to learn *timing spread,* and a *choice spread* which is helpful for making decisions. But be absolutely sure to study and practice the *Celtic Cross*. It is the most well-known *spread* in the world, and your clients will expect you to know it. We will skip origins and histories for the moment, as all of that is debatable and does not make you a better Tarot *reader* by knowing one version of the story or another.

Quick and Easy "Yes or No" Spreads

A lot of your *readings* will involve many "yes or no" questions. Having a good "yes or no" *spread* that you feel comfortable with (one you can trust for quality advice on a regular basis) will make your job—and life—a lot less stressful, and gain you a reputation as an expert card *reader* quickly. Most of the "accuracy factor" will come from your connection with your deck far more than the method you select for discerning how to divine a "yes" versus a "no." Anyone can play with cards. In fact, a computer can spit out *readings* and interpretations of cards faster than any ten professional *readers* put together. But speed is nothing compared to quality of the answer. Always remember that. You are not a computer. You need to develop a solid bond with your cards and sharpen your instincts so that your answers are <u>reliable</u>. So here are a few ways to pull "yes" or no" answers. Please try them all, invent new ones, ask your teacher what methods *they* like, and decide what works for you over time.

Aces-up

This is an incredibly old method that is rather time and energy consuming; but if you don't mind your clients <u>touching your deck</u> (or if you have a reliable deck that you *do* let them put their grubby little hands all over), this is good for them to have a feel in the action. Hand them the deck you want them to use. Ask them to focus an image of their question. Then have them shuffle the deck, or mix the cards from one hand to the other, thoroughly (give them 2-3 minutes) and have them explain what their question is and why they want to know. The point is to infuse *their energy* into the deck along with the energy of their question. When you feel they have shuffled enough, take the deck from them and flip over 40 cards, one at a time. Do this quickly. The whole point is to see how many *Aces* come up in the first 40 cards. If three or four *Aces* show themselves, the answer is a solid yes. If two *Aces* turn over, the answer is more of a "maybe" and doesn't look very good: <u>This calls for a reading why</u>. Try the *Roundabout Spread* to help them figure out how to get what they want to happen. If one or no *Aces* show up at all, the answer is a definite no and they should reconsider what they want or how they plan on going about getting it.

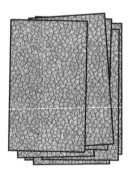

Tarot deck

"flipped card" pile

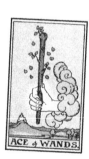

Hey! <u>Look at you!</u> Three Aces up means you are probably going to get your wish after all. Four Aces would qualify as an uncontested "Yes!!" But three Aces shows that <u>only a little effort</u> will be required on your part. Don't blow this opportunity!

"Up or Down Vote"

This *spread* requires that you *read* cards *reversed*, and that your deck is thoroughly shuffled. **Flip one card.** That's all there is to it.

Method One: "Up" means *yes*, "reversed" means *no*.

Method Two: You can also use suit meanings. *Wands* means yes, but you will have to work for it; *Cups* means that it will come to you naturally; *Coins* means it will come with a price—if at all; and *Swords* means no. "Major" Arcana cards mean, "It is in the hands of the gods," *(as in "good luck!")*.

Alternatively, you can consider if, "the card is generally positive or is it generally negative." Most of our students have found this method is a bit less reliable, but we mention it here in case you have better success with it. The whole point of a simple *one-card "yes or no" spread* is simplicity and accuracy. As you build your skill in this, you may even want to try *dowsing* with your cards, versus using a *witching stick*.

Examples:

Method One

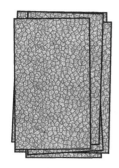    

Tarot deck   "Yes"   "No"   "Yes"   "No"

Method Two

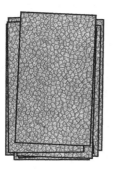    

Tarot deck   "Um . . . no"   "Yes. Now get to work!"   "It will cost you to get in."   "Bring some money . . ."

"Gyaaa! How long will this take?!!"

This is a fun little *spread* for your impatient clients. You have answered their question and now they want to know when. "When, when, when?!!" You will get asked that a lot over the years. When will I meet a guy I like? When will my husband finally learn to put the seat *down*? When will my stupid boss give me a *raise*? This quick *spread* will show you how soon something will come to pass. You have to know exactly what is that you want (or want to know), and a rough time frame you are asking about (the next 30 days, the next year . . .).

For example, you are at your favorite coffeehouse practicing your skills, and one of your best friends plops down and starts whining about her love life. She looks at you and asks you to, *"Ask the cards when I will finally meet a guy who's not a complete and total idiot!"* Being a saint (as well as a good friend), you smile at her and ignore the fact that she completely interrupted your practice, and you *toss out this spread,* looking out over the coming 12 months. Here are the results you get:

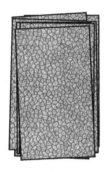

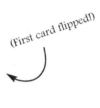

Tarot deck   *"flipped card" pile*

Well . . . that was easy. You explain to her that every card in <u>this</u> *spread* (being that you were looking out over the next 12 months) is approximately 4-5 days, so it looks like she should meet someone in the next few days. She nods and says something absently that sounds a lot like *"That's nice . . ."* and suddenly jumps up from the table to *"go talk to that hot guy at the counter."* The way this *spread* works is simply to pick a card from your knowledge of the Tarot that answers the question at hand. In this case, *The Lovers,* the *2 of Cups,* the *10 of Cups,* the *Ace of Cups,* or even the *6 of Cups* would have shown encounters that your friend might end up turning into relationships.

The process goes like this: Ask your question while shuffling and take the time to think of what cards you would consider a *strong* "positive" answer to your question. Also decide what time frame you are looking at. Once you are satisfied that you have passed the question into the deck and have shuffled thoroughly enough, draw the number of cards below. If one of your chosen cards shows up, you have your answer. ***If none of your cards show up,*** the answer is that you have to wait, or remedy the situation to make it more likely that *what you want* will come to pass. Make changes in your life and try again later. Here are the general guidelines for various time frames:

If you are asking about something you expect <u>within a week</u>, draw 7 cards to start with. If you are asking about something <u>over the next 30 days</u>, draw 15 cards, one at a time of course. <u>For a year</u>, flip no more than 21 cards. Flip each one over and mentally count until you reach your maximum draw or until you get one of your preselected cards.

This or That

Another dilemma your clients will come to you with regularly is the classic "this or that" scenario. *"Should I stay with my girlfriend or go after that actress I met at a party the other night?"* or *"Should I keep my current job or quit and start my own business this summer?"* or *"Should I move to Cleveland or Cincinnati?"* People want advice on how to live their lives, but they want credible answers, not guesswork or opinions. What you need is a reliable "this or that" *spread* for occasions such as this. Fortunately, we have one below. We hope you will like it as well as we do. The best part is that you already know how to do it. It is a simple *two-card reading* followed by *opening up* each card. This is why we wanted you to practice, practice, practice your *one-, two-, and three-card spreads*. Some of your best *spreads* will be combinations of *one-, two-* and *three-card readings*, and others will incorporate the blending, merging, comparing, contrasting, and *opening up* of one or more cards in the *spread* you throw. Don't ever mistake complexity for accuracy. Simplicity <u>works</u> (and it is a *lot* less stressful on you). You can always add cards to any *reading* if you feel the need at the time.

Step one: Select a significator card for <u>each</u> <u>choice</u> in the matter at hand. Lay them out face up, side by side, but with enough room between them for the rest of the reading. Tell your client that these represent the options they are considering. Make sure they understand this. Shuffle the deck (or have them shuffle if you are so inclined).

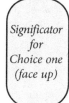

Step two: Flip one card over on top of each significator card as an "answer" to your client's question. Verify that these cards generally make sense before you proceed to the next step.

(In our example we have moved the flipped cards off to the side so you can clearly see the significator cards below.)

Step three: Now simply "open" each of the answer cards up for a better picture of "what and why" things are predicted to turn out this way. Ask questions and compare what your client says to what you see in your spread.

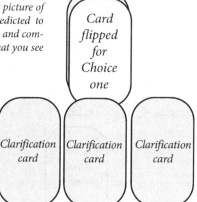 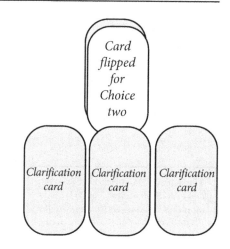

This is a great spread for picking elections. We know—we have been using it consistently in the past electoral cycles.

The Celtic Cross

This is the most popular *spread* in the world. Movie directors use it a lot, further increasing its fame. It is a reliable *spread*; certainly not the *best spread* ever created, but it works for most routine situations, and it is easy to remember. There are a few variations on this *spread* and you can use whichever one you fancy (they all work just as well as any other), but the version we will teach you here is the one we were taught, back in the Stone Age. We use it *because it makes sense*. Use your own best judgment in your *readings*. Here is the basic layout:

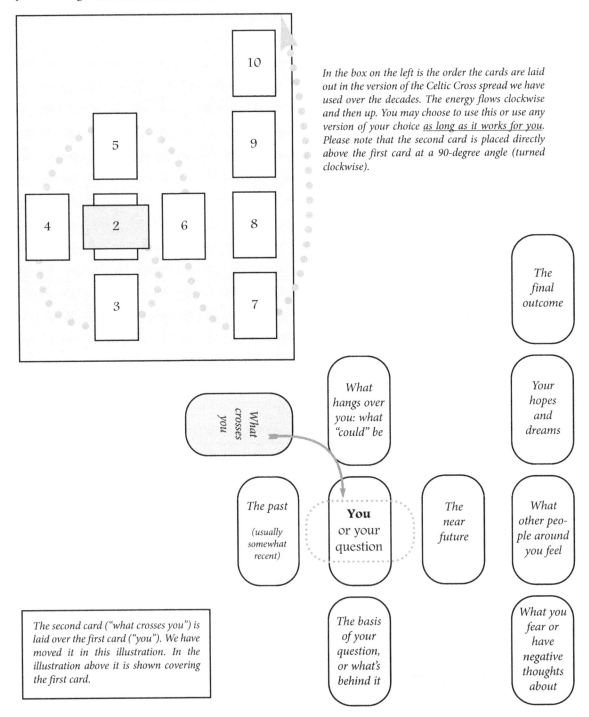

In the box on the left is the order the cards are laid out in the version of the Celtic Cross spread we have used over the decades. The energy flows clockwise and then up. You may choose to use this or use any version of your choice *as long as it works for you*. Please note that the second card is placed directly above the first card at a 90-degree angle (turned clockwise).

The second card ("what crosses you") is laid over the first card ("you"). We have moved it in this illustration. In the illustration above it is shown covering the first card.

> NOTE: To significate or not to significate? That is the question you will have to face every *reading*. If you talk to enough people, you will undoubtedly hear all sorts of passionate arguments about whether you "should always" (or not) use a special card to indicate or "significate" the person, place, or thing you are asking about. Use one if you like. <u>End of story</u>.
>
> Why use one at all? Well, they tend to make you look more professional to your clients. They also give you something to focus on (the card), and a placeholder for the rest of your *spread*. If you need help understanding the significance of the *significator* (sorry), please look up "Significator" in the Glossary for a full rundown on exactly what it is.
>
> One other thing about *significators:* You can use it as a placeholder to start your *spread,* or as the first card of your *spread*. Once again, if you talk to enough people, you will hear arguments on both sides of this issue. Do what your teacher says for now, and see how that works out. If you do not have a teacher at the moment, we recommend trying out *significators,* and placing the *spread* on top of them, as if they were part of the tablecloth. Then later on try using them as the first card of your *spread*. This is what practice is for: to find out what works for *you*. Never, ever, <u>ever</u> let anyone convince you that "practice" is simply repetition. "Practice" is your personal time where you sharpen your skills, experiment, and do <u>whatever you want</u> free from judgment.

Things you should know about the Celtic Cross spread . . .

First and foremost: Unlike other *spreads* you already know, this is a <u>general</u> *spread*. It provides an overview of a situation, looking at the various factors involved, including how everything came to be. This *spread* is good for general occasions and vague questions (like "Will I find love?"). Other times you will need more specific or targeted *spreads* to give you direct answers to your questions. Learn and practice this *spread* as it will serve you well, but do not rely solely on it.

Okay, let's go over what each *card position* of the *spread* entails. As noted earlier, the whole purpose of a *spread* is to assign set meanings to *card positions,* so that every time a card falls in that slot, you know exactly what that *position* means, and you simply apply that card's meaning to it. <u>This is why it is so important</u> for you to actually know how to *read* the cards, to have them talk to you, rather than simply memorize some meaning or symbolism someone or some book (like this one) once told you was "the only one true answer." If there were only one true answer, we could simply use computers to tell our fortunes. <u>You need to know what the cards say to *you*</u>. Any *spread* you *throw* (or *cast*) **is simply an organizational tool to make hearing what the cards are trying to tell you** infinitely more easy. That said, here is the breakdown for the version of the *Celtic Cross* we have found to work the best for us over the years:

Card 1: *(not the significator)* This card represents "you"; being the situation at hand, the event, place, person, thing, or whatever the issue is that you are *reading*. If you are using a *significator,* this is a *clarifying card* as to what is "really going on" to the *significator,* whether that is a person, place, or thing. If you are not using a *significator,* this card holds the same meaning. You simply have not used a card from the deck to *signify* the "thing" you are *reading*. **The importance of this card is** that it <u>verifies</u> the *spread*. This card should easily match your understanding or impressions of the matter at hand. If not, look at the second, third, and fourth cards. Unless those cards are <u>spot on</u>, then you haven't shuffled well enough, or were unclear in asking your question. You should reshuffle your deck (more carefully this time) and relax, focus on the matter at hand, and <u>listen</u> to what your cards tell you about "when to *cast the spread.*"

Card 2: *"What crosses you (for good or bad)."* This is the first "active" card of the *reading*. As an example: If your *significator card* were a baseball player, the first card would be him standing at home plate with a bat in his hand ready to swing at the next ball the pitcher throws at him. This card would be the actual ball flying at him (at 90 miles per hour). The act of being in the baseball park ready to have a baseball lobbed at you is "a situation." It is static, but it is in the present, or "ready to be acted upon." This card comes flying at you and WHAM! What happens next? This card reveals a lot of *why* your *querent* is asking you for answers. If they have been truthful with you and you have prepared your deck and yourself to answer that question, this card will tell you immediately what is *really going on*. One more metaphor: If the first card were a picnic your *querent* happened to be at, this card would tell you whether it was raining (or sunny, or whether they were generally having a good time, or if the potato salad had gone bad). Before anything else happens, this card screams out the immediate situation and provides the basis for every other card you will interpret.

Card 3: This is an interesting card because it shows the hidden or unseen forces behind the question. It reveals why your querent wants to know what's going on. It often works with the next card (the recent past) and can actually be something *from* the past. Other times it will be a suspicion they hold in their heads, or even something that is actually happening, whether they happen to actually know it or they simply suspect it right now. Use this card to help form a foundation of understanding of the situation before you get into any final predictions.

Card 4: *"The (usually recent) past."* Pretty straightforward location here. This is either something that has happened, a state of being, or the *cause* before the *effect*. This card location reflects something that directly affects the question or situation, so it may be something from the distant past if that thing was extremely powerful. Use this card as reference and/or verification of the *spread,* but don't fuss over it too much unless it obviously needs to be addressed to the querent.

Card 5: *"What could be."* This card is like the *Sword of Damocles**. It "hangs over your head" and *"could become if..."* This card is highly dependent upon circumstance and action, but it is a precursor to any "final result," and generally represents options for the near future, or what will happen (unless a direct change of course is undertaken). Compare this to *card 10* (the final outcome, or end-result) to see if there is continuity of philosophy, emotional connection, or direct physical action. Usually you will see parallels in these two card spots. NOTE: Some *readers* prefer the term *"this crowns you"* (and if that single strand of hair breaks, it just might!).

Card 6: *"This comes next."* This will happen. Before you get to your final result, this card must be crossed. Compare this card to *card 4* and then to *card 3*. Look casually for patterns and associations but don't force associations or make leaps of logic just yet. Do a quick comparison to *card 5* to see if there is a congruency of thought and action. Then do a quick look at *card 10* to see if there is a flow of action or a synchronicity of purpose. Ideally *cards 5, 6,* and *10* will all work together, but how often does life work that way? How often do any of us have resolute focus and consistent supportive action? As humans we are a bundle of conflicting desires and actions, each supporting and negating other actions and desires we carry simultaneously. So if *cards 5, 6,* and *10* are a jumble, explain to your client that they may need to refocus their desires and actions to work seamlessly together, not in conflict.

Card 7: This card represents the negative side of the question. This is what you are afraid of, what you are ignoring, or what you don't want to happen. This is the only card slot that is inherently negative, but even so, it can be a very positive card location. The ever-present counterbalance to *"the law of attraction"* is its sister *"the law of repulsion."* Pushing away is just as powerful as pulling toward psychically, as well as physically (and usually much easier as well). This card can represent anything we fear, can't see, or want gone from us in regards to the situation at hand. Compare it to all of the other cards to determine how your client is handling the overall situation at hand.

*Sword of Damocles: (See Glossary)

Card 8: This position shows us what other people are feeling. This card can be a general consensus from a large body of people or the direct influence of someone important to the querent or their question. It may even be why they are asking the question in the first place. People influence us every day. No matter how resolute our will, or how strong our desire (or need), someone will usually bend our opinions and actions along the way. We are all affected to some extent by the people around us. This position shows us how that social pressure is affecting the situation. In a simple question of marriage, this may be the mother (or mother-in-law) harping on some point or another. In a group or politically related question, this card could indicate the "popular opinion" among the masses. It shows us what we face from others both now and as a consequence of our actions.

Card 9: *"This is your hopes and dreams."* This spot represents your client's goals, their desires, and their positive associations with the question at hand (see *"Law of Attraction"*). Often it will reveal information your client has conveniently omitted, a secret desire they are afraid to voice lest you judge them too harshly, so don't be surprised if you see something a bit shocking.

Card 10: This is the final outcome or end result. In the end "something" has to happen. This card is not an absolute. It is the most likely outcome given the current set of actions and decisions by all parties involved. Compare this card directly to *cards 5 and 6* before settling on an answer. Do the current events and implications support or "help" this outcome? Do they stand in the way? Are there conflicting energies or obstacles before the final destination? Now look at the internal cards (*cards 7 and 9*). How do your client's feelings affect the outcome? Is their desire true and strong, or do they secretly wish for something else? Is their fear stronger than their desire? Do their fears of "this" prevent "that" from happening? People sabotage themselves every day. Is your client doing that right now? Is that why they came to you for a *reading* (whether they know it or not yet)?

Compare *card 10* to the rest of the *spread*. Is there a flow of energy to the end result? Does it make sense? Look for general patterns among cards that cloud or confirm the *reading*, but don't lose your focus on the question at hand. Once you have a pretty good feel of the reading, look for additional patterns by asking yourself the following questions:

Are there more than three "major" Arcana cards? This often indicates huge, impersonal forces at work, being decisions made that affect the querent they are powerless to change, and must deal with the consequences. For example: An economic recession or even a "first quarter sales slump" may cause the board of directors at the company your client works for to lay off half of its employees. This is an unavoidable circumstance that directly affects your client as surely as if it rained on their picnic. Of course, these outside forces can be favorable or unpleasant to your client, but an abundance of "major" Arcana cards often shows that someone or something else is pulling the strings of the overall situation and they have to accept that or change their place in the whole of it.

Are there more than two cards of the same number? If your *ten-card reading* has all four 7's in it *(Coins, Wands, Swords, Cups)*, then focus on the repetitive energy or "pattern behavior" the *"7 cards"* represent. Compare the *"7 cards"* to each other and then compare their location and proximity to each other. Also look to see if they flow. For example: They are in positions *3, 4, 6, and 10* (showing a linear progression) or they are in *5, 6, 9, and 10* (showing a congruency between thought and action, cause and effect), and so on. In the case of a "major" Arcana card adding its own weight, proceed with a slight bit of skepticism when looking for patterns. If you see two of the "minor" Arcana 4's and *The Emperor (IV)*, look to see if this is important but don't place as much emphasis as you would in the above ("7's") example.

Is there an abundance of any one particular suit? If you get four or more *Cups* in a *ten-card spread* about love, don't be surprised, but note how much of a highly charged emotional situation this is. No matter what suit you get, or what the nature of your *reading* is, if you see that approximately 40% or more of the cards are of a particular suit, then add this additional awareness to your considerations of the *reading*'s implications. Excluding the "major" Arcana, each suit represents 25% of the deck. The "minor" Arcana alone represents over 70% of the deck, so you will undoubtedly see more "minor" Arcana cards on a regular basis. Simple probability will throw out the occasional oddly disproportionate distribution of suits or Arcana; but when you see a definite pattern that enhances your collective impressions from the *spread* at large, make a note of it.

Are there more than three "face cards"? Almost every Tarot card has someone in it doing something or another. "Face cards" (or "court cards" if you prefer) specifically represent people by societal position. When you see a face card (court card) the emphasis is placed on their position as an authority, or the emphasis is pointing directly at their core personality or characteristics as they pertain to the situation at hand. An <u>abundance</u> indicates that people are more essential to the issue than any particular path of action. Ask yourself (and your client), "Who are these people and why are *they* so important to the question?" This is the direction you need to follow to get answers. Open up these cards if necessary.

Additionally

Expansion cards: Sometimes your *spread* will answer a lot of foundation questions, or verify what you already know, but it won't quite give you everything you *want* to know. You don't want to pick everything up and start fresh, but you want "just a little more" information. More often your client will allow you to answer their question in depth and without hesitation they will whine *"but what about . . .?"* This is when being able to "add a few cards" to the *spread* helps you keep the focus of the question at hand but draw out a bit more information. The most common method is simply to draw one to three more cards from the top of the deck to "expand upon" the final outcome. Alternatively, you can always reshuffle the deck (leaving the *spread* untouched), as you focus on what you know already and what you wish to find out as well.

Clarification cards: This is the process of "opening up a card" from earlier in the book, and this is exactly where you will use it. It works in exactly the same way as "expansion cards" (above), except that you can apply them to any card in the *spread* you wish to know more about. We *highly* recommend shuffling the deck, or drawing individual cards at random rather than simply from the top of the deck when doing this.

Astrological and time spreads

These *spreads* work <u>amazingly</u> <u>well</u>, but you really have to focus on your client and the matter at hand or you will just get an incoherent jumble of cards. Please note that these are "general *spreads*." They cover ALL areas of life, or all possible angles, so <u>these are not effective readings for simple "yes or no" or highly specific questions</u>. Practice these *spreads* a lot. Once you get the hang of it, you will find these to be some of your most resourceful (and most useful) *spreads*. Basic order of card distribution is below. Interpretations start on the next page. *Be sure to check out all of these spreads.*

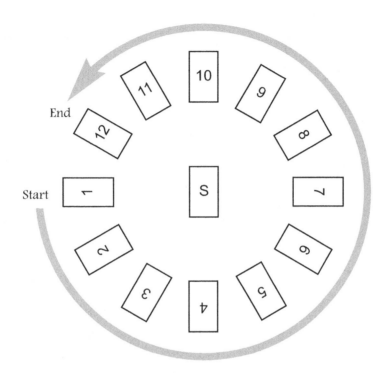

The diagram above illustrates the order to lay out the cards "astrologically." Each card position in this layout represents the energies of an astrological *house* or *sign,* whereas the cards themselves replace the *planets*. These *spreads* use a *significator card,* which is placed in the center of the circle. In these *spreads,* the *significator card* can be the querent, the situation, or the <u>end goal</u>. This is especially true of the second *spread* you will find on the following pages. In that particular *spread* we *strongly recommend* that you use a *significator card* to represent the <u>end goal</u>. It is possible to use it without a *significator* if you wish to leave that card in your deck and focus directly on your client or the object being questioned.

<u>This same basic layout can be used for other, non-astrological spreads as well</u>, such as a *time spread,* where each card represents one hour of a day or one month of the (solar) year, or even three cards to a season. In the latter case, the card layout remains the same, but in the *day* and *year spreads* the first card should be laid at the "one o'clock" position (where *card 9* resides in the above *spread*) and the rest of the cards would follow in a clockwise fashion. *Clarification cards* fit easily on the outer edge of the circle, as needed.

Please note: In this and following examples we have placed the cards so that each card reads upright <u>facing out</u> (the top of each card is on the outside edge of the circle). If you want to reverse this and place each card in your *spread* <u>facing in</u>, instead of <u>facing out</u> that works just as well.

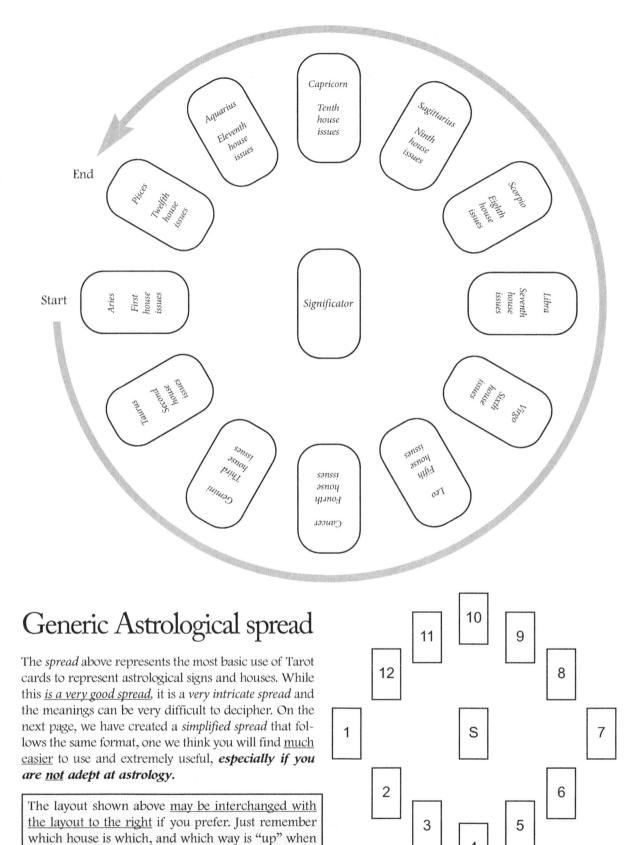

Generic Astrological spread

The *spread* above represents the most basic use of Tarot cards to represent astrological signs and houses. While this *is a very good spread*, it is a *very intricate spread* and the meanings can be very difficult to decipher. On the next page, we have created a *simplified spread* that follows the same format, one we think you will find <u>much easier</u> to use and extremely useful, ***especially if you are not adept at astrology.***

The layout shown above <u>may be interchanged with the layout to the right</u> if you prefer. Just remember which house is which, and which way is "up" when you are *reading. This is true of any "round" spread.*

The Roundabout spread

<u>You will love this spread</u>. *We promise*. This is a carefully researched and tested astrologically-correct *spread* that has been simplified <u>so that anyone with a good connection with their cards</u> can decipher any situation, no matter how complex. This *spread* does not invest as much card energy in predicting future events as ***it defines a map of how to get where you want to be from where you are now.*** Generally speaking, *astrological spreads* do not "predict" the future as much as they give an overall view of what is going on. In this *spread,* you will find easy-to-access answers that lead you directly to your goal. We hope you will master this *spread,* for it will work tirelessly for you for years to come. The order the cards are laid out is exactly the same as any other *astrological spread.*

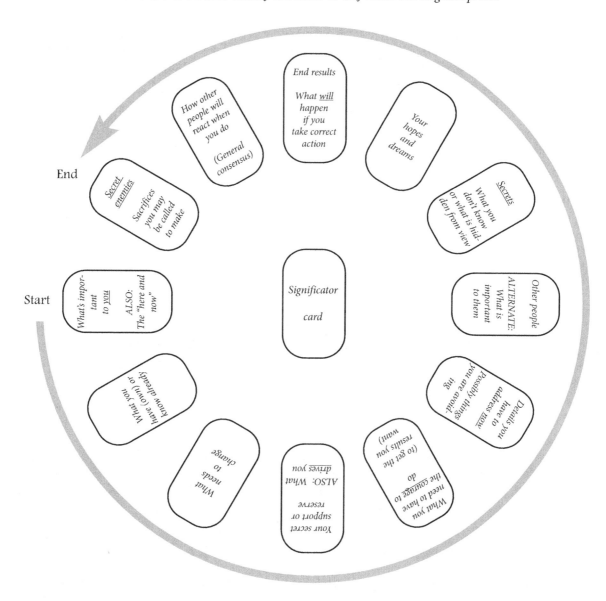

PLEASE NOTE: This spread is from the lesson plans of our own mystery school and you will not find it anywhere else. You are welcome to use it personally and professionally, and to teach it to your students, but please do not reprint the card layout or interpretations without prior written consent. If you have any questions or comments, please post us a note in the forums. We would love to hear from you. Expanded interpretation follows on the next page.

Card position meanings

Card 1: *What's important to you (right now). The "here and now." What you are focusing on. The situation at "face value."*

<u>As a setting or circumstance</u>: This card shows the situation "at face value." This also makes it a good *verification card* to determine if the *spread* is indeed accurate, or simply random cards. If this card does not tie in directly to the matter at hand, stop and examine the overall feel of the *spread* before spending any amount of time interpreting it. If every other card "makes sense," this card indicates self-deception on the part of your client—<u>or they are lying to you</u>.

<u>As an expression of the querent</u>: This shows the needs of the person or event that is at the center of the question. *"This is what is most important to you."* This card will show you what they want, need, or "can't live without." This is their *focus*. "Getting" comes from "doing," and "doing" requires knowing what to "do." If your client is not clear on *exactly* what they want, this card will reveal it.

<u>Any card reversed here</u> will reveal selfish, impatient, or explosively aggressive tendencies associated with or toward the card that occupies this spot.

Card 2: *What you have (own) right now, or what you "have to work with." What you know already. Habits you need to develop. Steps to take to get what you want.*

<u>As a setting or circumstance</u>: This card shows what you have to work with right now. It shows your current resources and possessions, or *what you have on hand that helps you* toward your goal. If you do not have these things yet, the card here will show you what habits you need to develop and what steps you need to take *now* to achieve your goal.

<u>As an expression of the querent</u>: This is your platform or your base of opinion and operations. This can also indicate your "strong points." Make sure that your client is not taking these things for granted, or ignoring their potential value.

<u>Any card reversed here</u> will reveal greed or possessiveness, *even jealousy,* over whatever is represented by the card occupying this position. Any obsession here must be overcome before progress can be made.

Card 3: *What needs to be said, <u>changes you need to make</u> to get what you want, alternative ways to g e t where you want to be.*

<u>As a setting or circumstance</u>: This position is dynamic. It shows you what is unstable in your life or what you need to change to get where you want to be. Occasionally in *readings* it will show you ideas instead of current actualities.

<u>As an expression of the querent</u>: This is what you need to get off of your chest, what you need to say to someone, or who you need to address regarding the question asked. It can also reveal beliefs and attitudes that need to be changed or new ones that need to be assumed in order to reach your goal. Due to the numerous variations possible here, please compare this card's message to the rest of the *spread* and be sure to get additional information from your client if you need to.

Any card reversed here tells us about uncertainties, inconsistencies, or delusions that are preventing acquisition of the goal. These can be people who are working against the wishes of the querent (by happenstance or by design) or they could even be the fallibilities of the querent themselves. Perhaps your client is "their own worst enemy." People do this every day. If you see a card reversed in this spot, tread carefully while you verify information before giving your client advice on how to proceed.

Card 4: *Your secret support or reserve. What (secretly) drives you. "Your secret weapon or allies."*

As a setting or circumstance: As a location, this is any safe place or a haven. For example, the *3 of Cups* here could indicate a celebration (family dinner, feast, or party) *at home*. But the *3 of Swords* would indicate infidelity from your spouse or an argument with your mother, any woman close to you, or even a confrontation with the security guard at your condo! The key points of identification for any *location* indicated here are security, privacy, and familiarity. Unfortunately, not all of life's motivations are positive. Sometimes the best motivators are fear and/or pain. We do not have to like what drives us forward, but we can always *use* it.

As an expression of the querent: These are your hidden talents or strengths that you may not be focusing on right now. *This is what keeps you going*, and you should *make it a point to* harness this energy. A person in this position will usually be a secret ally or a close friend, someone whose efforts behind the scenes help the querent make progress. If it is a negative card (see directly below), this still may be a positive motivational force ("moving toward" something and "moving away" from something are equally powerful motivational drives). This is the simultaneous *"law of attraction and repulsion"* in action.

Any card reversed here gives us *insecurity* (lack of safety—or—paranoia), jealousy among close ties, *a lack of* emotional support and any compassion at all, or inner turmoil.

Card 5: *What you need to have the courage to do; how to get support for your cause. What to project. How to take charge. Risks to take. What you will be praised for accomplishing.*

As a setting or circumstance: Like *Card 6*, these may be things you are avoiding, are putting off, or even feel you are "not ready for yet." This card represents demons you must face down or challenges you need to attempt in order to get the help (and recognition) you need from others.

As an expression of the querent: This shows risks you are willing to take, grand dreams you have. You still need to *do* these things.

Any card reversed here shows tyranny, egoic-*in*validation (bullying, low self-esteem, lack of courage, identity crises, scars, possibly outright fear).

Card 6: *Details you have to address now, possibly things you may be avoiding.*

As a setting or circumstance: It's time to tighten the belt a few notches, set the alarm clock earlier, burn some midnight oil, or buy a better book of clichés. No matter the case, this is "the devil you know" (being the devil in the details) whereas *card 12* reveals "the devil you don't." These are things you need to do (usually unpleasant, or you would already be doing them), or you need to do more of them, or do them *better*.

<u>As an expression of the querent</u>: These are things you are avoiding, ignoring, or have even *outsourced,* hoping that someone else will do them. Stop it. Address the matters at hand and move on—now.

<u>Any card reversed here</u> gives us confusion, or a lack of knowledge, even a lack of awareness. Fear could be hiding underneath all of this. These matters must be ferreted out <u>or they will continue</u> to hamper progress.

Card 7: *Other people (who are important to or are involved in) the situation. Other people's feelings toward you or the question at hand. What's important to them.*

<u>As a setting or circumstance</u>: This can be other people who are pressuring you, or are being directly affected by the situation; or it can be the *opinions* of these people. Whatever this card reveals will illustrate <u>what is most important at this time</u>: the actual people involved, their attitudes, or their actions.

<u>As an expression of the querent</u>: This is how you are affecting others. Alternately, this is someone or several people who are affecting you (see above).

<u>Any card reversed here</u> shows negative input from others or a negative impact *on* others. In most cases it will be clear; but when in doubt, describe to your client the effect you see and find out whether *they* are being pressured **or** *if they are actively working against another* in the situation the *reading* addresses. *Open this card up* to help your client find solutions.

Card 8: *Secrets. What you don't know or what's being hidden from view. What you can't see (for whatever reason).* <u>Things you need to find out</u> *if you are to succeed.*

<u>As a setting or circumstance</u>: There are things you need to find out. Secrets are being held from you, or you need certain information to make progress or a decision. This card points to what this information is or who is guarding it. You may have to do another *spread* to figure out exactly how to get that information, or you can *open this card up* for *clarification*.

<u>As an expression of the querent</u>: This card can *also* show <u>what your client is hiding</u>. This is a somewhat rare situation, but in *readings* involving deception (infidelity, divorce, business or political negotiations, etc.) you might find this card pointing directly back at your client, indicating that *they* are withholding vital information and that this will affect the outcome of the situation they are involved in.

<u>Any card reversed here</u> could indicate all sorts of sordid entertainment: deception, blackmail, conspiracy, theft, infidelity, extortion, secrets revealed, possibly scandals arising from this.

Card 9: *Your hopes and dreams, goals (and occasionally your contingency plans).*

<u>As a setting or circumstance</u>: This is what you are hoping to come about.

<u>As an expression of the querent</u>: Personal goals, grand ideas and *ideals*.

<u>Any card reversed here</u> shows a lack of creativity, drifting aimlessly, fears of dreaming big, taking on too much at once, scattered energies, lack of focus, or unrealistic expectations.

Card 10: *End results. What <u>will</u> happen if you take correct action.*
If you follow the advice of this spread, this is what you can expect.

<u>As a setting or circumstance</u>: This is what will happen if your client follows the advice of the *spread* (assuming that the *spread* is valid and your advice is solid).

<u>As an expression of the querent</u>: Congratulations! Whatever bed you made, here it is . . .

<u>Any card reversed here</u> indicates things not quite turning out as we had hoped. It can show sabotage (look carefully at *cards 8* and *12*), <u>self</u>-sabotage (study *cards 3, 5, 6* and *9*), or any other result stemming directly from not taking the necessary steps. Some "requests" will be <u>impossible</u> for that person to accomplish (a client may come to ask you how he can steal Angelina Jolie from Brad Pitt and you may get the *3 of Hearts reversed* as a result, with *Judgement* in the *11th position*). Any *reversed* card here immediately requires a careful study of the *spread*, most especially if the *reversed* card is "obvious and specific" in its relation to the querent or the question at hand. Often the very reason for the failure will be written all over the *spread*. People deceive themselves every day. It is possible one of your clients will come to you asking you to perform some kind of miracle for them or expect you to simply tell them the answers they want to hear—*even in the face of absolute proof that what they want cannot possibly be.*

Card 11: *What will happen as a result of your "results." How other people will react.*
General consensus or "resulting public opinion."

<u>As a setting or circumstance</u>: So much emphasis is placed on "the getting" of what we want (money, love, sex, popularity, fame, power, etc.) that the next part, or "what do we do now?" aspect of "having" anything is not considered until *after the fact.* This causes no end of fun and entertainment for us on the sidelines (it is a well-established fact that someone getting bonked on the head with an anvil in a cartoon, or a huge celebrity being hauled off to rehab, getting divorced, or losing their money is "fun and entertaining" to the public at large only *as long as it is happening to <u>someone else</u>*). The point of all of this is that *card 11* gives us a peek into the future to see what will happen after we "do everything right" and get results (revealed in *card 10*). The "and then . . ." comes to life and we get to see the consequences of our actions and machinations before we complete them. This is *invaluable* information.

If, for example, your client is working on an invention and they are seeking funding and the card in *position 10* shows them successfully patenting their new idea and the next card is either the *6 of Coins,* or the *Ace of Coins,* or even the *10 of Coins,* you will have some pretty good news for your client, but: the *6* shows an investor, the *Ace* shows a bank loan, and the *10* shows the possibility of selling the whole idea outright and retiring to Tahiti. Your interpretations may be slightly different, but the whole point of *card 11* is to show us how other people (who are important to the *spread*) <u>will</u> react.

<u>As an expression of the querent</u>: See above. Also, this is *what you will have to deal with.*

<u>Any card reversed here</u> is not a very good sign. Study the whole *spread,* especially *cards 9* and *10.* Without moralizing, are your client's desires honorable? Are they trying to cause pain and misery to others? Because a *reversed* card in this *position* shows you that their efforts *will bring* unpleasantries, <u>or even backfire on them</u>. Good to know *before* it happens.

Card 12: *Your secret enemies. Sacrifices you may be called to make. What is preventing you from succeeding. Obstacles in your way. What is standing between you and your goal.*

As a setting or circumstance: This is the "devil you *don't* know" *(see also card 6)*. What is revealed here is anything that is standing in your way that has not been addressed already. Often this will be something internal (see below). It could, however, uncover the plot of a false friend, someone who is nice to your face but is secretly trying to steal your money, your spouse, your idea, or someone who, for whatever reason they believe "justifiable," is working against you or your plans.

As an expression of the querent: This indicates (more) self-deception, laziness, bad habits, a secret wish to fail, or it reinforces fears already uncovered. The good news is that a proper *reading* and interpretation of this card will point out exactly what needs to be gotten rid of so that your client can make progress.

Any card reversed here can show an overcoming of said disability, or it shows *a lack of* the positive trait or energy needed to succeed.

Time Spreads: Twelve-hour or "one-day" forecast

The *spread* below can be *read* as "one card per hour," "one card for every two hours" (for a 24-hour *spread*), or you can break the whole thing up into four *three-card spreads,* each representing 6 hours, which you would *read* as morning, afternoon, evening, and night. The only thing you need to be certain of is exactly how you will *read* them before you *throw* the cards. The one cardinal sin in *casting spreads* is to change your mind on how you will *read* the cards <u>after</u> you have *cast* the *spread*.

This *spread* is useful for predicting the events or overall feel of the day, if you like.

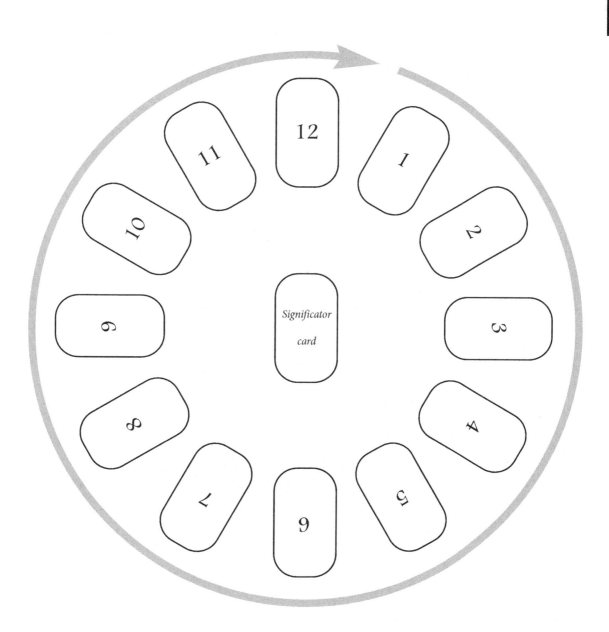

Time Spreads: A basic one-year forecast

The *spread* below is incredibly simple. It is simply four *three-card spreads* in succession. Start with any season and draw twelve cards from the deck to cover the next twelve months. In our illustration below we are starting with spring, but you can start anywhere in the year you like. You can *read* the *spread* as "one card for each month"; but we strongly recommend that you try *reading* the *spread* as "four *three-card spreads* in succession," as this gives a more in-depth view of each season, where as "one card per month" is a masochistic invitation for your client to ask you endless questions about how "one card" can dictate the entire happenings of a month, and "what else you see" (and so on). Of course, the most important thing you can do is to practice and <u>see what works best for you</u>.

In our example *spread* below we kept with the *astrological spread* feel and *threw* the cards counter-clockwise, starting at "spring." You can *throw* your cards clockwise, counterclockwise, left, right, backwards, however you like, as long as it makes perfect sense to you, because <u>you</u> have to *read* the cards, after all.

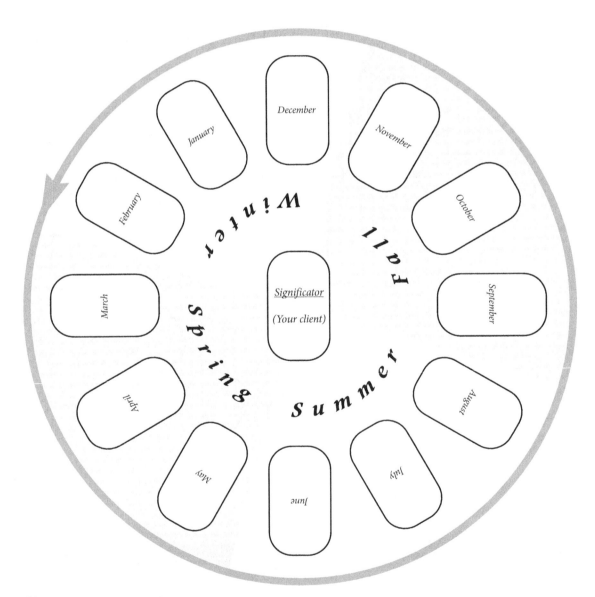

Fun Things You Can do to Your Tarot Deck!

(Write funny captions on them . . .)

Below are some examples of what we have done to our Tarot cards over the years. These will undoubtedly shock and enrage a few of the *purist sect* of Tarot aficionados, but that is not why we did them. We did them because we were bored at the time, it sounded like fun, it *was* fun (we made it a competition of who could write the funniest captions), and it was a way to become more attuned with our decks, understanding them more intimately. If you choose to write your own captions on your deck, we strongly recommend having a "caption deck" specifically, one that you may or may not *read* with regularly, but don't write on your *only* deck.

Join our community at *EasyTarotLessons.com* and share your ideas for funny captions and read many others as well.

It's not important what you scribble on your cards, or even that you do. The whole point of this exercise <u>is to get you to bond with your personal deck</u> in a light-hearted way, and to see the cards in ways you would never expect. Many of your readings will present you with your cards speaking to you in ways you could not begin to guess now. You <u>will</u> find this out.

These are just a few silly ideas we had fun with at one point or another. We hope that you will enjoy bringing your cards to life and light as well. Our own students have liked this part of the lessons on the Tarot the best. It's more fun than boring old "keywords" to memorize in any case.

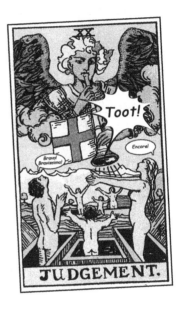

It should be painfully clear by now that these have not been decorated for comedy value, but to open your mind to unforeseen "alternate meanings" the cards will surprise you with over time. Still, we hope you enjoy them.

Quick and easy "Cheat Sheets"

On the following pages we have provided multiplication table-style charts for you to jot down your own personal meaning of each card. The boxes have been kept small to require you to summarize each card's "general meaning" (given allowances for variation *if and as needed* in each *reading*). We encourage you to use short descriptive sentences or multiple *keywords*. Simply fill in what you "know now" and add more when it comes to you. If you find certain cards are giving you trouble, please don't simply write something in just to fill that box. Spend some time with your cards and figure out what each card *says* to you.

We have provided three complete sets of tables so that you can fill these out now and do so again two more times in the future—after you have practiced with your deck and given quite a few *readings*. Fill out the first set of tables as soon as your teacher instructs you to, or if you are teaching yourself (and many of the best *readers* have, so you would be in good company), fill the first one out as soon as you have successfully completed all of the previous exercises in this book. Either way, make it a point to come back in three to six months and fill in the second set of tables (without peeking at your answers from the first set of tables until after you have completed all of the tables), and then six months after that, assuming that you are keeping up with your Tarot practice.

In the meantime, these charts will help serve to remind you of the general *card interpretations* (according to you, which is the most important authority when you are *reading*). Make sure to use these charts in your early *readings* as much as possible.

"Minor" Arcana
Ace through Ten

Number	Wands	Cups	Swords	Coins
Ace	explosive beginnings, new adventures	Births, new love, emotional renewal, spiritual cleansing	Victory! Well, a good start at least, leadership by force, authority	a raise, new job, winning lottery ticket, Christmas bonus, loans
2				
3		celebrations happiness among friends, good times		
4				
5	Conflict. Could be good natured or chaotic depending on surrounding cards			Loss of job, house, health. Grief and despair, lack of spiritual guidance
6			Travel by water, or, running away from problems or a bad situation. Lot from Sodom	
7		Choices. A fork in the path, decisions to make, new opportunities, inspirations, or even indecision if aspected badly		
8				
9	results of a lot of hard work, a tough road won, and scars to prove it, rest after struggle.	Passion for life and the freedom to pursue it. Being well cared for. Having favorite hobbies	Insomnia, lack of sleep due to stress, unhappiness due to circumstances	
10			retribution, victim of scams, character assassination, back trouble, bad endings	

"Minor" Arcana
"Face cards" (royal court)

Status	Wands	Cups	Swords	Coins
Page		new baby, romance, artistic lessons, time to create, also: new ideas, psychic insight	new challenges, baby boy, legal notices, bills, minor aggression, fearless attitude	
Knight	grandstanding, poseur, or, rallying the troops before action, wake-up call			Careful investment, caution with money, showing but not sharing wealth, slow progress, patience
Queen		emotional woman, artistic or psychic, deep meditation, careful consideration, compassion		
King				

Notes:

The Tarot is an allegory of the many paths we can take in life and how easily one path can be altered or changed by our loss of focus or distraction. It is not the path of one suit that is "the way" to success and happiness, but the careful blending of the suits as they represent our experiences. I am finding that ...

"Minor" Arcana
Ace through Ten

Number	Wands	Cups	Swords	Coins
Ace				
2				
3				
4				
5				
6				
7				
8				
9				
10				

"Minor" Arcana
"Face cards" (royal court)

Status	Wands	Cups	Swords	Coins
Page				
Knight				
Queen				
King				

Notes:

Fill in this cheat sheet after you have done all of the exercises in this book and cast a few spreads.

"Major" Arcana
Zero through Ten

Number	Interpretation	Reversed	Notes
0 *Fool*			
1 *Magician*			
2 *High Priestess*			
3 *Empress*			
4 *Emperor*			
5 *Hierophant*			
6 *Lovers*			
7 *Chariot*			
8 *Strength*			
9 *Hermit*			
10 *Wheel of Fortune*			

"Major" Arcana
Eleven through Twenty-one

Number	Interpretation	Reversed	Notes
11 *Justice*			
12 *Hanged Man*			
13 *Death*			
14 *Temperance*			
15 *Devil*			
16 *Tower*			
17 *Star*			
18 *Moon*			
19 *Sun*			
20 *Judgement*			
21 *World*			

"Minor" Arcana
Ace through Ten

Number	Wands	Cups	Swords	Coins
Ace				
2				
3				
4				
5				
6				
7				
8				
9				
10				

"Minor" Arcana
"Face cards" (royal court)

Status	Wands	Cups	Swords	Coins
Page				
Knight				
Queen				
King				

Notes:

"Major" Arcana
Zero through Ten

Number	Interpretation	Reversed	Notes
0 *Fool*			
1 *Magician*			
2 *High Priestess*			
3 *Empress*			
4 *Emperor*			
5 *Hierophant*			
6 *Lovers*			
7 *Chariot*			
8 *Strength*			
9 *Hermit*			
10 *Wheel of Fortune*			

"Major" Arcana
Eleven through Twenty-one

Number	Interpretation	Reversed	Notes
11 *Justice*			
12 *Hanged Man*			
13 *Death*			
14 *Temperance*			
15 *Devil*			
16 *Tower*			
17 *Star*			
18 *Moon*			
19 *Sun*			
20 *Judgement*			
21 *World*			

"Minor" Arcana
Ace through Ten

Number	Wands	Cups	Swords	Coins
Ace				
2				
3				
4				
5				
6				
7				
8				
9				
10				

"Minor" Arcana
"Face cards" (royal court)

Status	Wands	Cups	Swords	Coins
Page				
Knight				
Queen				
King				

Notes:

"Major" Arcana
Zero through Ten

Number	Interpretation	Reversed	Notes
0 *Fool*			
1 *Magician*			
2 *High Priestess*			
3 *Empress*			
4 *Emperor*			
5 *Hierophant*			
6 *Lovers*			
7 *Chariot*			
8 *Strength*			
9 *Hermit*			
10 *Wheel of Fortune*			

"Major" Arcana
Eleven through Twenty-one

Number	Interpretation	Reversed	Notes
11 *Justice*			
12 *Hanged Man*			
13 *Death*			
14 *Temperance*			
15 *Devil*			
16 *Tower*			
17 *Star*			
18 *Moon*			
19 *Sun*			
20 *Judgement*			
21 *World*			

Section Four

THE "MINOR" ARCANA

Here we examine the *"minor" Arcana*—the 56 cards that deal with the aspects of daily life. Please do not be fooled by the term "minor," as it is the affairs we attend to daily that shape the whole of our lives. If it helps, please take a moment and imagine *the whole of you* as a giant mosaic, where each day is one tile of thousands that reveal your essence to the world. Each stone of the mosaic that is you is painted *and* engraved with your thoughts and actions, your passions, and things that you surround yourself with. Over time these things shape you as surely as you decide what you will allow in your life and what goals and dreams you will fight for.

The so-called "minor" Arcana is a look at how we get where we want to go. It is who we are along the way, and it is the people we meet and interact with on our path. It is a representation of the sum total of our experiences and our reactions to them. Much like a hive of bees, the strength and beauty lies not so much in any one card, as it does in the harmony of concerted efforts of the totality working together to create the magical golden honey that is so highly prized.

A sneak peek at the royal family . . .

As a preface to each suit, we will offer tidbits of additional information on the royal family of that suit and their place in the Arcana. We will also offer various trivia on life in the feudal hierarchy as it clarifies the individual "face cards." Feel free to use or dispose of this information at your leisure. Trust the knowledge you have gained through study, but trust your instinct even more. Just don't start a *reading* without knowing what the cards say to you.

Fun nobility trivia

The page: attendant to the *squire, who, in turn,* was the knight's loyal and very personal *servant.*

Around the age of seven, boys (usually of noble birth) were often put into service to a squire as the beginning of their training to (eventually) become knights themselves. They were taught etiquette, basic fighting, and were for the most part errand boys (cheap labor). Even so, the underlying lessons of all of the mundane tasks were of character so that the page would grow up to be *a man of honor.* So the *Page* as a card represents more than just a young person or a student, but one with strengths (and weaknesses, *especially if the card is reversed*) of their respective suit.

In the case of the *Page of Wands,* these character strengths are often energy and drive, honesty, courage, and a sense of adventure, while the weaknesses are most likely to be impulsiveness, zealotry (fanaticism), exaggeration, and alpha tendencies of all sorts.

When it comes to representing events or incidents, you can use some, all, or even "none" of the following general guide to interpreting what you see in the cards. As a rule, *Knights* infer physical action, movement, or travel, including *the means* of travel: they can represent cars, planes, trains, auto accidents or breakdowns (this is just one possible meaning for a reversed *Knight* as an example), whereas *Pages* illustrate messages (invitations, news), the act of studying, education, or preparations. *Kings* and *Queens* show decision makers, and/or their decisions.

As to the ages of the court cards, don't get locked into this, but as an example, you may choose to see the various "face cards" represent people of these general age groups below. Remember that *aspecting* and *clarifying cards* will help identify these people much more than guesswork.

King: Adult male *(or authority figure)* generally over 30
Queen: Adult female *(or authority figure)* generally over 30
Knight: Late teen to early adulthood, to age 30-ish (depending on maturity)
Page: Child, pre-teen, tween, early teen (to age 13-15 at most, usually)

The House of Wands

The House of Wands is populated with ambitious, active, enterprising people who may appear to others as domineering or hyper-competitive. These cards represent the self-starting energy that lends itself to leadership so easily. *The overall theme* we would like you to focus on when you see *Wands* cards is that of action, energy, ambition, competition, and aggression.

Ace of Wands

(Prime Cardinal Fire)

Description: The "hand of God" appears from a small cloud, holding a budding branch while leaves reminiscent of Hebrew *yods* gently fall. The sky is otherwise calm, a tranquil river crosses the flat plains in the background, and a large castle sits atop a hillside fortification. This image is static *and* symbolic, and ethereal.

This card inherits its *cardinality* from being an *Ace,* or the first of the suit, and the suit of *Wands* is representative of the element of fire. This combination makes this a card of explosive energy.

Prime elements at work in this card

Number:	Ace (or One). Impetus, beginnings, or priority. Odd
Suit:	Wands. Action, adventure, vitality, *virility,* dominance, authority by might
Direction:	East. General beginnings. Mornings, dawn
Element:	Fire. Aggression, ambition, leadership, energy, competition

Traditional meaning: First off, this is a very *Aries* card. Let's cover this. The suit of *Wands* is equated with the metaphysical element of fire, and the number one is the "first" of anything. But take a moment and really think about the whole "Aries" thing. Love 'em or hate 'em, not much would get done without *Aries* people and *Aries* energy. The whole point of *Aries* energy is "something from nothing" (never confuse that as something *for* nothing—a popular concept which in reality just does not exist). Before *Aries* there is nothing. "Zero," or the null. *Aries* energy is the will imposing itself so forcibly on the universe that it simply springs into being. No other astrological sign can do that (sorry Scorpios). The sheer audacity required to say **"I _am_!"** and force yourself into existence is often downright barbaric, but it is the most powerful "impact" in all of reality. It is explosive and "pushy," "rude," and even "obnoxious," but it is the only way to drag anything from the ether into "reality." This card represents that wild, untamed, explosive energy that unleashes "new" onto the world. That "new" is often described by accompanying cards ("new" ideas, actions, beliefs, habits, cars, spouses, etc.), but this card is the catalyst to change. Keep that in mind when this card comes up in your *spreads*.

This is the card of new beginnings, enterprises, calculated risks, or taking renewed action after a period of rest. It is the energy similar to the Sun in *Aries* (Spring) and is inspirational and highly motivational. This card *also* often signifies opportunities (that you have to jump at) and actions that require physical effort. All in all it is a very positive card, but it can be combative due to its emphatic and forceful energy.

Traditional reversed meaning: This is still a high energy card, but when it comes up *reversed,* expect conflict, disagreements, obstacles, and general mayhem in any new venture. *Reversed,* this card can also reveal a new direction in life *(like being chased out of town by peasants armed with pitchforks!),* so be ready to adapt, or leave, as necessary.

Personal Notes:

Now it's your turn

Please note: *You can fill this in later if nothing comes to mind right away. It is far more important to get a good feel for this card than it is to write something in right away.*

What is your interpretation? What does this card say to you?

_____

_____

_____

What does it <u>say to you</u> when it is *reversed*?

_____

_____

_____

If you saw this card as an "end result," what would you say to your client?

_____

_____

_____

How would you use this card as an "affirmation helper"? Keep in mind that <u>each</u> <u>card</u> is extremely valuable as an assistant in your *"Laws of Attraction and Repulsion"* exercises. Any time you *desire* something intensely, **or** find yourself in a situation *you want out of,* you can use the imagery of your chosen card (or recommend this to your clients) to enhance your visualizations and "speed up" your results. Of course, much, much more of this is covered in depth in our *Advanced Tarot Secrets* course and workbook if you choose to learn even more about the Tarot.

_____

_____

_____

What other feelings, impressions, or uses do you want to note about this card?

_____

_____

_____

WANDS

Two of Wands
(Mutable Fire)

Description: A wealthy merchant looks out over the sea from the parapets of his estate. *This is a man of vision.* He is successful and confident, and he is in the midst of planning a new venture. He holds the world in his right hand, and his left holds a staff. Behind him a staff is firmly anchored in place. The lands below are fertile and populated with civilized people. This image is active and pragmatic.

This card is a direct, active response to the explosive creativity of the *Ace of Wands*. It is controlled action with a purpose.

Prime elements at work in this card

Number:	Two. Response to <u>initial</u> stimulus. Battle plans, first steps. Even
Suit:	Wands. *Controlled* action, adventure, vitality, competition
Direction:	South-Southwest. Visionary thought. Late night
Element:	Fire. Optimism, ambition, leadership, *channeled* energy

Traditional meaning: This is a card of beginnings and *calculated* risks, but instead of the spark of creativity or a burst of energy as seen in the *Ace,* this energy is a carefully planned effort to create a favorable outcome. <u>This is the card of planning</u>, coordinating, the *will* applied to physical action: the *"law of attraction" being applied.* This a card of doing and waiting. Results will come later. *Right now, plan carefully* and act decisively. Gather allies and support if you can, as well.

Traditional reversed meaning: Bad planning, or a complete lack of planning. Things NOT going at all according to plan, difficulties at the beginning of a venture, ideas without resources to put them into action. Possible weakness of will to take needed action (verify this by looking at associated cards). *Reversed,* this card represents *"the curse of inconvenience,"* which is an extremely powerful but subtle curse where countless "little things" just go wrong no matter what we do. *Persist.*

Personal Notes:

Now it's your turn

Please note: *You can fill this in later if nothing comes to mind right away. It is far more important to get a good feel for this card than it is to write something in right away.*

What is your interpretation? What does this card say to you?

_____

_____

_____

What does it <u>say to you</u> when it is *reversed*?

_____

_____

_____

If you saw this card as an "end result," what would you say to your client?

_____

_____

_____

How would you use this card as an "affirmation helper"? Keep in mind that <u>each</u> <u>card</u> is extremely valuable as an assistant in your *"Laws of Attraction and Repulsion"* exercises. Any time you *desire* something intensely, **or** find yourself in a situation *you want out of,* you can use the imagery of your chosen card (or recommend this to your clients) to enhance your visualizations and "speed up" your results. Of course, much, much more of this is covered in depth in our *Advanced Tarot Secrets* course and workbook if you choose to learn even more about the Tarot.

_____

_____

_____

What other feelings, impressions, or uses do you want to note about this card?

_____

_____

_____

WANDS

Three of Wands

(Fixed Fire)

Description: Late in the afternoon our friend from the *2 of Wands* stands on a perch overlooking his ships at sea. His plans have produced results and even now his affairs are in motion. It's not time to celebrate yet, but things go well. *Very* well.

The energy of this card is *fixed* as it represents the *management* of ongoing activities toward an important goal. It represents "active waiting," where circumstance, or the actions of others, move us closer to our goals, *but we remain productive* while these outside forces are working *with* us.

Prime elements at work in this card

Number: Three. Several people involved in this action, *teamwork*. Odd
Suit: Wands. Action, adventure, vitality, productivity, progress
Direction: Northwest. Governance, administration. Afternoon work stride
Element: Fire. Courage, ambition, charisma, *infectious and shared enthusiasm*

Traditional meaning: This is an extremely fortunate card to draw, although it can be frustrating because as you look closely at the boats in the bay they are sailing *away*, indicating the successful launch of a venture rather than the return (profits) of one. This card tells us that "things go well, *keep going.*" This card often appears when we are frustrated by a lack of "obvious results" and we need encouragement to persist. Other forces are at work and *we must also* apply our efforts intelligently while we are waiting for our results.

Traditional reversed meaning: Expect delays. Also: problems getting resources or the cooperation of others. Possible sabotage by a team member of a project early on. Make sure that team members are working together and that energies are not scattered. Don't sit around waiting for results or try to micro-manage the project at hand. Stop whining about "lack of progress" and *do* something.

Personal Notes:

Now it's your turn

__Please note__: *You can fill this in later if nothing comes to mind right away. It is far more important to get a good feel for this card than it is to write something in right away.*

What is your interpretation? What does this card say to you?

_____

_____

_____

What does it <u>say to you</u> when it is *reversed*?

_____

_____

_____

If you saw this card as an "end result," what would you say to your client?

_____

_____

_____

How would you use this card as an "affirmation helper"? Keep in mind that <u>each</u> <u>card</u> is extremely valuable as an assistant in your *"Laws of Attraction and Repulsion"* exercises. Any time you *desire* something intensely, **or** find yourself in a situation *you want out of*, you can use the imagery of your chosen card (or recommend this to your clients) to enhance your visualizations and "speed up" your results. Of course, much, much more of this is covered in depth in our *Advanced Tarot Secrets* course and workbook if you choose to learn even more about the Tarot.

_____

_____

_____

What other feelings, impressions, or uses do you want to note about this card?

_____

_____

_____

WANDS

Four of Wands

(Prime Fixed Fire)

Description: *Life is good.* A celebration is happening with musicians and dancing, feasting, and much merriment. The city fortress looms ominously overhead in the background, illustrating a powerful family in an era of prosperity. Flowers bloom and fruits ripen on garlands tied decoratively to staves planted into the foreground. Two women celebrate gaily with bouquets.

This potent card combines the strength and rigidity of the *square* with the fiery ambition of the suit of *Wands*. The resulting energy is an impressive bastillion of success and resultant prosperity.

Prime elements at work in this card

Number: Four. Fixed, solid, reinforced binding, resilience. Even, square
Suit: Wands. Action, adventure, vitality, conquest, fortitude, fortresses and safe havens
Direction: Northwest. Generosity, fun. Warm, lazy afternoons
Element: Fire. Dominance, self-governance, autonomy, summer, renewable energy

Traditional meaning: This is a prime *empire* card. The harvest is a good one and the fruits of labor are being enjoyed in a great feast. This is the time to celebrate. This card indicates parties and joyful gatherings of friends and associates. It also reflects the serenity of financial security, especially as a result of good long-term planning and careful application of efforts. This is not a card of *action* as much as it is a card of rest and recreation after much hard labor. Also: parties, a happy homelife.

Traditional reversed meaning: Don't start counting those chickens just yet. *(They have yet to actually hatch!)* Delays in payoffs and lost invitations are common here now (or worse, being excluded from celebrations). Possibilities of being disowned from the family fortune or losing one's cushy lifestyle. Best to start saving and spend cautiously while things get sorted out. <u>Watch your finances right now</u>.

Personal Notes:

Now it's your turn

Please note: You can fill this in later if nothing comes to mind right away. It is far more important to get a good feel for this card than it is to write something in right away.

What is your interpretation? What does this card say to you?

_____

_____

_____

What does it say to you when it is *reversed*?

_____

_____

_____

If you saw this card as an "end result," what would you say to your client?

_____

_____

_____

How would you use this card as an "affirmation helper"? Keep in mind that each card is extremely valuable as an assistant in your *"Laws of Attraction and Repulsion"* exercises. Any time you *desire* something intensely, **or** find yourself in a situation *you want out of,* you can use the imagery of your chosen card (or recommend this to your clients) to enhance your visualizations and "speed up" your results. Of course, much, much more of this is covered in depth in our *Advanced Tarot Secrets* course and workbook if you choose to learn even more about the Tarot.

_____

_____

_____

What other feelings, impressions, or uses do you want to note about this card?

_____

_____

_____

WANDS

Five of Wands

(Mutable Fire)

Description: *"Fight! Fight! Fight! Fight!..."* You knew this had to happen. Life was too good in the house of ambition and drive. Here we simply have too much testosterone, and too much money and ease, which led to people carving out their own mini-empires. Five young men, all shouting, glaring, worrying, and examining their "staves" as they each test the limits of their power, or prepare to be set upon by others.

Chaos meets ambition and excess energy in this card. The duality of the number five blends with fire to make times "interesting."

Prime elements at work in this card

Number:	Five. Duality of essence: chaos and structure. Odd
Suit:	Wands. Action, adventure, sports, vitality, competition, duels, showdowns
Direction:	East. Conflict, competition. Early mornings, dawn
Element:	Fire. Aggression, ambition, ferocity, unrest, discordant energy

Traditional meaning: Look closely at the players in this card. One man guards against another who makes a proclamation, while another looks up in worry. The central character wonders of the quality of his staff and his destiny with it while the last holds his staff high in defiance so as not to be left out of the "fun." *Everyone has their own idea of how things should be done,* and this is what happens when those ideas come into contact with each other. This card represents a madhouse, a situation that is devolving into a circus. Egos flare and while some work to find harmony, others prance and dance to their own tunes. Step lightly *(or run!)* at this time. Let cooler heads prevail.

Traditional reversed meaning: This is still not a very "positive" card, so remain vigilant. Usually this indicates a truce, or a rectification of earlier squabbles, but beware of political maneuvering and bruised egos looking for future opportunities to find vengeance.

Personal Notes:

Now it's your turn

Please note: You can fill this in later if nothing comes to mind right away. It is far more important to get a good feel for this card than it is to write something in right away.

What is your interpretation? What does this card say to you?

___

___

___

What does it say to you when it is *reversed*?

___

___

___

If you saw this card as an "end result," what would you say to your client?

___

___

___

How would you use this card as an "affirmation helper"? Keep in mind that each card is extremely valuable as an assistant in your *"Laws of Attraction and Repulsion"* exercises. Any time you *desire* something intensely, **or** find yourself in a situation *you want out of,* you can use the imagery of your chosen card (or recommend this to your clients) to enhance your visualizations and "speed up" your results. Of course, much, much more of this is covered in depth in our *Advanced Tarot Secrets* course and workbook if you choose to learn even more about the Tarot.

___

___

___

What other feelings, impressions, or uses do you want to note about this card?

___

___

___

WANDS

Six of Wands

(Fixed Fire)

Description: Well, someone had to win, and now they get to lord their victory over others. This is the card of the celebrated hero, the conqueror with his battle parade marching in celebration. Note also that the staves in the background are held high and straight with *pride*. Neither rider nor horse is dressed for battle. They are garmented for public celebration. If this card represents you, *then it is good to be you.*

This card is *a reaction* to previous events more than it is an original thought. It is a celebration of great deeds.

Prime elements at work in this card

Number: Six. Group empowerment toward commonality, recognition. Even
Suit: Wands. Action, adventure, vitality, competition, public accolades
Direction: South-Southwest. Nobility of character. Late night
Element: Fire. Aggression, ambition, leadership, shared energy, mobs, riots, instigators

Traditional meaning: Parades, accolades, victories, and celebrations of victories. If this card is *an outcome,* expect good things—and then expect a public spectacle of the victory. Possible raise, promotion, awards won, public affection, and even perhaps a little boasting are bound to happen very soon. Occasionally this card also represents a leader *rallying his or her troops,* organizing for a major cause. If that is the case, the surrounding cards will support that notion quite clearly.

Traditional reversed meaning: Ugh! All this work and does *anyone* notice at all? Sometimes you work, and work, and work, and *of course* someone else steals your thunder, your credit, or kisses up to the powers-that-be to make it look like *they* are the noble *hero du jour.* Time to buy yourself a cheap voodoo candle (or just grin and bear it). Occasionally this card may indicate outright defeat. Verify this before proceeding.

Personal Notes:

Now it's your turn

Please note: You can fill this in later if nothing comes to mind right away. It is far more important to get a good feel for this card than it is to write something in right away.

What is your interpretation? What does this card say to you?

_____

_____

_____

What does it <u>say to you</u> when it is *reversed*?

_____

_____

_____

If you saw this card as an "end result," what would you say to your client?

_____

_____

_____

How would you use this card as an "affirmation helper"? Keep in mind that <u>each</u> <u>card</u> is extremely valuable as an assistant in your *"Laws of Attraction and Repulsion"* exercises. Any time you *desire* something intensely, **or** find yourself in a situation *you want out of,* you can use the imagery of your chosen card (or recommend this to your clients) to enhance your visualizations and "speed up" your results. Of course, much, much more of this is covered in depth in our *Advanced Tarot Secrets* course and workbook if you choose to learn even more about the Tarot.

_____

_____

_____

What other feelings, impressions, or uses do you want to note about this card?

_____

_____

_____

Seven of Wands

(Fixed Fire)

Description: A man stands defensively on the edge of a cliff, staff raised both to ward off attacks as well as to physically intercept them. His back is to the proverbial wall (or cliff) and *he knows he has no <u>choice</u> left* but to fight (or at least look menacing and determined enough to scare off his pursuers). We see their staves in the foreground, as a group, but so far *not one* has ascended to face this man personally.

This is the card of *active defense*. It is *fixed* in nature, as it is the holding of a position against an imminent onslaught.

Prime elements at work in this card

Number:	Seven. Signifies challenge to one's beliefs, defensive preparations. Odd
Suit:	Wands. Physical action, vitality, competition, determination
Direction:	Northwest. Courage, fortitude. Afternoon
Element:	Fire. Aggression, defiance, making a stand, "second wind"

Traditional meaning: *"This may hurt a bit . . ."* Sun Tzu advocates in *The Art of War* holding the higher ground in battle if one desires to be victorious. This may take the form of a mental process (being smarter in battle), an emotional one (remaining calm while whipping your opponent into a frenzy), or a physical one (where you can throw rocks *down* on your enemies). This card indicates attackers ganging up on one who is above, more powerful, or better than they are (verify with other cards to discern which). The defender here has the advantage of the high ground, and the *confidence* and *determination* to win. Skill is also implied, foretelling victory after strife.

Traditional reversed meaning: *Don't expect an easy victory.* In fact, victory at all may not be possible along the present course. Sometimes it is best to retreat and find more solid ground. Occasionally, this card may indicate weakness or paranoia.

Personal Notes:

Now it's your turn

Please note: You can fill this in later if nothing comes to mind right away. It is far more important to get a good feel for this card than it is to write something in right away.

What is your interpretation? What does this card say to you?

___

___

___

What does it say to you when it is *reversed*?

___

___

___

If you saw this card as an "end result," what would you say to your client?

___

___

___

How would you use this card as an "affirmation helper"? Keep in mind that each card is extremely valuable as an assistant in your *"Laws of Attraction and Repulsion"* exercises. Any time you *desire* something intensely, **or** find yourself in a situation *you want out of,* you can use the imagery of your chosen card (or recommend this to your clients) to enhance your visualizations and "speed up" your results. Of course, much, much more of this is covered in depth in our *Advanced Tarot Secrets* course and workbook if you choose to learn even more about the Tarot.

___

___

___

What other feelings, impressions, or uses do you want to note about this card?

___

___

___

WANDS

Eight of Wands

(Mutable Fire)

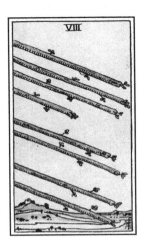

Description: Eight wands fly through the air. This may, in fact, be the most annoying Tarot card ever drawn. It has caused no small amount of confusion and consternation among teachers and students alike over the years. If the artwork of this card bothers you, you are in the vast majority. Nonetheless, it is generally a good omen.

This card has no attachments and the staves are unanchored, and thus stated by all commentaries to be "in flight." This bequeaths a sense of mutability or impermanence to the energies of these staves.

Prime elements at work in this card

Number:	Eight. Cycle of completion, time for a change, travel, sudden movement. Even
Suit:	Wands. Action, adventure, vitality, competition, rebirth, change of location
Direction:	South-Southwest. Idealism, enthusiasm. Late night
Element:	Fire. Change, excitement, enthusiasm, optimism, "electric" energy

Traditional meaning: Quick, sudden burst of energy and/or action. Adventure is afoot in the realm and there is no time for rest or sloth. The flight of the staves indicates unified sources of action (unseen causes) leading to change and possible travel. Be ready to change, move, adjust, or fly (literally or even physically) at a moment's notice. The alignment of the wands in this picture indicates a certain uniformity of action, so expect a reasonably orderly process rather than a chaotic mess. This is generally assumed to be a mildly lucky card.

Traditional reversed meaning: Stagnation or missed opportunities. Not being able or ready to take action when fortune calls. Canceled plans or vacations, inconsistency in action. Reckless action taken without adequate forethought. <u>Alternatively</u>: scattered and wasted energies. If paired with any *Sword* card (but especially the *7 of Swords*), this could indicate an ambush or even a call to retreat.

Personal Notes:

Now it's your turn

Please note: You can fill this in later if nothing comes to mind right away. It is far more important to get a good feel for this card than it is to write something in right away.

What is your interpretation? What does this card say to you?

_____

_____

_____

What does it <u>say to you</u> when it is *reversed*?

_____

_____

_____

If you saw this card as an "end result," what would you say to your client?

_____

_____

_____

How would you use this card as an "affirmation helper"? Keep in mind that <u>each</u> <u>card</u> is extremely valuable as an assistant in your *"Laws of Attraction and Repulsion"* exercises. Any time you *desire* something intensely, **or** find yourself in a situation *you want out of,* you can use the imagery of your chosen card (or recommend this to your clients) to enhance your visualizations and "speed up" your results. Of course, much, much more of this is covered in depth in our *Advanced Tarot Secrets* course and workbook if you choose to learn even more about the Tarot.

_____

_____

_____

What other feelings, impressions, or uses do you want to note about this card?

_____

_____

_____

Nine of Wands

(Fixed Fire)

Description: A man stands watchful guard over a small forest of staves. The man is a veteran and has recently been called upon to defend his charge. He does not allow his bandaged head to serve as an excuse to abandon his post. He is tired and worn, but watchful, conserving his energy for a fight, or the duration of his watch, whichever comes first.

Here we have another defensive card, yet, unlike the *7 of Wands,* this is guard duty: protection of material possessions, rather than being accosted by upstarts.

Prime elements at work in this card

Number:	Nine. Fruition of ideas and labors, waiting. Weapon or tool collection. Odd
Suit:	Wands. Strength, endurance, vitality, competition, total market dominance
Direction:	Northwest. Duty, honor, endurance. Storage sheds or silos. Afternoon
Element:	Fire. Determination, "turf," defensiveness, reserve energy

Traditional meaning: Dedication, trustworthiness, a sense of duty and the will to carry it out. Loyalty to a cause. Endurance in the face of challenges. Victory through perseverance and determination. Inner strength and a solid conviction in one's beliefs. A very worthy adversary. Also: physical or emotional "solid fortress" (bastillion). Something worth defending. Successfully defending your "stuff" (your beliefs, possessions, job, spouse, or anything that is in question) against all opposition. The person in question has *backbone*.

Traditional reversed meaning: Weakness of character. Shifty and shifting alliances. Someone who tries to evade responsibility, or even deserts outright. Fear of standing up for what is most important to yourself or your needs. Escapism.

Personal Notes:

Now it's your turn

Please note: You can fill this in later if nothing comes to mind right away. It is far more important to get a good feel for this card than it is to write something in right away.

What is your interpretation? What does this card say to you?

_____

_____

_____

What does it <u>say to you</u> when it is *reversed*?

_____

_____

_____

If you saw this card as an "end result," what would you say to your client?

_____

_____

_____

How would you use this card as an "affirmation helper"? Keep in mind that <u>each</u> <u>card</u> is extremely valuable as an assistant in your *"Laws of Attraction and Repulsion"* exercises. Any time you *desire* something intensely, **or** find yourself in a situation *you want out of,* you can use the imagery of your chosen card (or recommend this to your clients) to enhance your visualizations and "speed up" your results. Of course, much, much more of this is covered in depth in our *Advanced Tarot Secrets* course and workbook if you choose to learn even more about the Tarot.

_____

_____

_____

What other feelings, impressions, or uses do you want to note about this card?

_____

_____

_____

WANDS

Ten of Wands

(Mutable Fire)

Description: A man is bent over in an effort to carry his burden of wands to the distant town. He is labored but shows no sign of quitting and uses his momentum to carry him toward his goal. His load of sticks is both valuable and an albatross around his neck. Whether harvest or punishment, the weight of the wands remains the same.

This card is the fulfillment of a lifetime of efforts and energies along the path of *Wands*. From *Ace* to *Nine* <u>our heroes have progressed to this point</u>: the culmination and the reward of ambition and competition.

Prime elements at work in this card

Number:	Ten. End results. System reset. Sum total. End of the day. Even
Suit:	Wands. Action, adventure, vitality, endurance, competition, drive
Direction:	South-Southwest. Over-zealousness, travel. Late night
Element:	Fire. Aggression, ambition, refusal to quit, dominance, energy

Traditional meaning: *Be careful what you wish for.* This powerful card reminds us, as does the *10 of Swords,* that at the end of the day, all we have said and done catches up with us. The luxuries we crave are our burdens in turn. This man has "lots of sticks" but he has to carry them to his destination *or lose them.* <u>Success has a price</u>, and you may have to bear it once you get everything you desire. Fame, power, and wealth are seldom what we thought they would be when we first started along our path. Know exactly what you want before you invest a lifetime pursuing it so that when you get it you are still happy to carry the load. This card shows heavy labor or emotional burdens one chooses (or is forced) to carry for a time.

Traditional reversed meaning: Release of burdens or responsibilities. A weight being lifted off of your shoulders. Perhaps shirking responsibilities (check any aspecting cards to verify if this is so).

Personal Notes:

Now it's your turn

__Please note:__ You can fill this in later if nothing comes to mind right away. It is far more important to get a good feel for this card than it is to write something in right away.

What is your interpretation? What does this card say to you?

_____

_____

_____

What does it <u>say to you</u> when it is *reversed*?

_____

_____

_____

If you saw this card as an "end result," what would you say to your client?

_____

_____

_____

How would you use this card as an "affirmation helper"? Keep in mind that <u>each</u> <u>card</u> is extremely valuable as an assistant in your *"Laws of Attraction and Repulsion"* exercises. Any time you *desire* something intensely, **or** find yourself in a situation *you want out of,* you can use the imagery of your chosen card (or recommend this to your clients) to enhance your visualizations and "speed up" your results. Of course, much, much more of this is covered in depth in our *Advanced Tarot Secrets* course and workbook if you choose to learn even more about the Tarot.

_____

_____

_____

What other feelings, impressions, or uses do you want to note about this card?

_____

_____

_____

WANDS

Page of Wands
(Weak Cardinal Fire)

Description: A young man dressed in the royal court's yellow tunic holds up a staff for inspection. Overall, he looks to be pretty satisfied with his find. His stance and attire indicate a relaxed state, prior to a journey or adventure. The feather in his cap tells us that he is indeed at the beginning of his journey through life, but is schooled and experienced (at least enough to warrant the feather). Do notice though how his feather *is just a lick of flame.*

This card is *cardinal* as it is instigatory, representing initiations, arrivals, or "edges of."

Prime elements at work in this card

Status:	Page. Apprentice, attendant, student, youth, messenger
Suit:	Wands. Action, adventure, vitality, competition, verbal challenges
Direction:	East. General beginnings, taunts or threats. Early morning, dawn
Element:	Fire. Aggression, ambition, leadership, *budding* energy

Traditional meaning: *Pages* are "catch-all" cards in *readings*. Most often <u>this Page</u> is used to indicate a male baby, or a young boy or girl with blonde hair. It can also indicate a young boy or girl of a *Fire* sign *(Aries, Leo, Sagittarius)*, news of, or an invitation to, a new adventure, or even the study (apprenticeship) of an active or dangerous field of employment (firefighting, police work, sports, military school, etc.). If this *Page* shows up in a *reading* strongly associated with an *Ace* or a *Queen,* it often portends a birth. If this *Page* shows up in connection with *The Empress,* it almost assuredly represents pregnancy with a male child, or a baby who will be one of the *Fire* signs.

Traditional reversed meaning: Unhappy news suddenly, arguments, unruly children, mild danger (if regarding any of the employment listed above), problems with pregnancy or small children. Rebel or minor rebellion. Also: Impotence.

Personal Notes:

Now it's your turn

Please note: You can fill this in later if nothing comes to mind right away. It is far more important to get a good feel for this card than it is to write something in right away.

What is your interpretation? What does this card say to you?

_____

_____

_____

What does it say to you when it is *reversed*?

_____

_____

_____

If you saw this card as an "end result," what would you say to your client?

_____

_____

_____

How would you use this card as an "affirmation helper"? Keep in mind that each card is extremely valuable as an assistant in your *"Laws of Attraction and Repulsion"* exercises. Any time you *desire* something intensely, **or** find yourself in a situation *you want out of,* you can use the imagery of your chosen card (or recommend this to your clients) to enhance your visualizations and "speed up" your results. Of course, much, much more of this is covered in depth in our *Advanced Tarot Secrets* course and workbook if you choose to learn even more about the Tarot.

_____

_____

_____

What other feelings, impressions, or uses do you want to note about this card?

_____

_____

_____

WANDS

Knight of Wands
(Intense Mutable Fire)

Description: *"Mister Adventure."* The *Knight of Wands* is shown rearing his horse up on two legs. This controlled maneuver requires a *lot* of training between rider and mount, and is a highly symbolic announcement of action <u>before</u> <u>action</u>. It is also *grandstanding*. His feathers are symbolic of the fiery sexual energy that burns through his entire being. He is ever the "knight in shining armor" charging off to some adventure or danger to embrace. Something big is <u>about</u> to happen.

This card is testosterone feeding the brain. The result is a *need* for action, danger, and fun.

Prime elements at work in this card

Status:	Knight. Youthful, warrior, bravado, adventure, danger, machismo
Suit:	Wands. Action, adventure, vitality, competition, masculinity
Direction:	South-Southwest. Zealotry, travel, promiscuity. Late night
Element:	Fire. Aggression, ambition, leadership, energy, drive, testosterone

Traditional meaning: *"No time for explanations! We have to move <u>now</u>! . . .* Okay, maybe a quick explanation, but then we have to *take action!"* This is a card of rallying. Swift, sudden movement, decisive action, high adventure, sudden movement (especially "road trips"), impromptu vacations, hyperactivity, active, danger-seeking young men, *"the hunt."* Occasionally this card pairs with the *6 of Swords* or *The Chariot* to indicate travel, or relocation. This card can also be used to signify a young man with red hair or an aggressive/impulsive personality, should you wish to do so.

Traditional reversed meaning: Charging ahead without forethought. Impulsive behavior (usually detrimental), <u>uncontrolled</u> anger or sexual desires, bullying, domineering young "alpha" males. Also: abruptness of personality, rudeness, bad planning, grandstanding, attention-getting antics of little useful value. Need for public attention and validation.

Personal Notes:

Now it's your turn

Please note: You can fill this in later if nothing comes to mind right away. It is far more important to get a good feel for this card than it is to write something in right away.

What is your interpretation? What does this card say to you?

_____

_____

_____

What does it say to you when it is *reversed*?

_____

_____

_____

If you saw this card as an "end result," what would you say to your client?

_____

_____

_____

How would you use this card as an "affirmation helper"? Keep in mind that each card is extremely valuable as an assistant in your *"Laws of Attraction and Repulsion"* exercises. Any time you *desire* something intensely, **or** find yourself in a situation *you want out of,* you can use the imagery of your chosen card (or recommend this to your clients) to enhance your visualizations and "speed up" your results. Of course, much, much more of this is covered in depth in our *Advanced Tarot Secrets* course and workbook if you choose to learn even more about the Tarot.

_____

_____

_____

What other feelings, impressions, or uses do you want to note about this card?

_____

_____

_____

Queen of Wands

(Fixed Fire)

Description: The *Queen of Wands* sits on her throne gazing off at some unknown point of interest, delicately holding aloft a sunflower in her left hand, and her staff of rulership in her right. A mangy black cat sits before her like a guardian.

This is a queen whose passion is ruling, not intrigue and scandal. She rules comfortably from her stone throne and aspires to oneness with nature. She will always connect more to her animal side than her *anima* or any plant she cares for. She is *fixed* in her ways, as they work well for her kingdom.

Prime elements at work in this card

Status:	Queen. Mother, boss, athlete, entrepreneur, *coach,* woman
Suit:	Wands. Action, adventure, vitality, competition
Direction:	Northwest. Honor, nobility, reliability. Mid-afternoon
Element:	Fire. Radiance, warmth, nobility, leadership, energy

Traditional meaning: There are several ways to *read* the *Queens*. For ease and consistency (as well as accuracy), we *strongly* recommend the following. *Queen of Wands: Aries, Leo,* or *Sagittarius* woman. Primary characteristics are courage, assertiveness, confidence, often open and friendly, outgoing, adventurous, honest, frank, resolute, reliable, hard working. Also could be used for any self-assured, pleasant woman, preferably with a strong fondness for animals and nature. Possible tomboy.

Traditional reversed meaning: Same woman: (could be any of the following) Impatient, demanding, self-obsessed, intolerant, angry, flaky, *drama queen,* commanding or bossy, tactless, *un*feminine, headstrong, tyrannical, fixed opinions.

Personal Notes:

Now it's your turn

Please note: You can fill this in later if nothing comes to mind right away. It is far more important to get a good feel for this card than it is to write something in right away.

What is your interpretation? What does this card say to you?

_____

_____

_____

What does it say to you when it is *reversed*?

_____

_____

_____

If you saw this card as an "end result," what would you say to your client?

_____

_____

_____

How would you use this card as an "affirmation helper"? Keep in mind that each card is extremely valuable as an assistant in your *"Laws of Attraction and Repulsion"* exercises. Any time you *desire* something intensely, **or** find yourself in a situation *you want out of,* you can use the imagery of your chosen card (or recommend this to your clients) to enhance your visualizations and "speed up" your results. Of course, much, much more of this is covered in depth in our *Advanced Tarot Secrets* course and workbook if you choose to learn even more about the Tarot.

_____

_____

_____

What other feelings, impressions, or uses do you want to note about this card?

_____

_____

_____

King of Wands

(Fixed Fire)

Description: The *King of Wands* sits slightly forward on his throne, left hand clenched into a relaxed fist, as if he is looking for, even begging someone to step out of line in *his* kingdom. Even his pet lizard is attentive to the court in front of him. This man reeks action held in place only by duty, from his golden crown of flames to his staff which rests diagonally across him, ready to be flipped up into his left hand for a fight. His cape is thrown back on his left side to allow freedom of movement, should he need to jump up and attack someone.

Prime elements at work in this card

Status:	King. Boss, overlord, *alpha-male,* coach, athlete, authority figure
Suit:	Wands. Action, adventure, vitality, sports, military, options, and opportunity
Direction:	Northwest. Honor, nobility. Mid-afternoon
Element:	Fire. Ambition, courage, nobility, leadership, generosity, competition

Traditional meaning: This is a *"man's man,"* one of adventure, action, and machismo. Usually quick to anger with a fiery, intense personality, he is usually too impatient to invest his valuable time scheming. His way is direct, forceful, and to the point, so he is often honest simply from the lack of cunning. Choose this card for a leader, a boss, or any highly-dangerous profession. Alternatively, you can use this card to represent any man of the *Fire* signs *(Aries, Leo, Sagittarius),* a fiery-tempered man, or a redheaded man over 30.

Traditional reversed meaning: Tyrant, rude, bully, domineering boss, violent criminal, self-obsessed megalomaniac, basically a real jerk. Could also represent a glory-seeking poseur masquerading as the positive side of this card. Alternatively, this card *reversed* could show possible misfortune to an otherwise good man *if it is heavily aspected by negative cards* in the *reading.*

Personal Notes:

Now it's your turn

Please note: You can fill this in later if nothing comes to mind right away. It is far more important to get a good feel for this card than it is to write something in right away.

What is your interpretation? What does this card say to you?

_____

_____

_____

What does it say to you when it is *reversed*?

_____

_____

_____

If you saw this card as an "end result," what would you say to your client?

_____

_____

_____

How would you use this card as an "affirmation helper"? Keep in mind that each card is extremely valuable as an assistant in your *"Laws of Attraction and Repulsion"* exercises. Any time you *desire* something intensely, **or** find yourself in a situation *you want out of*, you can use the imagery of your chosen card (or recommend this to your clients) to enhance your visualizations and "speed up" your results. Of course, much, much more of this is covered in depth in our *Advanced Tarot Secrets* course and workbook if you choose to learn even more about the Tarot.

_____

_____

_____

What other feelings, impressions, or uses do you want to note about this card?

_____

_____

_____

WANDS

A sneak peek at the royal family . . .

As a preface to each suit, we will offer tidbits of additional information on the royal family of that suit and their place in the Arcana. We will also offer various trivia on life in the feudal hierarchy as it clarifies the individual "face cards." Feel free to use or dispose of this information at your leisure. Trust the knowledge you have gained through study, but trust your instinct even more. Just don't start a *reading* without knowing what the cards say to you.

Fun nobility trivia

The knight was more than a member of the king's army. He was a field commander, a leader of men, and a rallying point. Therefore, he needed to be a hero. Unfortunately, heroes aren't *born*. Heroes are forged in the fires of pain and tempered in the icy waters of sacrifice. You don't get to be a hero by putting on a team jersey and getting paid millions of dollars a year to be "really good at a sport" (well, in the old days you didn't). In the days of knights and kings, you had to get out there and hunt down groups of bandits and actually "win" when you fought (or else you were dead). You had to protect the peasants (the "common people") and build an impressive list of deeds witnessed by credible persons. Moreover, when the king decided it was time to fight some other country, you didn't get to stay home sick: you would fight whoever the king (or queen) pointed at whenever the fancy struck him (or her).

Assuming you lived through all of that and had some impressive stories to tell, you got to train the sons of various noble families sent to learn from you (see "Page"). Because you had proven your character and skill-at-arms, you were often granted a part of the king's realm to govern (thereby saving him the chore of doing it himself). You gained the respect of men and the admiration of women, but in every way you had to earn this exalted position: You had to be of sterling moral character, a pious man, a brave *and* skilled warrior, wise enough to govern well when needed, compassionate to the poor, and relentless in your punishment of those who would harass or bully the people of your land. It wasn't an easy job by any stretch of the imagination, which is why it was reserved for *highly*-trained professionals of noble character. **But you did get a horse,** which was a nice perk, because horses, especially the well-bred (and well cared-for) horses that knights got, ate a lot of food. Not everyone could own and properly care for a horse. You also had a squire (personal attendant) and a page to help you care for your horse, armor, weapons, and whatnot, which was nice.

In the case of the *Knight of Cups,* character strengths are often highly emotional, which can be "good" *(romantic, loyal, friendly)* or "bad" *(stalker, alcoholic, abusive)* depending on the person in question this is representing. Also, remember that *Knights* can also represent action (the act of doing, as related to powerful emotional states), travel or the means of travel (car, boat, plane), as well as young men. The problem with *Knights* is that they create a "gender gap" where young men are represented but young women are not. Usually *Queens* have traditionally taken up the slack, but if you would like to have the *Knight of Coins* and the *Knight of Cups* represent young women, that is fine as well.

As to the ages of the court cards, don't get locked into this, but as an example, you may choose to see the various "face cards" represent people of these general age groups below. Remember that *aspecting* and *clarifying cards* will help identify these people much more than guesswork.

- King: Adult male *(or authority figure)* generally over 30
- Queen: Adult female *(or authority figure)* generally over 30
- Knight: Late teen to early adulthood, to age 30-ish (depending on maturity)
- Page: Child, pre-teen, tween, early teen (to age 13–15 at most usually)

The House of Cups

The House of Cups is populated with emotional, sensual, poetic, musical, and artistic people who may occasionally appear to others as whiny, controlling, manipulative, or needy. These cards represent the deep capacity for emotion that lends itself to nurture so easily, but can represent either compassion or hatred, depending on how these people perceive you. *The overall theme* we would like you to focus on when you see *Cups* cards is that of emotional response, intuition, and instincts (versus things like, say . . . "logic"), happiness and the lack thereof (when indicated), moodiness, and needs for things like security, comfort, friends, and food.

Ace of Cups

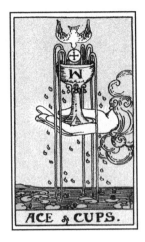

(Cardinal Water)

Description: The "hand of God" appears from a cloud, holding a fountain aloft for a dove to dip a *Catholic communion wafer* into. Water droplets shaped like *Hebrew yods* fall to the water below. The essence implied here is the absolute purity of the spiritual waters that are the source for all human emotion (the large body of water below).

Being an *Ace,* this card is *cardinal,* or bold and forceful in leadership by nature, and the suit of *Cups* is representative of the metaphysical element of water, indicating spiritual purity (or lack thereof) and raw emotions.

Prime elements at work in this card

Number:	Ace (or One). Source, infusion, endless supply, origin(s). Odd
Suit:	Cups. Emotional capacity, need, fertility, receptacle
Direction:	North. Domesticity, matriarchy. Noon. Midday meal
Element:	Water. Spirituality, emotion, faith, inspiration, purity, instinct

Traditional meaning: As with all *Aces* of the Tarot, this card reflects new beginnings, *purity of form and purpose,* and the elemental intensity required to successfully manifest something from nothing. This *Ace,* however, indicates *the wellspring,* or source, of what is to follow in this suit. This places it parallel in prominence with any of the "major" Arcana cards. Easy interpretations are: anything *new* on an emotional level; love, hope, "a miracle cure" of any sort, a surge of happiness, a birth (likely a girl), engagement, or even a marriage (if aspected by the *2 of Cups, The Lovers,* or other obvious indication). The deeper implications show a potential *soul bonding,* spiritual awakening or deep religious devotion, a peace offering in war, or a miracle *offered* (longshot hope). Being an *Ace,* this card is the essence of the suit of *Cups* without the burden of outside influence or representation. As such, all of the *Aces* can amplify the energy of similar, related cards. **All *Aces* are amplifiers:** they empower related and congruent card energies to illustrate powerful events and circumstances.

Traditional reversed meaning: Depression. Unhappiness and malaise, potentially devastating news (with any *Page,* or *Swords*), loss of love, faith, or happiness. Separation from one's personal *source* of inspiration and hope. Drug overdose in a medical *spread* or if aspected negatively by *Sword* cards or cards akin to the *5 of Cups.* Poison.

Personal Notes:

Now it's your turn

Please note: You can fill this in later if nothing comes to mind right away. It is far more important to get a good feel for this card than it is to write something in right away.

What is your interpretation? What does this card say to you?

_____

_____

_____

What does it say to you when it is *reversed*?

_____

_____

_____

If you saw this card as an "end result," what would you say to your client?

_____

_____

_____

How would you use this card as an "affirmation helper"? Keep in mind that each card is extremely valuable as an assistant in your *"Laws of Attraction and Repulsion"* exercises. Any time you *desire* something intensely, **or** find yourself in a situation *you want out of,* you can use the imagery of your chosen card (or recommend this to your clients) to enhance your visualizations and "speed up" your results. Of course, much, much more of this is covered in depth in our *Advanced Tarot Secrets* course and workbook if you choose to learn even more about the Tarot.

_____

_____

_____

What other feelings, impressions, or uses do you want to note about this card?

_____

_____

_____

Two of Cups

(Intense Fixed Water)

Description: Look closely at this card. *Two become one here.* The man wears a wreath of roses while the woman wears a laurel (traditionally a masculine adornment) in a sacred ritual of gender communion. This is *soul bonding*. Cups are exchanged and a peaceful cottage in the distance alludes to a happy family to come, but the true symbolism here are the twin serpents of *curiosity* and *desire* balanced below the lion's head of nobility flanked by wings of purity of intent. This is not "ordinary love," although this card often refers to its lesser, more commonplace form of companionship people enjoy.

Prime elements at work in this card

Number: Two. Elements joining together. Blended energies, covenants. Even
Suit: Cups. Capacity for compassion, sharing, loyalty, friendship
Direction: Southwest. Tantra, depth of commitment. Evening
Element: Water. Spirituality, love, faith, seduction, chemistry, bonding agents

Traditional meaning: Everyday meanings—A date, chance meeting, new romance, an engagement (if supported by enhancing cards), proposal or handfasting, agreement or truce between two parties, law settlement, or man asking woman out (he is approaching her). Deeper meanings—Tantric union, soul mate card. Use this card in your meditations *to attract* the right person for you. Conversely, this card *can indicate* successful contract signings in business (if supported by *Wands*), conflict resolution (if supported by *Swords*), or a promotion, raise, or loan (if supported by *Coins*). This is a *very* lucky, or fortunate, card. It is also the physical manifestation of the concept of *The Lovers* "major" Arcana card.

Traditional reversed meaning: *Trouble in Paradise.* A separation; two people going their own way, or refusing to hear each other out. Compassion dissolves into bitterness. Spurned love. Rejection. If coupled with the *3 of Swords,* this card *(reversed)* specifically indicates infidelity.

Personal Notes:

Now it's your turn

Please note: *You can fill this in later if nothing comes to mind right away. It is far more important to get a good feel for this card than it is to write something in right away.*

What is your interpretation? What does this card say to you?

_____

_____

_____

What does it <u>say to you</u> when it is *reversed*?

_____

_____

_____

If you saw this card as an "end result," what would you say to your client?

_____

_____

_____

How would you use this card as an "affirmation helper"? Keep in mind that <u>each card</u> is extremely valuable as an assistant in your *"Laws of Attraction and Repulsion"* exercises. Any time you *desire* something intensely, **or** find yourself in a situation *you want out of,* you can use the imagery of your chosen card (or recommend this to your clients) to enhance your visualizations and "speed up" your results. Of course, much, much more of this is covered in depth in our *Advanced Tarot Secrets* course and workbook if you choose to learn even more about the Tarot.

_____

_____

_____

What other feelings, impressions, or uses do you want to note about this card?

_____

_____

_____

Three of Cups

(Mutable Water)

Description: Three maidens dance happily together celebrating a good harvest. Adorned in wreaths of flowers and fruits, they gaily raise their cups high and hold bouquets of *even more* flowers. This card is *disgustingly happy*. Good friends, good food, good times, effervescent youth, and not a care in the world. Even the sky is a nauseatingly pleasant shade of baby blue. The only way one could possibly make this card any happier would be to paint smiley faces all over it.

This card is *the product* of earlier efforts to create a state of serenity and peace, and is *mutable* in energy.

Prime elements at work in this card

Number: Three. Joyful union of many. *Fertility*. Positive results. Odd
Suit: Cups. Capacity for understanding, need, desire, loyalty
Direction: East-Southeast. Community, sisterhood. Late-night celebrations
Element: Water. Felicity, emotional fulfillment, deep friendships, bonding

Traditional meaning: This is *the* pregnancy card, especially with any *Ace,* any *Page,* or *The Empress.* Alternately it shows celebrations and parties, close friendships, and happiness among like-minded people. If you draw this card, expect good things to happen. This card is not the victory itself; it is the *victory dance*. If following an illness or surgery, this card shows rapid and complete recovery. *In aspect to any card it enhances the level of happiness* by a factor of three.

Traditional reversed meaning: If you draw this card *reversed,* simply place it back in the deck and draw another card. Obviously you have made a mistake. If you stubbornly refuse to admit making a mistake, look carefully at the surrounding and *aspecting cards* in relation to this card. *When reversed,* this card reveals a deep unhappiness *brought on by* solitude, loneliness, abandonment, ruined plans, disappointment, alcoholism, drug addiction, withdrawing from society, and the loss of friends. It can also indicate excess hedonism in search of a "deeper connection" if it is aspected badly by insinuating cards.

Personal Notes:

Now it's your turn

__Please note:__ You can fill this in later if nothing comes to mind right away. It is far more important to get a good feel for this card than it is to write something in right away.

What is your interpretation? What does this card say to you?

_____

_____

_____

What does it <u>say to you</u> when it is *reversed*?

_____

_____

_____

If you saw this card as an "end result," what would you say to your client?

_____

_____

_____

How would you use this card as an "affirmation helper"? Keep in mind that <u>each</u> <u>card</u> is extremely valuable as an assistant in your *"Laws of Attraction and Repulsion"* exercises. Any time you *desire* something intensely, **or** find yourself in a situation *you want out of,* you can use the imagery of your chosen card (or recommend this to your clients) to enhance your visualizations and "speed up" your results. Of course, much, much more of this is covered in depth in our *Advanced Tarot Secrets* course and workbook if you choose to learn even more about the Tarot.

_____

_____

_____

What other feelings, impressions, or uses do you want to note about this card?

_____

_____

_____

Four of Cups

(Prime Fixed Water)

Description: A young man sits discontentedly under the shade of a tree on a pleasant day. Before him are three cups he can choose from, and if that weren't enough, flying in the face of all probability, a fairy hand reaches out from a conveniently placed nearby cloud to offer him a "wish cup" of whatever he desires. <u>Yet he resists</u>, arms crossed in passive defiance. Or perhaps, like too many of us, he is merely asleep at the time, not realizing what wonders he is missing out on.

Absolutely fixed. Our friend would not budge if the world stopped spinning suddenly. *"S-s-some men, you just can't reach . . ."*

Prime elements at work in this card

    Number: Four. Resoluteness, emotional fortress, resistance, walls. Even
    Suit: Cups. Despondence, unmet needs, withdrawal, silence
    Direction: Southwest. Secrecy, inability to "open up." Evening.
    Element: Water. Things hidden, depth of thought, meditation, astral travel

Traditional meaning: <u>Immovable object</u>—Discontent (phase). *Malcontent* (person). It is hard to be this disappointed with life, but some people find ways to become so. This card represents <u>resistance to</u> any help, advice, compassion, charity, or compromise. This is more than unhappiness. *This is a solid wall* one builds up around themselves and shuts the world out. It is absolute refusal to listen to, interact with, or even recognize the efforts of others. The subtext of this card is that *everything* has been offered to the person this card represents. Therefore, this card is *supremely dependent* on associated cards for causality. One cannot reach this state of withdrawal without reason or circumstance. Look closely for these reasons before offering up solutions.

Traditional reversed meaning: This is still not the most pleasant card, but it can indicate "coming out of one's shell," or a release from despondence and an ending of hiding away from the world.

Personal Notes:

Now it's your turn

Please note: *You can fill this in later if nothing comes to mind right away. It is far more important to get a good feel for this card than it is to write something in right away.*

What is your interpretation? What does this card say to you?

_____

_____

_____

What does it <u>say to you</u> when it is *reversed*?

_____

_____

_____

If you saw this card as an "end result," what would you say to your client?

_____

_____

_____

How would you use this card as an "affirmation helper"? Keep in mind that <u>each</u> <u>card</u> is extremely valuable as an assistant in your *"Laws of Attraction and Repulsion"* exercises. Any time you *desire* something intensely, **or** find yourself in a situation *you want out of,* you can use the imagery of your chosen card (or recommend this to your clients) to enhance your visualizations and "speed up" your results. Of course, much, much more of this is covered in depth in our *Advanced Tarot Secrets* course and workbook if you choose to learn even more about the Tarot.

_____

_____

What other feelings, impressions, or uses do you want to note about this card?

_____

_____

_____

Five of Cups
(Mutable Water)

Description: A man stands mourning his fortunes. His focus is on the three spilled cups (an obvious loss), but he either ignores, or cannot see, the two behind him. His modest estate lies in the distance, but before he gets there he has a bridge to cross, one that will force him to leave the scene of his loss, and in doing so leave behind a piece of him: his now shattered plans and expectations of *what was to be*.

This card is simultaneously *dependent on* and also a reaction to unfortunate events. As such, it is both unpleasant and *mutable* in nature.

Prime elements at work in this card

Number:	Five. Broken structure/routine. Forced changes. Odd
Suit:	Cups. Deep emotions, loyalty, regret, sadness, pain
Direction:	East-Southeast. Sacrifice, secret enemies. Just before dawn
Element:	Water. Resignation, despair, endure, propitiation, aby (penance)

Traditional meaning: *Sacrifice*. This is a card of loss and of mourning. The loss itself is usually a very real and tangible thing (find what it is by looking at the aspecting and associated cards). The subtext of this card is hope, but respect the loss before dismissing it altogether. It is quite possible that your client is feeling very strongly about their loss and is not ready to be told that *"two out of five cups are still standing."* In time the loss will be left behind, and the mess will be cleaned. Perhaps that time is now. Proceed gently here in your advice: This card is not a total loss *(see 10 of Swords)*, but it does entail emotional despair, and a need for support and healing.

Traditional reversed meaning: Recovering from distant wounds and pain. Can also indicate a recovering alcoholic. It's time to forget the past and take positive action. A renewing of faith after hard times. Courage against loss. "<u>Damn</u> the torpedoes! Full speed ahead!!"

Personal Notes:

Now it's your turn

Please note: You can fill this in later if nothing comes to mind right away. It is far more important to get a good feel for this card than it is to write something in right away.

What is your interpretation? What does this card say to you?

_____

_____

_____

What does it say to you when it is *reversed*?

_____

_____

_____

If you saw this card as an "end result," what would you say to your client?

_____

_____

_____

How would you use this card as an "affirmation helper"? Keep in mind that each card is extremely valuable as an assistant in your *"Laws of Attraction and Repulsion"* exercises. Any time you *desire* something intensely, **or** find yourself in a situation *you want out of,* you can use the imagery of your chosen card (or recommend this to your clients) to enhance your visualizations and "speed up" your results. Of course, much, much more of this is covered in depth in our *Advanced Tarot Secrets* course and workbook if you choose to learn even more about the Tarot.

_____

_____

_____

What other feelings, impressions, or uses do you want to note about this card?

_____

_____

_____

Six of Cups

(Cardinal Water)

Description: A strangely dressed boy gives a cup filled with white, star-shaped flowers to a little girl. A guard makes his rounds off to the side. *As far as these two are concerned,* the world is at peace, home is at hand, and the sky is blue. What more could anyone ask for (except perhaps a nice cup of white, star-shaped flowers to brighten up one's window sill)?

This card is exactly what it looks like and very little more. It is a pleasant thing to experience, in a pleasant, secure, location, on a very pleasant day.

Prime elements at work in this card

Number:	Six. Sharing, balance, enduring harmony. Even
Suit:	Cups. Consideration, trust, friendship, kindness
Direction:	North. Domesticity, nurturing, familial. Early afternoon
Element:	Water. Empathy, graciousness, serenity, care

Traditional meaning: Much has been written about this card by various writers, and most of it is contradictory. The meaning of this card is the simple act of *giving*. This is one of the very few Tarot cards that illustrate children at all. Here, they are a visual stylus used to illustrate, *or emphasize,* the natural innocence of the act of giving without expectation, machination, or hidden inference. This is a card of simple kindness that is all too rare in this world. No fierce battles are fought this day. No glories are won or honors bestowed. Expect a gift from a friend, or perhaps *you* will be the giver of gifts. This card can also mean a reunion with old friends.

Traditional reversed meaning: Reversed, this card often indicates a longing for everything this card represents (upright). It also indicates stress, lack of close, deep relationships with considerate people, false friends, and a need for a deeper connection with "self."

Personal Notes:

Now it's your turn

__Please note:__ You can fill this in later if nothing comes to mind right away. It is far more important to get a good feel for this card than it is to write something in right away.

What is your interpretation? What does this card say to you?

_____

_____

_____

What does it <u>say to you</u> when it is *reversed*?

_____

_____

_____

If you saw this card as an "end result," what would you say to your client?

_____

_____

_____

How would you use this card as an "affirmation helper"? Keep in mind that <u>each</u> <u>card</u> is extremely valuable as an assistant in your *"Laws of Attraction and Repulsion"* exercises. Any time you *desire* something intensely, **or** find yourself in a situation *you want out of,* you can use the imagery of your chosen card (or recommend this to your clients) to enhance your visualizations and "speed up" your results. Of course, much, much more of this is covered in depth in our *Advanced Tarot Secrets* course and workbook if you choose to learn even more about the Tarot.

_____

_____

_____

What other feelings, impressions, or uses do you want to note about this card?

_____

_____

_____

Seven of Cups

(Cardinal Water)

Description: A man stands in silhouette in apparent surprise and apprehension at the abundance of choices presented to him. Before him are life's great choices: beauty (spouse), mystery, knowledge, glory, power, fame, wealth. <u>Each is a temptation</u>, but the subtext of this card is that *his focus will become his destiny* (as in "you take the good with the bad"). It is not "a choice of one" he faces, but rather a choice of how focused will he be, and at what cost?

This card is *cardinal*, as it requires us to make choices *now*. Indecision is loss here.

Prime elements at work in this card

Number:	Seven. Destiny, evolution, spiritual choices. Odd
Suit:	Cups. Desires, life choices, possibilities, wishes
Direction:	North. Indecision, emotional vacillation. Noon
Element:	Water. Fog (physical and mental), prognostication

Traditional meaning: You have opportunities and possibilities before you. The world is at your feet (whether you know it or not), and you may even be overwhelmed by the choices you face now. *But a choice is called for,* and the clock is ticking. This is a very fortunate card as you have options, but the pressure on you to *choose and act* may be overwhelming. Take a deep breath, do some quick research, decide what you want most from life *right now,* and "strike while the iron is (still) hot." If you wait too long, the moment will pass, and the opportunity may be gone. "Choose; but choose wisely."

Traditional reversed meaning: Reversed, this card most often indicates indecision, or worse, being paralyzed by the inability to choose. It can also indicate *a lack of focus* or not knowing what one wants, and occasionally it will indicate being forced into a decision against one's will. Aspecting cards will clearly illustrate what is happening.

Personal Notes:

Now it's your turn

__Please note:__ You can fill this in later if nothing comes to mind right away. It is far more important to get a good feel for this card than it is to write something in right away.

What is your interpretation? What does this card say to you?

_____

_____

_____

What does it say to you when it is *reversed*?

_____

_____

_____

If you saw this card as an "end result," what would you say to your client?

_____

_____

_____

How would you use this card as an "affirmation helper"? Keep in mind that each card is extremely valuable as an assistant in your *"Laws of Attraction and Repulsion"* exercises. Any time you *desire* something intensely, **or** find yourself in a situation *you want out of,* you can use the imagery of your chosen card (or recommend this to your clients) to enhance your visualizations and "speed up" your results. Of course, much, much more of this is covered in depth in our *Advanced Tarot Secrets* course and workbook if you choose to learn even more about the Tarot.

_____

_____

_____

What other feelings, impressions, or uses do you want to note about this card?

_____

_____

_____

Eight of Cups

(Mutable Water)

Description: A man has placed his affairs in order and heads away to distant lands, and hopefully greener pastures. <u>A note on the symbolism used in this card</u>: *Correct symbolism would show a full moon in the sky with a crescent moon reflected in the water, revealing his emotional desire for more from life (full moon) and the emptiness of his psyche's current state (new moon).*

<u>Nonetheless</u>, his red cloak and boots illustrate he has clothed himself with purpose and resolve of action. He will *not* be coming back, no matter what he finds over the distant mountains he must traverse. This card is *a reaction to* a life of unhappiness and, therefore, is *mutable*.

Prime elements at work in this card

Number: Eight. Cycle of completion, time for a change. Even
Suit: Cups. Unfulfilled needs, desires and longings, change
Direction: East-Southeast. Escape, travel, greener pastures. Pre-dawn
Element: Water. Spiritual needs, vision quests, solitude, withdrawal

Traditional meaning: "I'm taking my ball and I'm going *home!*" Sometimes it seems like anything has got to be better than what you have now, and you just get the urge to go find out. You may (from all *outward* appearances) have everything you want in life, but inside you feel the need to get away from everything and scrub your *soul* clean. This is different from the *4 of Cups,* as it is a need for something different *and taking action on it,* versus shutting everyone out. This card indicates *life changes*: a move across state, country, or even continent, a relocation for a new job, a new career; but changes *you* make from a deep desire to get away from where you are now. Much clarity can be found by looking at aspecting cards.

NOTE: If you really want to get snooty (although we prefer the term "precise"), this card indicates travel over land, whereas the *6 of Swords* illustrates travel over water, and the *8 of Wands* suggests travel by air. This comes in handy when planning a vacation.

Traditional reversed meaning: Inability to leave a bad situation. Imprisonment or a situational mess that needs to be resolved or "cleaned up" before you can make progress toward your goals.

Personal Notes:

Now it's your turn

Please note: You can fill this in later if nothing comes to mind right away. It is far more important to get a good feel for this card than it is to write something in right away.

What is your interpretation? What does this card say to you?

_____

_____

_____

What does it <u>say to you</u> when it is *reversed*?

_____

_____

_____

If you saw this card as an "end result," what would you say to your client?

_____

_____

_____

How would you use this card as an "affirmation helper"? Keep in mind that <u>each</u> <u>card</u> is extremely valuable as an assistant in your *"Laws of Attraction and Repulsion"* exercises. Any time you *desire* something intensely, **or** find yourself in a situation *you want out of,* you can use the imagery of your chosen card (or recommend this to your clients) to enhance your visualizations and "speed up" your results. Of course, much, much more of this is covered in depth in our *Advanced Tarot Secrets* course and workbook if you choose to learn even more about the Tarot.

_____

_____

What other feelings, impressions, or uses do you want to note about this card?

_____

_____

_____

Nine of Cups

(Mutable Water)

Description: A well-fed man sits contentedly on his bench posing before his collection of nine cups. His future is assured and he knows it. There is more to be had from life, but he is smart enough to know when to get off of the merry-go-round and say, *"I have my health and my wealth, and I am going to spend the rest of my days enjoying what I have. I leave the rest of life's temptations and treasures to you."* He is downright smug in his striped shirt, fancy red cap (of pride), and folded arms.

This card is *mutable* because it is dependent upon other actions to bring it into reality. It is most often a *results* card or one indicating a *state of being*.

Prime elements at work in this card

Number:	Nine. Fruition of hopes and dreams, manifestation. Odd
Suit:	Cups. Emotional satiation, being fulfilled, abundance
Direction:	East-Southeast. Jupiter in Pisces—*dreams can come true*
Element:	Water. Happiness, indulgence, comfort, dreams

Traditional meaning: This is the fabled "wish card." It represents getting almost everything you want, "quitting the game on top," and taking your winnings home. <u>*You win!*</u> This is you getting your wish, or living your passions (ideally this is what the *8 of Cups* leads to), or just being supremely happy with what you have and not needing to toil or risk to gain anything more. This is an idealistic card of satiation and sensual pleasure, so it is a good idea to have a clear vision of your wish before you have it delivered.

Traditional reversed meaning: Some argue that "too much of a good thing can be bad." If by that they mean *too much* indulgence in wine, food, luxury, and ease of life, they may be right; at least as far as this card offers *in reverse*. Beware of the "sugar crash" brought on by too much indulgence: unhappiness, and possible health issues. Also indicative of unfulfilled wishes and dreams.

Personal Notes:

Now it's your turn

Please note: You can fill this in later if nothing comes to mind right away. It is far more important to get a good feel for this card than it is to write something in right away.

What is your interpretation? What does this card say to you?

___

___

___

What does it say to you when it is *reversed*?

___

___

___

If you saw this card as an "end result," what would you say to your client?

___

___

___

How would you use this card as an "affirmation helper"? Keep in mind that each card is extremely valuable as an assistant in your *"Laws of Attraction and Repulsion"* exercises. Any time you *desire* something intensely, **or** find yourself in a situation *you want out of,* you can use the imagery of your chosen card (or recommend this to your clients) to enhance your visualizations and "speed up" your results. Of course, much, much more of this is covered in depth in our *Advanced Tarot Secrets* course and workbook if you choose to learn even more about the Tarot.

___

___

___

What other feelings, impressions, or uses do you want to note about this card?

___

___

___

Ten of Cups

(Mutable Water)

Description: A man and his wife enjoy the splendor of their own personal rainbow high overhead their cottage estate. It looks as if our friends from the *2 of Cups* actually made it work as a couple, and now they have two happy and healthy children to add to their family bliss. This is life as it should be. Life, love, and enough land to be able to enjoy the view.

This is the end of the road along the path of *Cups*. It is the "happily ever after" card, and is one of the very best cards you can draw from the deck.

Prime elements at work in this card

Number: Ten. End results. System reset. Sum total. Even
Suit: Cups. Contentment, emotional needs, longevity
Direction: East-Southeast. Jupiter in Pisces—*dreams can come true*
Element: Water. Emotional security, faith, family, hopes and dreams

Traditional meaning: It's hard to find a more pleasant scene than this one. While there are no extravagant displays of wealth found in other cards, or accolades tossed about, it is hard to beat lasting love, health, and genuine serenity. This card indicates a happy marriage, a happy home, a stable family, and good friends.

Unlike the 9 of Cups, this "ending" is less sensually oriented, less personally indulgent, and more communally-centered, representing a larger base of happiness, with a longer endurance.

Traditional reversed meaning: Broken dreams. Illusion of happiness. Disruption of the home. Loss of security or home ownership. Broken marriages and dysfunctional families.

Personal Notes:

Now it's your turn

Please note: You can fill this in later if nothing comes to mind right away. It is far more important to get a good feel for this card than it is to write something in right away.

What is your interpretation? What does this card say to you?

_____

_____

_____

What does it say to you when it is *reversed*?

_____

_____

_____

If you saw this card as an "end result," what would you say to your client?

_____

_____

_____

How would you use this card as an "affirmation helper"? Keep in mind that each card is extremely valuable as an assistant in your *"Laws of Attraction and Repulsion"* exercises. Any time you *desire* something intensely, **or** find yourself in a situation *you want out of,* you can use the imagery of your chosen card (or recommend this to your clients) to enhance your visualizations and "speed up" your results. Of course, much, much more of this is covered in depth in our *Advanced Tarot Secrets* course and workbook if you choose to learn even more about the Tarot.

_____

_____

What other feelings, impressions, or uses do you want to note about this card?

_____

_____

_____

Page of Cups

(Weak Cardinal Water)

Description: A stylish young man dressed primarily in blue and pink poses poetically as he listens to the fish who resides in his cup dispense valuable, but routine, wisdom. His casual, matter-of-fact demeanor at being lectured to by his scaly friend belies their long-standing acquaintance, symbolizing his acceptance of the creative voices in his head occasionally presenting him with tidbits of *life advice*.

This card is *cardinal* and indicative of the gentle whispers of creative inspiration and psychic awareness.

Prime elements at work in this card

Status:	Page. Apprentice, attendant, student, youth, messenger
Suit:	Cups. Creativity, psychic awareness, artistic talent
Direction:	North. Emotional nature, inspiration. Noon. Light lunch
Element:	Water. Birth weight, imagination, subconscious mind

Traditional meaning: Keeping in mind that *Pages* have numerous meanings, this particular card can represent the birth of a baby girl, or a *Cancer, Scorpio,* or *Pisces* baby of either gender if aspected by other pregnancy cards, or in direct response to a pregnancy-related question. Otherwise, usual meanings include psychic flashes, artistic impulses, musical talent (or study), or even artistically gifted children. This *Page* also often indicates "good news" regarding some part of the *reading*. Due to the various possibilities all Pages can represent in a reading, it is best to read around them at first to glean what meaning this particular card will take.

Traditional reversed meaning: Lack of creativity, depression, anxiety, hearing voices in one's head *(not the "good kind")*, possible autism, low birth weight, unhappy childhood (if representing the past). Also: drug overdoses, alcoholism, or conversely *simple indigestion*. This is why you really need to verify what you see in *aspecting cards* or by *opening up cards* before you start handing out advice.

Personal Notes:

Now it's your turn

Please note: You can fill this in later if nothing comes to mind right away. It is far more important to get a good feel for this card than it is to write something in right away.

What is your interpretation? What does this card say to you?

_____

_____

_____

What does it say to you when it is *reversed*?

_____

_____

_____

If you saw this card as an "end result," what would you say to your client?

_____

_____

_____

How would you use this card as an "affirmation helper"? Keep in mind that each card is extremely valuable as an assistant in your *"Laws of Attraction and Repulsion"* exercises. Any time you *desire* something intensely, **or** find yourself in a situation *you want out of,* you can use the imagery of your chosen card (or recommend this to your clients) to enhance your visualizations and "speed up" your results. Of course, much, much more of this is covered in depth in our *Advanced Tarot Secrets* course and workbook if you choose to learn even more about the Tarot.

_____

_____

What other feelings, impressions, or uses do you want to note about this card?

_____

_____

_____

Knight of Cups

(Fixed Water)

Description: The *Knight of Cups* is in no rush today. He patiently approaches a wide river bisecting a stretch of desert, ignoring the heat of the day, his heavy armor, and his plodding pace. He reins his horse in tightly, to the point that the horse cannot even lift her head. His mount is not at all happy about this and shows it by laying her ears flat, kicking up her back leg mid-stride* and bobbing her head. But the Knight pays no attention to this, as all of his attention is firmly planted on keeping the contents of his cup *in* his cup.

His *fixed* nature fortifies his stern resolve.

Prime elements at work in this card

Status:	Knight. Youthful, protector, chivalry, self-discipline
Suit:	Cups. Quests, sense of duty, high-mindedness, patience
Direction:	Southwest. Obsession, dedication to a cause. Evening
Element:	Water. Inner turmoil, deep emotions, cautious, obsessive

Traditional meaning: This cards represents a young man with the ability to focus or obsess completely on a task at hand. In this card he is focusing on keeping his drive and emotions under control and contained. This card often refers to men who are either "emotionally unavailable" or simply cautious (as compared to the reckless *Knight of Swords* or the high-spirited *Knight of Wands*). This card also indicates an average or better intellect and strong musical or artistic talents. This card can represent entering into any relationship slowly and with caution.

Traditional reversed meaning: Obsessive, jealous man, *one ruled by his emotions*. Generally unreliable and dishonest. If you are in doubt as to the character of this man, use much caution in dealing with him.

* Horses walk with three of their hooves on the ground at all times. This knight is restraining his own biological urges even as his body tries to rebel from his obsessive self-control.

Personal Notes:

Now it's your turn

Please note: You can fill this in later if nothing comes to mind right away. It is far more important to get a good feel for this card than it is to write something in right away.

What is your interpretation? What does this card say to you?

_____

_____

_____

What does it <u>say to you</u> when it is *reversed*?

_____

_____

_____

If you saw this card as an "end result," what would you say to your client?

_____

_____

_____

How would you use this card as an "affirmation helper"? Keep in mind that <u>each</u> <u>card</u> is extremely valuable as an assistant in your *"Laws of Attraction and Repulsion"* exercises. Any time you *desire* something intensely, **or** find yourself in a situation *you want out of,* you can use the imagery of your chosen card (or recommend this to your clients) to enhance your visualizations and "speed up" your results. Of course, much, much more of this is covered in depth in our *Advanced Tarot Secrets* course and workbook if you choose to learn even more about the Tarot.

_____

_____

_____

What other feelings, impressions, or uses do you want to note about this card?

_____

_____

_____

Queen of Cups

(Mutable Water)

Description: A fair-haired woman sits on her seaside throne staring intently at an ornate cup of Eastern design, with handles topped with standing angels whose wings are arched far over their heads. Her cup is far more intricate than any other in the entire Tarot and illustrates the complexity of her emotions. She is examining herself at the moment, lost to the private realms of introspection.

Her external nature is *mutable* and passive as she exists more within the confines of her mind than she does the physical world.

Prime elements at work in this card

Status:	Queen. Mother, artist, writer, artist, designer, woman
Suit:	Cups. Capacity for understanding, need, desire, loyalty
Direction:	East-Southeast. Psychic, sensitive, ethereal, imaginative
Element:	Water. Spirituality, emotion, faith, inspiration, visions

Traditional meaning: This is the card of an emotionally sensitive woman, usually gifted either with some level of psychic abilities or a strong creative talent: artistic, musical, or design. Her primary traits are her imagination, sensitivity to the needs and desires of others, her caring nature, and love of animals or nature. Astrologically, use this card to represent *Cancer, Scorpio,* or *Piscean* women.

Traditional reversed meaning: The *Queen of Cups reversed* indicates a woman whose emotions tend to escape her control on a regular basis. Additionally, her sanity may come into question. Potential for drug or alcohol abuse. Potentially jealous, unreliable, dishonest, and dangerous to herself and those around her. Approach with caution.

Personal Notes:

Now it's your turn

<u>Please note:</u> You can fill this in later if nothing comes to mind right away. It is far more important to get a good feel for this card than it is to write something in right away.

What is your interpretation? What does this card say to you?

_____

_____

_____

What does it <u>say to you</u> when it is *reversed*?

_____

_____

_____

If you saw this card as an "end result," what would you say to your client?

_____

_____

_____

How would you use this card as an "affirmation helper"? Keep in mind that <u>each</u> <u>card</u> is extremely valuable as an assistant in your *"Laws of Attraction and Repulsion"* exercises. Any time you *desire* something intensely, **or** find yourself in a situation *you want out of,* you can use the imagery of your chosen card (or recommend this to your clients) to enhance your visualizations and "speed up" your results. Of course, much, much more of this is covered in depth in our *Advanced Tarot Secrets* course and workbook if you choose to learn even more about the Tarot.

_____

_____

_____

What other feelings, impressions, or uses do you want to note about this card?

_____

_____

_____

King of Cups

(Cardinal Water)

Description: We find the *King of Cups* on his throne not on the shore, like his queen, but far out at sea. The waters out here are ever turbulent and toss ships around like toys, but not a drop stains the monarch's robe. A fish jumps out of the water in the background, but his eyes are focused off in the distance and he sits on the edge of his throne at a pronounced angle, one foot forward, as if he's ready to make a move at any moment.

This man's spirit is as *cardinal* and restless as the waters surrounding his throne.

Prime elements at work in this card

Status:	King. Priest, artist, author, cook, fisherman, sailor
Suit:	Cups. Psychic, religious, loyal, family man, friendly
Direction:	North. Hard worker, provider, creative. Noon
Element:	Water. Spirituality, emotional depth, possessive, security

Traditional meaning: Notice this man's posture. This is a solid key to understanding him. Behind those eyes rage a storm of emotion, just like the fish behind him who finds that the entire sea can't contain him. This man is restless and energized with emotion. Supportive man with good character. Highly creative and could well be psychically or artistically gifted. A passion burns deep within him, and whether he releases it or not is a measure of his character. Astrologically this card represents *Cancer, Scorpio,* or *Pisces* men.

Traditional reversed meaning: The *King of Cups reversed* is a shifty devil. His word is not to be trusted as his mind (and loyalties) changes with the tide of his emotions. Potential alcohol and drug abuse, also often emotionally unstable. Before having any serious dealings with this man, ensure that you have done some investigative research to determine the extent of his character flaws and how they affect you.

Personal Notes:

Now it's your turn

Please note: *You can fill this in later if nothing comes to mind right away. It is far more important to get a good feel for this card than it is to write something in right away.*

What is your interpretation? What does this card say to you?

_____

_____

_____

What does it <u>say to you</u> when it is *reversed*?

_____

_____

_____

If you saw this card as an "end result," what would you say to your client?

_____

_____

_____

How would you use this card as an "affirmation helper"? Keep in mind that <u>each</u> <u>card</u> is extremely valuable as an assistant in your *"Laws of Attraction and Repulsion"* exercises. Any time you *desire* something intensely, **or** find yourself in a situation *you want out of,* you can use the imagery of your chosen card (or recommend this to your clients) to enhance your visualizations and "speed up" your results. Of course, much, much more of this is covered in depth in our *Advanced Tarot Secrets* course and workbook if you choose to learn even more about the Tarot.

_____

_____

_____

What other feelings, impressions, or uses do you want to note about this card?

_____

_____

_____

A sneak peek at the royal family . . .

As a preface to each suit, we will offer tidbits of additional information on the royal family of that suit and their place in the Arcana. We will also offer various trivia on life in the feudal hierarchy as it clarifies the individual "face cards." Feel free to use or dispose of this information at your leisure. Trust the knowledge you have gained through study, but trust your instinct even more. Just don't start a *reading* without knowing what the cards say to you.

Fun nobility trivia

The queen is an interesting part of the royal family unlike any other. She is both sovereign (leader) and wife to her king, except when she is unmarried (see Queen Elizabeth I, arguably one of the *best* queens in recorded history). But most queens are married and have children. This means she is wife and mother, and shares this commonality with the backbone of her kingdom: that being the wives and mothers of her "king's men." She may not have to till the field and milk the cows, and such like that, but she is still both representationally and, in fact, a mother and has the appropriate duties to perform as well as those of reigning monarch and socialite (when you are the queen *every* foreign dignitary wants to befriend you—especially if you are "hot").

This is a complex social position requiring a complex (and usually highly intelligent) woman. Oh sure, history is littered with queens who fell short of their people and their "job responsibilities," but they are far outweighed by the unsung heroines of countries and empires, the women who "stood beside" their emperors and kings (who usually got the "lion's share" of the glory in the history books). All of that makes this a particularly complex card. This card (the *Queen* of any suit) has to indicate a woman, a boss, a woman of certain character qualities (or when *reversed* possibly a woman who lacks those redeeming qualities in relation to the *spread*), **and/or** a female of a specific age range. Queens usually need to be clarified if there is any vagueness in the *reading*. Most of the time your *Queens* will refer to women who possess (or do not) the qualities of the suit in question.

In the case of the *Queen of Swords,* these character strengths are usually decisiveness, inner strength and personal authority, intelligence, responsibility, and clarity of thought. Weaknesses (if *reversed*) show up as aggressiveness, maliciousness, heartlessness, cunning, ill-tempered, selfish, and rude.

As to the ages of the court cards, don't get locked into this, but as an example, you may choose to see the various "face cards" represent people of these general age groups below. Remember that *aspecting* and *clarifying cards* will help identify these people much more than guesswork.

King: Adult male *(or authority figure)* generally over 30
Queen: Adult female *(or authority figure)* generally over 30
Knight: Late teen to early adulthood, to age 30-ish (depending on maturity)
Page: Child, pre-teen, tween, early teen (to age 13–15 at most usually)

The House of Swords

The House of Swords is populated with highly ambitious, domineering and/or deceptive people who delight in causing others pain. Most of the family members of this house are corrupt and amoral. The rest suffer at their hands. This suit represents "at face value" many of the woes society faces from its most unenlightened populace. However, this suit also represents the element of Air, which has nothing to do with violence and treachery inherently. The meanings of this suit are taken "at face value" as they were originally designed, allowing for cross-interpretation on an "as-needed" basis.

Ace of Swords

(Cardinal Air)

Description: The "hand of God" appears from a cloud, grasping a short, stout sword upright encircled at its tip by a gold crown of rulership draped with a frond of palm and a branch of olive. The lands below are desolate and barren, with harsh, jagged edges slicing angrily into the tepid sky. Six blazing *yods* of fire dance above the guard of the sword indicating righteous valor.

This card inherits its *cardinality* from being an *Ace,* or the first of the suit, and the suit of *Swords* is representative of violence, deception, victory and defeat, change, and conversely: the element of *Air*.

Prime elements at work in this card

Number:	Ace (or One). ***"No other . . ."*** Fanaticism, tyranny, authority <u>by force</u>. Odd
Suit:	Swords. Violence, decisiveness, dominance, force of will, courage
Direction:	West. Leadership, a rallying point, justice, balance, purity. Sunset
Element:	Air. Change, unpredictability, swiftness, sharp intellect, acerbic wit

Traditional meaning: This card predicts victory against any obstacle and dominance over all adversaries through aggression. It's hard to imagine any Tarot card being more phallic, or more metaphysically worshipful of the male anatomy. God himself decrees virility *über alles* here. This card indicates the rise of a new order, a new power, or leader, usually by force, or force of will. It also foretells the onset of conquest, challenges issued, macho displays of testosterone, and righteousness. This card further reveals *a lack of fear* that is downright religious in its zeal. This is a *very* powerful card to have on your side. As a *"result,"* it shows a <u>decisive</u> victory.

Traditional reversed meaning: Among professional *readers* this is quietly referred to as the *real* death card. This indicates <u>sharp</u>, <u>sudden</u> violence and <u>defeat</u>, usually accompanied by vehement rage. Before you accept this, be sure to verify any and all *aspecting cards*.

Personal Notes:

Now it's your turn

Please note: You can fill this in later if nothing comes to mind right away. It is far more important to get a good feel for this card than it is to write something in right away.

What is your interpretation? What does this card say to you?

_____

_____

_____

What does it <u>say to you</u> when it is *reversed*?

_____

_____

_____

If you saw this card as an "end result," what would you say to your client?

_____

_____

_____

How would you use this card as an "affirmation helper"? Keep in mind that <u>each</u> <u>card</u> is extremely valuable as an assistant in your *"Laws of Attraction and Repulsion"* exercises. Any time you *desire* something intensely, **or** find yourself in a situation *you want out of,* you can use the imagery of your chosen card (or recommend this to your clients) to enhance your visualizations and "speed up" your results. Of course, much, much more of this is covered in depth in our *Advanced Tarot Secrets* course and workbook if you choose to learn even more about the Tarot.

_____

_____

_____

What other feelings, impressions, or uses do you want to note about this card?

_____

_____

_____

SWORDS

Two of Swords

(Fixed Air)

Description: A woman sits on a plain stone bench, blindfolded and holding two large swords crossed high over her shoulders. The image suggests the lady *Justice*. In fact, this woman is guarding the fertile, life-giving ocean behind her. Her blindfold reveals that she allows *no one to pass;* without prejudice. The crescent moon further illustrates the restriction of *the feminine,* and of the vast emotional storehouse held within.

This is a <u>highly</u> defensive card and is of a *fixed* nature.

Prime elements at work in this card

Number:	Two. Opposing forces, diverging ideologies, indecision. Even
Suit:	Swords. Defensiveness, force of will, restriction, crossroads
Direction:	Southeast. Defiance, headstrong, opposition to any use of *force*. Late night
Element:	Air. Harsh winds, harsh words, restriction of emotions

Traditional meaning: There is no winning here. The balance created is a thinly veiled stalemate where no meaningful action can take place. This card indicates an *impasse*. Without some sort of compromise there will be no progress, no real or lasting peace, and certainly no possibility of effective change. <u>Everything is at a standstill</u>. Additionally, parties involved are defensively engaged, unwilling or unable to let their defenses down and expose themselves emotionally or to any new ideology that will precipitate a breakthrough. This card foretells labor disputes or negotiations breaking down. In artistic or literary endeavors it indicates creative or *writer's block*.

Traditional reversed meaning: Swords are sheathed and hands come out to grasp each other in agreement *(in the ancient rite of checking to make certain that the other's hands are indeed devoid of sharp objects as well)*. Settlements are reached, and action can proceed. The "creatively dead" come back to life as fresh new ideas come suddenly and in force. Breakthroughs in research. Critical problem solving. Ancient secrets are revealed.

Personal Notes:

Now it's your turn

Please note: You can fill this in later if nothing comes to mind right away. It is far more important to get a good feel for this card than it is to write something in right away.

What is your interpretation? What does this card say to you?

_____

_____

_____

What does it say to you when it is *reversed*?

_____

_____

_____

If you saw this card as an "end result," what would you say to your client?

_____

_____

_____

How would you use this card as an "affirmation helper"? Keep in mind that each card is extremely valuable as an assistant in your *"Laws of Attraction and Repulsion"* exercises. Any time you *desire* something intensely, **or** find yourself in a situation *you want out of*, you can use the imagery of your chosen card (or recommend this to your clients) to enhance your visualizations and "speed up" your results. Of course, much, much more of this is covered in depth in our *Advanced Tarot Secrets* course and workbook if you choose to learn even more about the Tarot.

_____

_____

_____

What other feelings, impressions, or uses do you want to note about this card?

_____

_____

_____

Three of Swords

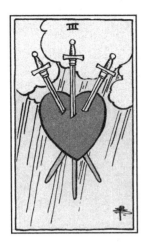

(Cardinal Air)

Description: A healthy, plump red heart, full of zest for life and love for everyone and everything is viciously stabbed, not once, but three times (three being the number of repetition designed to illustrate that something is utterly and completely done and all duties fulfilled: as in the term *threefold*).

And it's raining.

This attack on the defenseless innocent is *cardinal* (decisive and forceful) in nature and excessive due to the suit's nature.

Prime elements at work in this card

Number:	Three. Multiple people involved, triangles. Odd
Suit:	Swords. Pain, savage attacks, emotional cruelty
Direction:	West. Affairs of the heart, romantic liaisons. Sunset
Element:	Air. Fickleness, drama, scorn, inconsistency

Traditional meaning: *Ouch.*

<u>Emotionally speaking</u>: heartbreak, despair, despondence, depression, betrayal *but by someone very close to you,* abandonment, jealousy, infidelity. "Love triangle."

<u>Verbally, literally</u>: slander, libel, public humiliation, lawsuits, breach of contract, severe arguments with loved ones, rejection, treason, blasphemy.

<u>Physically</u>: heart attacks, stroke, blood diseases. See a doctor—*now*.

Traditional reversed meaning: Swift, healthy recovery after surgery, rectifications of injuries sustained, emotional healing after brutal heartache, restitutions offered under command of authority figures.

Personal Notes:

Now it's your turn

Please note: You can fill this in later if nothing comes to mind right away. It is far more important to get a good feel for this card than it is to write something in right away.

What is your interpretation? What does this card say to you?

___

___

___

What does it say to you when it is *reversed*?

___

___

___

If you saw this card as an "end result," what would you say to your client?

___

___

___

How would you use this card as an "affirmation helper"? Keep in mind that each card is extremely valuable as an assistant in your *"Laws of Attraction and Repulsion"* exercises. Any time you *desire* something intensely, **or** find yourself in a situation *you want out of,* you can use the imagery of your chosen card (or recommend this to your clients) to enhance your visualizations and "speed up" your results. Of course, much, much more of this is covered in depth in our *Advanced Tarot Secrets* course and workbook if you choose to learn even more about the Tarot.

___

___

___

What other feelings, impressions, or uses do you want to note about this card?

___

___

___

Four of Swords

(Fixed Air)

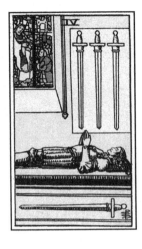

Description: A small chapel of a keep holds the final resting place of a valiant knight, presumably to whom the family is indebted. His effigy is carved in stone on the lid of his sarcophagus. A replica of his personal sword is carved on the side of his sarcophagus to serve him in the afterlife. Three swords are mounted on the wall above, next to a stained-glass window set high in the wall to bathe his monument in late-afternoon sun at the end of the day. This is a *high honor* bestowed only on a handful of men at arms. It simply is not possible, nor cost-effective, to go to the efforts to do this for everyone.

Prime elements at work in this card

Number:	Four. Rest, structure, Masons, honor. Even
Suit:	Swords. Valor, warrior, war memorials, statues, recouping from injuries
Direction:	Southeast. Public places, service to humanity. Late night
Element:	Air. Stillness, silence, stagnant, eulogies and inscriptions

Traditional meaning: This is not a card of death *(there are several of those already—if this were yet another card of death, that would be redundant)*. This card symbolizes a few different but related *fixed energy* concepts. Most often it shows a rest after protracted effort: a retirement, or putting something to rest finally. It could also indicate rest after surgery. An alternative set of meaning is that of legacies, monuments, and honors bestowed rather belated. This card could indicate an inheritance if aspected by any of several cards. Physical locations indicated are quite naturally funeral parlors, crypts, and the morgue. Occasionally this will indicate actual funerals.

Traditional reversed meaning: Dishonor. Someone is digging up the past, or things that are better left alone. No rest from prying eyes and searching hands. Lack of recognition for one's efforts and deeds.

Personal Notes:

Now it's your turn

<u>Please note:</u> You can fill this in later if nothing comes to mind right away. It is far more important to get a good feel for this card than it is to write something in right away.

What is your interpretation? What does this card say to you?

_____

_____

_____

What does it <u>say to you</u> when it is *reversed*?

_____

_____

_____

If you saw this card as an "end result," what would you say to your client?

_____

_____

_____

How would you use this card as an "affirmation helper"? Keep in mind that <u>each</u> <u>card</u> is extremely valuable as an assistant in your *"Laws of Attraction and Repulsion"* exercises. Any time you *desire* something intensely, **or** find yourself in a situation *you want out of,* you can use the imagery of your chosen card (or recommend this to your clients) to enhance your visualizations and "speed up" your results. Of course, much, much more of this is covered in depth in our *Advanced Tarot Secrets* course and workbook if you choose to learn even more about the Tarot.

_____

_____

What other feelings, impressions, or uses do you want to note about this card?

_____

_____

_____

SWORDS

Five of Swords

(Cardinal Air)

Description: A red-headed young man grins wickedly over his shoulder at his vanquished foes. He holds two swords he has recently added to his own collection, and two more swords lie carelessly dropped on the ground before him. The man is a petty tyrant, one of no consequence, except that individually he has intimidated, or beaten, others into submission. His will dominates theirs and thus everyone's destiny changes.

This act of bullying is *cardinal,* even though all action has ceased since any possible opposition has surrendered the means to do so.

Prime elements at work in this card

Number:	Five. Disorder, vigilantism, disruption of plans. Odd
Suit:	Swords. Violence, intimidation, oppression, dominance
Direction:	West. Ego validation through others. Early evening
Element:	Air. Change in direction, verbal challenges, threats

Traditional meaning: Open intimidation by a bully. Physical, mental, or verbal assault by someone who carries the need within themselves to dominate others in order to gain self-worth. This intimidation may be due to actual skill, or it may be empty words and posturing. What matters is the effect it has. Verify the actuality of the threat by *opening up* the card, and comparing this card to aspecting cards. Note the high winds blowing on the bully that do not affect any of his victims. The rage that blows the clouds across the sky feeds his ego but does nothing to soothe or invigor those who have given up their hope. This card can also show weakness among the masses (fear of a dictator or "strong leader").

Traditional reversed meaning: An end to subjugation, freedom from oppression. Conflict resolution comes after someone has the nerve to stand up to false authority. More than likely this will be a concerted (team) effort rather than any one individual *(e.g., David vs. Goliath).*

Personal Notes:

Now it's your turn

__Please note:__ You can fill this in later if nothing comes to mind right away. It is far more important to get a good feel for this card than it is to write something in right away.

What is your interpretation? What does this card say to you?

_____

_____

_____

What does it <u>say to you</u> when it is *reversed*?

_____

_____

_____

If you saw this card as an "end result," what would you say to your client?

_____

_____

_____

How would you use this card as an "affirmation helper"? Keep in mind that <u>each</u> <u>card</u> is extremely valuable as an assistant in your *"Laws of Attraction and Repulsion"* exercises. Any time you *desire* something intensely, **or** find yourself in a situation *you want out of,* you can use the imagery of your chosen card (or recommend this to your clients) to enhance your visualizations and "speed up" your results. Of course, much, much more of this is covered in depth in our *Advanced Tarot Secrets* course and workbook if you choose to learn even more about the Tarot.

_____

_____

What other feelings, impressions, or uses do you want to note about this card?

_____

_____

_____

SWORDS

Six of Swords

(Mutable Air)

Description: A ferryman poles his skiff across a short distance of water. His cargo today is a woman and her child, leaving for the distant shore. The water on his right is choppy and agitated, but the waters on his left are placid all the way to his destination. The swords in the boat coupled with the woman's hunched over, hooded countenance in contrast to the ferryman's light clothing indicate her taking flight from oppression. Vaguely reminiscent of *Charon* of Greek mythology who ferried the recently dead (who could *pay*) safely to the lands of Hades, where all rest eventually, thus *leaving* discord and *entering* harmony.

Prime elements at work in this card

Number: Six. Creating order from chaos. Even
Suit: Swords. Retreat, seeking allies, regrouping
Direction: North-Northeast. Short trips, sudden travel. Late morning
Element: Air. Change in plans, disappearing, taking flight

Traditional meaning: Journey by water. This could be a move or a vacation, but given the nature of the suit of *Swords*, this would more often point to an escape, or separation *(from an abusive spouse for example)*, or a relocation from a poor economy or other harsh environments to safer locales. This card is similar to the *8 of Cups*, except that (aside from a journey over water versus land) this image implies leaving in something of a hurry, *and things left behind*. In the *8 of Cups* the man has set his affairs in order before skipping town. Here the woman did not even have time to pack. The symbolism of the mother and child alone also suggests leaving without a spouse.

<u>Special note</u>: One half of *the Laws of Attraction and Repulsion* paradigm is *"the Law of Repulsion."* This card exemplifies this energy in action as **the ferryman** (*Captain* of the ship—e.g., the brain, will, magical efforts and workings, and so forth. For vastly extended information on this please consult your local mystery school or apply to ours <u>when</u> we are accepting students.) **pushes <u>away</u> from** the *experienced** turbulence <u>toward</u> the calmer waters of distant shores. Motivationally speaking this is "moving away from," whereas the other half of *the law* (most commonly known as "attraction" or seduction of) is "moving towards." (Here see the hidden meaning of the *7 of Cups*.)

Traditional reversed meaning: Journey or escape is delayed. No way out of the present situation. Being forced to endure current circumstances or make changes from within the system rather than running away. Possibly returning to the location of previous despair for whatever reasons.

*(experienced) When you are working your *Laws of Attraction and Repulsion* exercises you will find your ability to manifest your desires quickly and easily <u>strengthened by the act of</u> *experiencing* versus a simple visualization. Anything "experienced" fully will resonate a much greater force to pull or push away from, but does not need to be "physically" a reality. By carefully developing your imaginative capacity and your skill with "visualization aids," you will often gain the benefits of "experience" without the burden of direct active physical stimulus. Ask your teacher for help with this if you need to.

Personal Notes: *(write in your journal if you need additional room)*

Now it's your turn

__Please note:__ You can fill this in later if nothing comes to mind right away. It is far more important to get a good feel for this card than it is to write something in right away.

What is your interpretation? What does this card say to you?

_____

_____

_____

What does it <u>say to you</u> when it is *reversed*?

_____

_____

_____

If you saw this card as an "end result," what would you say to your client?

_____

_____

_____

How would you use this card as an "affirmation helper"? Keep in mind that <u>each</u> <u>card</u> is extremely valuable as an assistant in your *"Laws of Attraction and Repulsion"* exercises. Any time you *desire* something intensely, **or** find yourself in a situation *you want out of,* you can use the imagery of your chosen card (or recommend this to your clients) to enhance your visualizations and "speed up" your results. Of course, much, much more of this is covered in depth in our *Advanced Tarot Secrets* course and workbook if you choose to learn even more about the Tarot.

_____

_____

_____

What other feelings, impressions, or uses do you want to note about this card?

_____

_____

_____

SWORDS

Seven of Swords

(Cardinal Air)

Description: A thief cautiously makes his way from a war camp, taking the swords of his enemies from their armory, thus reducing their ability to do his people damage. As risky as this venture is, the warriors in the background do not seem to notice him. It looks as if the day is his after all.

Please Note: Aleister Crowley labels this card (in his *Thoth* deck) "Futility," which shifts the protagonist from the thief to the band of warriors in the background. This changes the implications of this card from *action,* to being *acted upon.*

Prime elements at work in this card

Number:	Seven. Luck is on your side, changes of fortune. Odd
Suit:	Swords. Deception, dangerous professions, pride
Direction:	West. Passive aggression, misdirection. Early evening
Element:	Air. Adapting to circumstance, clever ideas, impulse

Traditional meaning: The easiest association is a thief in your camp. A false friend, backstabbing and machinations against you by cowards, outright theft, and general deception. Usually this is the case. In more esoteric *readings* this card will indicate some clever action taken to circumvent an existing situation for personal gain, or the act of using an oppressor's own words or devices against them, and getting away with it. In any case this card *almost always* deals directly with the issues of deception and schemes or manipulation. Check all of the cards that aspect this, and compare them carefully to your client's question to ascertain how this card fits in. Usually the answer will be fairly obvious.

Traditional reversed meaning: The return of stolen merchandise or "borrowed" items, uncovering of plots and conspiracies, "the bad guy gets caught." *Conversely:* unfounded accusations and paranoia.

Personal Notes:

Now it's your turn

Please note: You can fill this in later if nothing comes to mind right away. It is far more important to get a good feel for this card than it is to write something in right away.

What is your interpretation? What does this card say to you?

_____

_____

_____

What does it <u>say to you</u> when it is *reversed*?

_____

_____

_____

If you saw this card as an "end result," what would you say to your client?

_____

_____

_____

How would you use this card as an "affirmation helper"? Keep in mind that <u>each</u> <u>card</u> is extremely valuable as an assistant in your *"Laws of Attraction and Repulsion"* exercises. Any time you *desire* something intensely, **or** find yourself in a situation *you want out of,* you can use the imagery of your chosen card (or recommend this to your clients) to enhance your visualizations and "speed up" your results. Of course, much, much more of this is covered in depth in our *Advanced Tarot Secrets* course and workbook if you choose to learn even more about the Tarot.

_____

_____

_____

What other feelings, impressions, or uses do you want to note about this card?

_____

_____

_____

SWORDS

Eight of Swords

(Fixed Air)

Description: A young woman stands bound and blindfolded on a featureless flat plain. She is surrounded by eight swords and the wind slashes at her. In the background, set high on a rocky cliff, sits the fortress house of a powerful lord, perhaps her oppressor. She cannot escape, as she cannot see where to go. She cannot see because her eyes are covered tightly. She cannot remove her blindfold because her hands are tied. So even if she takes a few steps, she will most likely fall in the mud she stands in now.

The energy of this card is stagnant. Fixed.

Prime elements at work in this card

Number: Eight. Containing structure, prison, strong walls, *lack* of progress. Even
Suit: Swords. Constriction, imprisonment, bondage, solitude, inaction
Direction: Southeast. Opposition to the ruling elite. Late night
Element: Air. Strong winds, quiet time, time to reflect on life, sensory deprivation

Traditional meaning: This card obviously illustrates being *trapped* in a situation. Incarceration, feeling emotionally closed off, creatively stifled, being held hostage by unseen forces (most often a mediocre job, few viable options for betterment, trapped in a bad marriage, etc.). But the thinly veiled underlying message behind this card is that all of these possibilities are merely the *totality* of a wall of stone that surrounds you at this time. To effect your escape from this imprisonment *certain stones* must be removed. To take down a wall quickly and easily *only a few select stones need to be removed* for the weight of the wall to collapse in on itself. You don't have to take each and every stone down by hand. This card is a wake-up call to selectively remove things from your life that are collectively causing greater harm than they could individually.

Traditional reversed meaning: Escape or release from anything that has been holding you down so far. A chance for freedom is coming. Re-entering society.

Personal Notes:

Now it's your turn

Please note: You can fill this in later if nothing comes to mind right away. It is far more important to get a good feel for this card than it is to write something in right away.

What is your interpretation? What does this card say to you?

_____

_____

_____

What does it <u>say to you</u> when it is *reversed*?

_____

_____

_____

If you saw this card as an "end result," what would you say to your client?

_____

_____

_____

How would you use this card as an "affirmation helper"? Keep in mind that <u>each</u> <u>card</u> is extremely valuable as an assistant in your *"Laws of Attraction and Repulsion"* exercises. Any time you *desire* something intensely, **or** find yourself in a situation *you want out of,* you can use the imagery of your chosen card (or recommend this to your clients) to enhance your visualizations and "speed up" your results. Of course, much, much more of this is covered in depth in our *Advanced Tarot Secrets* course and workbook if you choose to learn even more about the Tarot.

_____

_____

_____

What other feelings, impressions, or uses do you want to note about this card?

_____

_____

_____

SWORDS

Nine of Swords

(Mutable Air)

Description: A person sits up in bed, having woken from a horrible dream only to find that the bed they have made for themselves is steeped in violence and bloodshed. The blanket that covers them is decorated with roses intermittent with the symbols of the zodiac. Many swords loom overhead, but unlike *Damocles,* they do not point directly at her. The part of the bed frame that lies exposed shows a woodcut of one man running through another with a sword in the forest.

As a reaction to events already passed, or of even worse to come, this card is *mutable.*

Prime elements at work in this card

Number:	Nine. Culmination, subconscious mind saturation, overwhelming fear. Odd
Suit:	Swords. Emotional pain, fear, worry, implied threats, nightmares, regrets
Direction:	North-Northeast. Over-analyzing, anxiety. Late morning
Element:	Air. Uncertainty, difficulty breathing, banshees, insomnia

Traditional meaning: Anxiety, concern over matters that seem to be out of your control, nightmares, and sleepless nights, or inability to sleep due to a physical condition. Overwhelming stress, despair over events passed or yet to come (compare this to your client's question), emotional pain, even general paranoia. Worries may be unfounded. You will have to sort through the *reading* to find if this is the case or not. *This is a card of culmination:* these feelings did not simply appear from "nowhere." Look for the root causes of this *effect* to locate the solution. Occasionally this card may even represent an uncomfortable bed or sleeping arrangement.

Traditional reversed meaning: Emotional release. Letting go of old pain and moving on. A release of tension that you can physically *feel.* You have endured great stresses and now the causes of those are being lifted. It's time to forget the past and create new, better memories.

Personal Notes:

Now it's your turn

Please note: You can fill this in later if nothing comes to mind right away. It is far more important to get a good feel for this card than it is to write something in right away.

What is your interpretation? What does this card say to you?

_____

_____

_____

What does it say to you when it is *reversed*?

_____

_____

_____

If you saw this card as an "end result," what would you say to your client?

_____

_____

_____

How would you use this card as an "affirmation helper"? Keep in mind that each card is extremely valuable as an assistant in your *"Laws of Attraction and Repulsion"* exercises. Any time you *desire* something intensely, **or** find yourself in a situation *you want out of,* you can use the imagery of your chosen card (or recommend this to your clients) to enhance your visualizations and "speed up" your results. Of course, much, much more of this is covered in depth in our *Advanced Tarot Secrets* course and workbook if you choose to learn even more about the Tarot.

_____

_____

_____

What other feelings, impressions, or uses do you want to note about this card?

_____

_____

_____

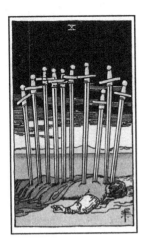

Ten of Swords

(Cardinal Air)

Description: Under a dismal coal-black sky of clouds, so thick they completely block out any sunshine or happiness, a man lies in his own blood, impaled by ten swords, all of which were conveniently delivered to his back. It seems that his past deeds have finally caught up to him. Too bad for his attackers; he left a clue to their identity.

Something *happened* to this man. Something forceful, sudden, and with enough will and determination to change his life forever. Thus the energy of this card is unmistakably *cardinal*.

Prime elements at work in this card

Number:	Ten. Endings and evolution. System reset. Results. Even
Suit:	Swords. Violence, deception, rage, betrayal, hidden enemies, injuries
Direction:	West. Revenge, mob justice, retaliation. Early evening
Element:	Air. Change, storms, "clearing the air," death rattle, *character* assassination

Traditional meaning: Live by the word, *die* by the sword. This is the undoing of a person. In extremely rare cases it may be the assault of an innocent; but as this is the summation of a life sworn to the fair and impartial virtues of the sword, the *fait accompli* visited upon this person is usually somehow apropos. This card is not a judgment on a person. It is an action befalling them, but this card rarely comes out when it has not been *earned*. In the case where it has honestly not been (earned karmically), this represents the analogous *"death of a thousand cuts"* or slightly less known, but more appropriate, "curse of inconvenience." The old saying that starts with, *"Ever have one of those days . . .?"* This card indicates one of those days (or weeks, months . . .) where it just seems like any tiny thing that can be an annoyance suddenly decides that you look like the perfect target for their aggression. In this case, the actual damage is much less than in other interpretations of this card (see above), but the real and complete damage is the incessant pin-pricking to the point of throwing you into a frenzy of anger and carelessness so that you ended up doing incalculable damage to yourself and your future, especially in ways that you cannot see.

Additionally: Absolute betrayal, financial ruin, treachery, overthrow by many hands. All of these may be physical or emotional, and they may apply to *situations,* as well as people (e.g., the sudden, ugly ending of a covenant, relationship, or business). Finally, this card may indicate chronic back pain or back *surgery.*

Traditional reversed meaning: Dodging the bullet. Danger passes so close by that you can feel the breeze of it passing. Making an "impossible" recovery from certain "death" (physical, financial, etc.). *Resurrection.*

Personal Notes:

Now it's your turn

__Please note:__ You can fill this in later if nothing comes to mind right away. It is far more important to get a good feel for this card than it is to write something in right away.

What is your interpretation? What does this card say to you?

_____

_____

_____

What does it say to you when it is *reversed*?

_____

_____

_____

If you saw this card as an "end result," what would you say to your client?

_____

_____

_____

How would you use this card as an "affirmation helper"? Keep in mind that each card is extremely valuable as an assistant in your *"Laws of Attraction and Repulsion"* exercises. Any time you *desire* something intensely, **or** find yourself in a situation *you want out of,* you can use the imagery of your chosen card (or recommend this to your clients) to enhance your visualizations and "speed up" your results. Of course, much, much more of this is covered in depth in our *Advanced Tarot Secrets* course and workbook if you choose to learn even more about the Tarot.

_____

_____

_____

What other feelings, impressions, or uses do you want to note about this card?

_____

_____

_____

Page of Swords

(Weak Cardinal Air)

Description: A young squire stands on a small mound of "high ground" practicing with his sword on a windy day. He looks dead into the wind daring someone—anyone—to attack his position. His stance is relaxed and practiced, for he has undergone years of training to become proficient with his sword, and now he faces an imaginary foe for his next duel. His clothes are light and his hair is pulled back. He has come prepared for this day's activities.

This card is active and *cardinal,* but not overly powerful. It is still "in training."

Prime elements at work in this card

Status:	Page. Apprentice, assistant, student, youth, messenger
Suit:	Swords. Defensiveness, verbal abuse, bad news
Direction:	West. Debate, opinionated, devil's advocate. Early evening
Element:	Air. Exchange of ideas, important news, urgent messages

Traditional meaning: As representative of a *person,* this card indicates a young boy or girl, or a student, either of the qualities of the suit of *Swords* (rash, loud, defensive, angry, potentially violent), or of the element of Air (intelligent, studious, [hyper] active, razor wit). If this card indicates a *message,* expect the wording to be sharp and pointed, like unpleasant news, or something delivered with disdain. When this card indicates a situation or a state of being, it reflects the act of taking the moral high ground, vehemently arguing a point, speaking from a platform (teaching, lecturing), or preaching. It does not indicate a "war of words," but rather a spirited exchange *(unless negatively aspected).*

Traditional reversed meaning: This implies a self-righteousness, or demeaning manner, poor communications, ill-chosen words leading to arguments, impatience, demotion, evisceration, irrationality, *brat.*

Personal Notes:

Now it's your turn

Please note: You can fill this in later if nothing comes to mind right away. It is far more important to get a good feel for this card than it is to write something in right away.

What is your interpretation? What does this card say to you?

___

___

___

What does it <u>say to you</u> when it is *reversed*?

___

___

___

If you saw this card as an "end result," what would you say to your client?

___

___

___

How would you use this card as an "affirmation helper"? Keep in mind that <u>each</u> <u>card</u> is extremely valuable as an assistant in your *"Laws of Attraction and Repulsion"* exercises. Any time you *desire* something intensely, **or** find yourself in a situation *you want out of,* you can use the imagery of your chosen card (or recommend this to your clients) to enhance your visualizations and "speed up" your results. Of course, much, much more of this is covered in depth in our *Advanced Tarot Secrets* course and workbook if you choose to learn even more about the Tarot.

___

___

___

What other feelings, impressions, or uses do you want to note about this card?

___

___

___

Knight of Swords
(Ultimate Cardinal Air)

Description: A young man pushes his horse hard across rough terrain. His well-trained horse is terrified, and is more concerned about what is on top of him than what lies before him. None of this matters to the myopic knight as he sees only his rage and desire for vengeance. His red cape of valor and helmet plume of righteous indignation broadcast his impatience to see justice (at the edge of a sword) done *"now!"* Even the sky is angry.

This may be the *angriest* card of the Tarot. It is full of youthful impetuousness, testosterone, and zeal. It is more *cardinal* than thou.

Prime elements at work in this card

Status: Knight. Youthful, warrior, vehemence, daring, rush of testosterone
Suit: Swords. Aggression, haste, fearlessness, force of will
Direction: West. Challenge, sense of duty, honor, military code. Sunset
Element: Air. Strong winds, hurricanes, tornadoes. Birds of prey

Traditional meaning: <u>Unstoppable force</u>. *Young alpha male:* active, decisive, even overbearing sometimes. Fearless. Natural born leader, or one thrust into it by circumstance. Either way though, things will happen "his way." This also shows a man who is quick to act, and often just as quick to leave, as well. Even so, this person will almost always have a certain charisma that draws others to him like flies to honey. As a character or personality trait, this card reveals extreme courage in the face of danger, or the act of violently forcing others to conform to one's personal beliefs. This can be either verbal or physical. Also: rushing heedlessly into action or rescue from peril.

Traditional reversed meaning: Negative aspects of the above—bully, abusive, quick to anger, loud, someone with a large personal collection of weapons, instigator, loudmouth, impatience, lack of foresight, religious fervor, zealot.

Personal Notes:

Now it's your turn

Please note: *You can fill this in later if nothing comes to mind right away. It is far more important to get a good feel for this card than it is to write something in right away.*

What is your interpretation? What does this card say to you?

_____

_____

_____

What does it say to you when it is *reversed*?

_____

_____

_____

If you saw this card as an "end result," what would you say to your client?

_____

_____

_____

How would you use this card as an "affirmation helper"? Keep in mind that each card is extremely valuable as an assistant in your *"Laws of Attraction and Repulsion"* exercises. Any time you *desire* something intensely, **or** find yourself in a situation *you want out of,* you can use the imagery of your chosen card (or recommend this to your clients) to enhance your visualizations and "speed up" your results. Of course, much, much more of this is covered in depth in our *Advanced Tarot Secrets* course and workbook if you choose to learn even more about the Tarot.

_____

_____

What other feelings, impressions, or uses do you want to note about this card?

_____

_____

_____

Queen of Swords

(Fixed Air)

Description: The *Queen of Swords* sits on her carved throne, her sword held aloft in her right hand, ready for action, her left hand beckoning to one of her minions to step forward for "judgment." She is *not* happy today.

This is a woman who is used to having things brought *to* her, or to her *attention,* to be dealt with presently. She is resolute, *fixed,* and immovable once she sets her mind to something.

Prime elements at work in this card

Status:	Queen. Mother, judge, teacher, nurse, policewoman, executive, woman
Suit:	Swords. Constriction, imprisonment, dominatrix, ice queen
Direction:	Southeast. Opposition to traditional ruling elite. Female politicians. Late night
Element:	Air. Storms, intense mental activity, being devoid of emotional clutter

Traditional meaning: This is a decisive woman, one who often gains enemies among others who do not understand her or cannot abide her stern ways. She is strong-willed and tends to keep her reasoning to herself, finding explanations of her behavior a nuisance, or even a question of her judgment, rather than a motivating factor in her underlings. She is highly intelligent, capable, and not overly swayed by emotional displays or tantrums. She represents the concept that *real power lies behind the throne,* as she is not always the one "officially" in charge, as that position comes with too much "shaking hands and kissing babies," and not nearly enough actual hands-on management of affairs.

Alternatively: If used to indicate "the element of *Air,*" this card will be either a *Gemini, Libra,* or an *Aquarius* woman, a doctor, nurse, executive, decision maker, *any type* of female authority figure, a politician, monarch, matriarch, architect, designer, engineer (etc.)—none of which are "heartless" or "emotionally distant" by nature. Remember that all of the cards in the suit of *Swords* have to pull "double duty," alternating between elemental interpretations and suit interpretations. *Clarifying cards* will solve any confusion instantly.

Traditional reversed meaning: Insufferably evil or mean-spirited, selfish woman. Tyrannical boss, corrupt politician, or harsh mother figure. Black widow or *femme fatale.* Heartless, critical, stern, and unforgiving. Could indicate the downfall of an otherwise good woman. Open this card up if you need additional information before deciding firmly on a set meaning.

Personal Notes:

Now it's your turn

Please note: *You can fill this in later if nothing comes to mind right away. It is far more important to get a good feel for this card than it is to write something in right away.*

What is your interpretation? What does this card say to you?

_____

_____

_____

What does it <u>say to you</u> when it is *reversed*?

_____

_____

_____

If you saw this card as an "end result," what would you say to your client?

_____

_____

_____

How would you use this card as an "affirmation helper"? Keep in mind that <u>each</u> <u>card</u> is extremely valuable as an assistant in your *"Laws of Attraction and Repulsion"* exercises. Any time you *desire* something intensely, **or** find yourself in a situation *you want out of,* you can use the imagery of your chosen card (or recommend this to your clients) to enhance your visualizations and "speed up" your results. Of course, much, much more of this is covered in depth in our *Advanced Tarot Secrets* course and workbook if you choose to learn even more about the Tarot.

_____

_____

_____

What other feelings, impressions, or uses do you want to note about this card?

_____

_____

_____

SWORDS

King of Swords
(Fixed Air)

Description: The *King of Swords* stares right out of the card at us. He is the only one to do so. He is challenging *us,* <u>inspecting</u> us. While other kings focus on what is most important to them *in their realms,* this man stares us down as if we are a part of *his realm.* His sword is held at a relaxed angle slightly off of the vertical, indicating that he is not as uptight as his wife. He waits for us to make the next move.

This energy of this card is *fixed,* not hesitant in any way, but unlike the *Knight,* the *King* has the wisdom to *observe* before taking action.

Prime elements at work in this card

Status:	King. Boss, overlord, alpha male, doctor, police, judge
Suit:	Swords. Establishment and established authority, "The man"
Direction:	Southeast. Politicians and "public servants." Late night
Element:	Air. Clear thought, justice, "the letter of the law," judgment

Traditional meaning: A strong leader or an authority figure, such as a police officer, lawyer, judge, businessman, military officer, corporate executive, or perhaps a stern father. Alternatively a highly intelligent professional such as a doctor, professor, scientist, or writer. Personality usually runs on the conservative side: judicious, aggressive, ambitious, reserved, distrusting of unproven ideas or people.

Astrologically: *Gemini, Libra,* or *Aquarius,* as these are all *Air* signs.

Traditional reversed meaning: A patient man with a cruel, calculating mind. Criminal mastermind or ringleader. Iron-fisted tyrant. Dictator.

Personal Notes:

Now it's your turn

Please note: *You can fill this in later if nothing comes to mind right away. It is far more important to get a good feel for this card than it is to write something in right away.*

What is your interpretation? What does this card say to you?

_____

_____

_____

What does it say to you when it is *reversed*?

_____

_____

_____

If you saw this card as an "end result," what would you say to your client?

_____

_____

_____

How would you use this card as an "affirmation helper"? Keep in mind that each card is extremely valuable as an assistant in your *"Laws of Attraction and Repulsion"* exercises. Any time you *desire* something intensely, **or** find yourself in a situation *you want out of,* you can use the imagery of your chosen card (or recommend this to your clients) to enhance your visualizations and "speed up" your results. Of course, much, much more of this is covered in depth in our *Advanced Tarot Secrets* course and workbook if you choose to learn even more about the Tarot.

_____

_____

_____

What other feelings, impressions, or uses do you want to note about this card?

_____

_____

_____

A sneak peek at the royal family . . .

As a preface to each suit, we will offer tidbits of additional information on the royal family of that suit and their place in the Arcana. We will also offer various trivia on life in the feudal hierarchy as it clarifies the individual "face cards." Feel free to use or dispose of this information at your leisure. Trust the knowledge you have gained through study, but trust your instinct even more. Just don't start a *reading* without knowing what the cards say to you.

Fun nobility trivia

The king is more than "the boss," although that fact is lost on the world at large today, and in many ways that explains the downfall of our greatest societal advancements. Too many of today's leaders (corporate, governmental, even family "leaders") enjoy the sensation of power but dodge the inherent responsibility that follows it like a shadow. In times of old (when we actually *had ruling* kings), the king was one with the land. This holds true for elected officials by the way: it is not an argument for the privileges of "divine right of birth." The essence of a true monarch (president or king) is his or her (when a queen was sovereign ruler) union with the land and its people. The unity and bonding of these two elements are at the center of the alchemical law of "as above, so below." When the king and country are *not* "one" (the ruler turns a blind eye to the needs of the people who are the heart and soul of any country) and he attempts to turn his country (or business, family, religious congregation, or any other "organization" he is put in custodial charge of) into a massive support mechanism for his ego and his luxury, the greatness of that entity starts to wither.

It is easy to see the opulence and decadence far too many self-proclaimed "emperors" narcissistically bathe themselves in at the expense of the very enterprise that supports them, and the unwillingness of the abused people to do anything about it. Therefore, the term *king* (or even *queen*) has acquired an occasionally sour taste when rolling off of the tongue. All too rare is the "honorable king" (or queen, as noted above) who realizes that his charge is to protect and enhance the land (entity: family, business, congregation, etc.) he has been en*trusted* with. And that is a shame, for as the king goes, so does the land (and its people). One good man as king can raise a whole nation of heroes.

As to our "friend" here . . . Mr. Smugness, the *King of Coins,* is an enigma. If we look at the fact that he is a representative of the element of *Earth,* it would seem that he is patient, strong, reliable, fertile, and a good manager. But one look at his face examining the size of his wealth is enough to make us pause and wonder, *"Are you a Good King? . . . or a BAD King?"* His strong points are those we just mentioned, or any of the best qualities of the astrological signs of *Earth*: decisive, good financial sense, warm, sensual ("moderately so"), wise, blah, blah, blah. *Reversed,* he is a smug, self-righteous, domineering, ultra-conservative hypocrite who uses his money to buy elections for the express purpose of making him even more money and ("just for fun") punishing anyone who dares defy him. Obviously, when he comes up, it is important to ascertain exactly which side of the tree he fell out of, *quickly.*

As to the ages of the court cards, don't get locked into this; but as an example, you may choose to see the various "face cards" represent people of these general age groups below. Remember that *aspecting* and *clarifying cards* will help identify these people much more than guesswork.

King: Adult male *(or authority figure)* generally over 30
Queen: Adult female *(or authority figure)* generally over 30
Knight: Late teen to early adulthood, to age 30-ish (depending on maturity)
Page: Child, pre-teen, tween, early teen (to age 13–15 at most usually)

The House of Coins

The House of Coins is populated with people who enjoy their money. Some are generous, others are miserly, but all of them are earthy and respect <u>the power of the coin</u> to "make things happen" in the world around them. "Coin" energy is not as volatile as "Sword," "Wand," or "Cup" energy, so it can be a little slower to "take effect," but the cardinal "Coin" energy can strike faster than a snake and hold one in its grip like a stone fortress. Coin energy tends to run a bit more permanent than other suits.

<u>Please note</u>:

While we have refrained from discussing any of the highly controversial aspects of the Tarot here (as the basis of this text is to make learning the Tarot <u>easy</u> and uncomplicated by too much advanced Tarot philosophy), unfortunately it is necessary to correct a misnomer that has befuddled far too many students throughout the past century. We are teaching this suit using the term "Coins" instead of "Pentacles" for a few simple reasons. The origin of the suit was "Gold" (as in gold coins), and the addition of pentacles inside of the disks shown in each card was an unnecessary embellishment by one artist, copied by others, and thoroughly dismissed by the master adept Aleister Crowley when he "improved" on Waite's design. The addition of pentagrams to the coins (making them pentacles) looks pretty, but it confuses the meaning and causes much self-doubt in students all over the world, as they wonder what the secret "hidden inference" of the star is that they are missing. This practice stops here. Too many otherwise able students have been needlessly confused by this. Call the suit what you will, but the interpretation is wealth, not paganism. It is impossible to contain the entirety of a religion in one "minor" Arcana suit, and the highly incompatible and contradictory religious symbolism of the Ace of Coins would render the card useless and indecipherable.

So while the pentagram inside the coins is an interesting decoration, <u>please do not read too much into the symbolism</u> of the artist who added it. Some decks alter or do away completely with the notion of the star, leaving the suit to remain gold coins, as the emphasis of this suit is, after all, <u>money</u>, and everything you can do with it. The problem of changing the suit representational of wealth into a suit representational of the pagan religion is that it removes the clarity of purpose of the illustrations, changes the meanings of ALL of the cards of that suit, and leaves the question of money completely unanswered.

Ace of Coins

(Cardinal Earth)

Description: The "hand of God" appears from a small cloud, holding a large gold coin this time. Ignore the pentagram inscribed in it for the moment. The *gold* and the *coin* part are the primary Tarot symbolism. The addition of a pentagram to the coin in this image does not change the Tarot symbolism, nor does it imply that a *Christian* "God" is a heathen (pagan). The grounds below are lush and luxurious in contrast to other *Aces,* reinforcing the fertility of the earth and the raw power of Nature.

The energy of this card is *cardinal,* as are all of the other *Aces.* It shows us the foundation of all wealth and worldly power.

Prime elements at work in this card

Number:	Ace (or One). Source, foundation, prime fertility. Odd
Suit:	Coins. Wealth, abundance, growth, raw materials
Direction:	South. Leadership, regimen, acquisition, *Kronos.* Midnight
Element:	Earth. Stability, strength, reliability, responsibility, nutrients

Traditional meaning: This card signifies the beginning of any fortunate enterprise or undertaking. "If you do *this 'thing,'* you will get money." This could mean buying a lottery ticket, marrying a wealthy spouse, earning a university degree, starting a new business, or taking a certain job. This card betokens new money, but to determine exactly where and how that money will appear, it helps to know the question asked, or have aspecting cards reveal to you their connection with this card. The timing on *Aces* is usually "imminent," with occasional exception that will be obvious in your *readings;* but aspecting cards can and will narrow down the time frame in exact proportion to your familiarity with your cards and the exact specifics of the question asked.

Traditional reversed meaning: Delays in getting paid, missed opportunities, *not* getting the "big raise," being written out of the inheritance, warning not to speculate or gamble, time to conserve your money.

Personal Notes:

Now it's your turn

Please note: *You can fill this in later if nothing comes to mind right away. It is far more important to get a good feel for this card than it is to write something in right away.*

What is your interpretation? What does this card say to you?

_____

_____

_____

What does it <u>say to you</u> when it is *reversed*?

_____

_____

_____

If you saw this card as an "end result," what would you say to your client?

_____

_____

_____

How would you use this card as an "affirmation helper"? Keep in mind that <u>each</u> <u>card</u> is extremely valuable as an assistant in your *"Laws of Attraction and Repulsion"* exercises. Any time you *desire* something intensely, **or** find yourself in a situation *you want out of,* you can use the imagery of your chosen card (or recommend this to your clients) to enhance your visualizations and "speed up" your results. Of course, much, much more of this is covered in depth in our *Advanced Tarot Secrets* course and workbook if you choose to learn even more about the Tarot.

_____

_____

_____

What other feelings, impressions, or uses do you want to note about this card?

_____

_____

_____

Two of Coins

(Mutable Earth)

Description: A man juggles his coins as a ship in the background is tossed about carelessly by the ever-changing sea. By the man's garb and spritely dance, we can see that he is a professional; and he is not overly concerned, yet pensive, as if trying to find the perfect balance. The ribbon that surrounds his coins is reminiscent of the infinity symbol, suggesting that his is an ongoing struggle for balance through constant adjustment and analysis.

The symbolism of this card strongly suggests ongoing emotional and physical imbalance, and is of a *mutable* nature.

Prime elements at work in this card

Number:	Two. Options, possibilities, differing needs and desires. Even
Suit:	Coins. Budgets, financial responsibilities, risks and gambling
Direction:	West-Northwest. Flexibility, adaptation, accounting. Early afternoon
Element:	Earth. Tremors, quicksand, mud, muck, murk, swamps, scandal

Traditional meaning: To truly get this card, simply angle it slightly to the right (clockwise) so that the boat is "level." Now imagine that the boat is "steady," and that *it is the entire earth that is rolling around under this man's feet* as he tries to juggle, and dance, and keep his balance without dropping either of his coins or his ribbon. This card has one central meaning that can manifest in several different ways: At best it reveals clever accounting and tricky cash flow to keep everything afloat, even against the stormy seas of volatile economic times. On a slightly less happy note, *it more often reveals a financial struggle,* literally the "juggling of one's finances" by borrowing money from this area of the budget to pay for that, and scrambling to make ends meet. In a worst case scenario, it is a dire warning that one's current money management style is about to explode in their face. Could indicate financial insolvency, gambling, even scams.

Traditional reversed meaning: Finances in complete disarray, overspending, disorganization leads to chaos, instability, nervous breakdown, hypochondria, trying to fulfill too many obligations, physical accidents.

Personal Notes:

Now it's your turn

Please note: *You can fill this in later if nothing comes to mind right away. It is far more important to get a good feel for this card than it is to write something in right away.*

What is your interpretation? What does this card say to you?

___

___

___

What does it say to you when it is *reversed*?

___

___

___

If you saw this card as an "end result," what would you say to your client?

___

___

___

How would you use this card as an "affirmation helper"? Keep in mind that each card is extremely valuable as an assistant in your *"Laws of Attraction and Repulsion"* exercises. Any time you *desire* something intensely, **or** find yourself in a situation *you want out of,* you can use the imagery of your chosen card (or recommend this to your clients) to enhance your visualizations and "speed up" your results. Of course, much, much more of this is covered in depth in our *Advanced Tarot Secrets* course and workbook if you choose to learn even more about the Tarot.

___

___

___

What other feelings, impressions, or uses do you want to note about this card?

___

___

___

COINS

Three of Coins

(Cardinal Earth)

Description: A master stonemason is doing some finishing work on an intricate arch he has been commissioned to create for a local monastery. He is interrupted by a friar and a bureaucrat who happen to have an *artistic rendition* of what the arch "should" look like. They simply have some questions or concerns about the project. This can be seen as forcing him to stop work to answer some questions that could easily be addressed after the daylight hours have passed, since he can't do this at night, or it may be taken as a commendation of his skills.

Whether this represents the master or the critic, it is *cardinal* in energy.

Prime elements at work in this card

Number:	Three. Additional input, "three's a crowd," structural analysis. Odd
Suit:	Coins. Work stoppage, quality control, commendations, clients, referrals
Direction:	South. Corporate executives, management, structure, detail. Midnight
Element:	Earth. Mastery of skill, contracts and *"contracts awarded,"* self-reliance

Traditional meaning: This is the card of *the master;* whether that is a master artist, swordsman, magus, stonecutter, or any other occupation, this card shows great skill and achievement. Compare this to the *8 of Coins,* which shows us the *apprentice.* This may indicate the master himself, his masterpiece work, his studio, or even a visit from clients. Similarly it can represent artistic criticism, or a critique of one's work, an employee evaluation, quality assessment, even a promotion or a raise. *All of these possibilities are positive in nature.* Look to the surrounding cards and the nature of the question to determine exactly what is at play here. This card can occasionally indicate unexpected assistance once you have earned your "sweat equity" (you have made your bandwagon and people want to jump on it, which is not necessarily a *bad* thing at all).

Traditional reversed meaning: The same basic principles for this card apply in *reverse,* except that they are far more negative. Now we see complaints about your work: unhappy bosses or clients, meddling in your affairs, or nagging and micro-managing to great detriment, even lack of recognition for your efforts. Conversely: *shoddy workmanship.*

Personal Notes:

Now it's your turn

Please note: *You can fill this in later if nothing comes to mind right away. It is far more important to get a good feel for this card than it is to write something in right away.*

What is your interpretation? What does this card say to you?

_____

_____

_____

What does it <u>say to you</u> when it is *reversed*?

_____

_____

_____

If you saw this card as an "end result," what would you say to your client?

_____

_____

_____

How would you use this card as an "affirmation helper"? Keep in mind that <u>each</u> <u>card</u> is extremely valuable as an assistant in your *"Laws of Attraction and Repulsion"* exercises. Any time you *desire* something intensely, **or** find yourself in a situation *you want out of,* you can use the imagery of your chosen card (or recommend this to your clients) to enhance your visualizations and "speed up" your results. Of course, much, much more of this is covered in depth in our *Advanced Tarot Secrets* course and workbook if you choose to learn even more about the Tarot.

_____

_____

_____

What other feelings, impressions, or uses do you want to note about this card?

_____

_____

_____

Four of Coins
(Fixed Earth)

Description: A merchant lord sits on a simple stone block *throne* in the middle of a thriving metropolis. This man is so cheap he doesn't even have his throne embellished beyond the most basic indications that it is a platform. He tightly grips a coin in an *"infinite loop,"* and prevents two from escaping while boastfully proclaiming his sovereignty of wealth by wearing yet another coin on top of his self-stylized crown. This man *needs* to display his smallness as much as he needs to display his wealth and "power." He is as *fixed* as his pose. Please do note that this is the *only* metropolis setting in the entire Tarot.

Prime elements at work in this card

Number:	Four. Walls, *glass ceiling*, restriction, stability, possessiveness. Even
Suit:	Coins. Budget cuts, savings, bank vaults, loan officers, businessman, greed
Direction:	Northeast. Heartless boss, tyrant, landlord, white-collar thief. Morning
Element:	Earth. Embezzlement, hoard and one who hoards, "conservative"

Traditional meaning: Money works best when it *flows*. The idea of great wealth is not to *stop* the flow at all. It is the process of diverting some of the vast flow of golden coins to jingle your way as you create a small pool for them to circulate in before they flow out to parts unknown, <u>preferably at a much slower rate than they come in</u>. Having large amounts of money *and not being able to spend it* (on food, clothing, luxuries, or necessities) is not wealth. It is hell. This card presents us with the complete stoppage of the *flow* of money. This man hoards what little he has, <u>and so he gets no more</u>. This card indicates being *too controlling* with any resources, to the point of being locked in a box. This card says, "There is no money available. Period." *End of story.*

Traditional reversed meaning: Tight-fisted boss or landlord, or someone who publicly wears excessive amounts of gold or other status and wealth indicators to intimidate and impress others. Obsessively greedy people, corporate feudal lords and their political cronies. Dictators.

Personal Notes:

Now it's your turn

__Please note:__ You can fill this in later if nothing comes to mind right away. It is far more important to get a good feel for this card than it is to write something in right away.

What is your interpretation? What does this card say to you?

_____

_____

_____

What does it say to you when it is *reversed*?

_____

_____

_____

If you saw this card as an "end result," what would you say to your client?

_____

_____

_____

How would you use this card as an "affirmation helper"? Keep in mind that each card is extremely valuable as an assistant in your *"Laws of Attraction and Repulsion"* exercises. Any time you *desire* something intensely, **or** find yourself in a situation *you want out of,* you can use the imagery of your chosen card (or recommend this to your clients) to enhance your visualizations and "speed up" your results. Of course, much, much more of this is covered in depth in our *Advanced Tarot Secrets* course and workbook if you choose to learn even more about the Tarot.

_____

_____

_____

What other feelings, impressions, or uses do you want to note about this card?

_____

_____

_____

Five of Coins

(Mutable Earth)

Description: A destitute woman and a leper *(notice the bell around his neck)* struggle through a snowstorm at night just outside the foot-thick towering stone walls of a fortress-like church, whose magnificent buttressed stained-glass window radiates brightly with the proclamation that all is well in the "house of God." No one comes out to greet them, no door stands open to welcome them in to the warmth and "compassion" of religion. This is the institution of religion failing, as it caters to its own wealth at the expense of the downtrodden it claims to serve. This is the destruction of the bonds of society.

Prime elements at work in this card

Number: Five. <u>Duality of essence</u>; chaos and structure, lies and machinations. Odd
Suit: Coins. Corporate spirituality, religion for sale, devastation, false gods
Direction: West-Northwest. Illness, financial insolvency, despair. Early afternoon
Element: Earth. Health issues, homelessness, eviction, lack of opportunity or ability

Traditional meaning: This is a very unpleasant side of any society. This card addresses poverty, homelessness, lack of health and health insurance. This card signifies a lack of ability to pay one's way in life after a tragedy. It shows the physical and emotional despair of ruin and the view of much of society that *the poor* are merely indolent, lazy, and deserve their fate. This card reflects more than a simple lack of funds. It reveals a lack of compassion, and a refusal to assist those in need, whether they brought their afflictions upon themselves, or they are victims of the abuse of others. All in all, this card is one of loss and despair. If this card comes up in a *reading*, look to aspecting cards to determine causes and solutions, or preventions.

Traditional reversed meaning: Materialism to the point of spiritual starvation and disconnect. Wealth at the cost of lasting happiness and any of the virtues. False gods or spiritual leaders, cults.

Personal Notes:

Now it's your turn

Please note: You can fill this in later if nothing comes to mind right away. It is far more important to get a good feel for this card than it is to write something in right away.

What is your interpretation? What does this card say to you?

_____

_____

_____

What does it say to you when it is *reversed*?

_____

_____

_____

If you saw this card as an "end result," what would you say to your client?

_____

_____

_____

How would you use this card as an "affirmation helper"? Keep in mind that each card is extremely valuable as an assistant in your *"Laws of Attraction and Repulsion"* exercises. Any time you *desire* something intensely, **or** find yourself in a situation *you want out of,* you can use the imagery of your chosen card (or recommend this to your clients) to enhance your visualizations and "speed up" your results. Of course, much, much more of this is covered in depth in our *Advanced Tarot Secrets* course and workbook if you choose to learn even more about the Tarot.

_____

_____

_____

What other feelings, impressions, or uses do you want to note about this card?

_____

_____

_____

COINS

Six of Coins

(Cardinal Earth)

Description: A man holds a scale in his left, or *sinister*, hand while dispensing alms to a pair of men unable to earn their way through life at this time. He is bathed in red: his hat of decisive action, his robe of purpose, his collar of vociferous piety, his leggings of applied effort, and his belt of self-discipline. His own robe is threadbare and fraying from much use, and his tunic is as white and pure as his motives. He acts independently, without the need of praise, sanction, nor accolades of any temple or government.

He is his own authority, which lends him the autonomy of being *cardinal*.

Prime elements at work in this card

Number: Six. Sharing, balance, give and take, equilibrium, social responsibility. Even
Suit: Coins. Charity, community investment, public policy, welfare, loans
Direction: South. Decision-making ability, scholarships and grants, lottery. Midnight
Element: Earth. Second chances, balanced thought, karma, careful decisions

Traditional meaning: This card illustrates a good person and a solid *citizen*. This person contributes more to society than their labors, or their DNA (offspring), and the taxes they pay for the public good. *They take action on their own initiative to help those in need,* create art and gardens for the public, clean up their neighborhoods, and in other ways make their area more livable. This card also refers to the act of charity, or selfless giving, stopping to help someone, or the giving and receiving of presents.

Traditional reversed meaning: Individual selfishness and narcissism. The person or action indicated are so concerned with their own well-being that they refuse to look out for the needs of others unless it benefits them directly somehow, usually insisting on payment before any services are rendered. That makes this the card of the *scam; also blackmail, or extortion.* If this card comes up *reversed,* look at aspecting cards to see if your client is being pressured or deceived.

Personal Notes:

Now it's your turn

Please note: You can fill this in later if nothing comes to mind right away. It is far more important to get a good feel for this card than it is to write something in right away.

What is your interpretation? What does this card say to you?

_____

_____

_____

What does it <u>say to you</u> when it is *reversed*?

_____

_____

_____

If you saw this card as an "end result," what would you say to your client?

_____

_____

_____

How would you use this card as an "affirmation helper"? Keep in mind that <u>each</u> <u>card</u> is extremely valuable as an assistant in your *"Laws of Attraction and Repulsion"* exercises. Any time you *desire* something intensely, **or** find yourself in a situation *you want out of,* you can use the imagery of your chosen card (or recommend this to your clients) to enhance your visualizations and "speed up" your results. Of course, much, much more of this is covered in depth in our *Advanced Tarot Secrets* course and workbook if you choose to learn even more about the Tarot.

_____

_____

_____

What other feelings, impressions, or uses do you want to note about this card?

_____

_____

_____

COINS

Seven of Coins
(Mutable Earth)

Description: A young man rests on his hoe, staring down despondently at the crop he has grown from seed. The harvest this year is beyond excellent. Large, full, rich leaves reveal the health of the stalk beneath, and bright golden disks grow in tight clusters, but for all of that the results seem disappointing to him, as if he dreams of life as an acrobat rather than a farmer, even a farmer of gold coins. This card is proof that if money really did grow on trees, *someone* would still wish they were strawberries.

This card is the result, or yield of previous actions, therefore, it is *mutable*.

Prime elements at work in this card

Number:	Seven. Realization, rest, overview, rewards and results. Odd
Suit:	Coins. Successful harvest, questionable results, high expectations
Direction:	West-Northwest. Disappointment, analysis, servile labor. Early afternoon
Element:	Earth. Fertility, unexpected pregnancy, indecision, slow or steady growth

Traditional meaning: No matter how good your situation may look to others, or even how comfortable and entertaining it may actually be, it is simply not for you. Your heart is not in your work. This card shows a boring job, or one that has become boring, if it ever had any gleam and luster to begin with. Daydreaming of distant places and adventures to be found there comes easily now, often to the cost of the quality of work you do *right now*. It's time for a change. Time to leave the nest and take risks, see the world and sample its varied pleasures. This place has nothing left for you.

Traditional reversed meaning: *Reversed,* this card indicates that you are missing the point—you have something worthwhile, something you will miss dearly if you let it die off, or walk away from. Before you neglect what you have into obscurity, you should take some time and think very seriously and carefully about your next move.

Personal Notes:

Now it's your turn

Please note: *You can fill this in later if nothing comes to mind right away. It is far more important to get a good feel for this card than it is to write something in right away.*

What is your interpretation? What does this card say to you?

_____

_____

_____

What does it say to you when it is *reversed*?

_____

_____

_____

If you saw this card as an "end result," what would you say to your client?

_____

_____

_____

How would you use this card as an "affirmation helper"? Keep in mind that each card is extremely valuable as an assistant in your *"Laws of Attraction and Repulsion"* exercises. Any time you *desire* something intensely, **or** find yourself in a situation *you want out of,* you can use the imagery of your chosen card (or recommend this to your clients) to enhance your visualizations and "speed up" your results. Of course, much, much more of this is covered in depth in our *Advanced Tarot Secrets* course and workbook if you choose to learn even more about the Tarot.

_____

_____

_____

What other feelings, impressions, or uses do you want to note about this card?

_____

_____

_____

COINS

Eight of Coins

(Fixed Earth)

Description: A young man carefully taps a large pentagram into a gold coin. He seems to enjoy his job, but his focus is on his precision, *on the task at hand*. Mounted on the wall next to him are several finished coins, and others rest on the ground next to him. He wears the apron of a *trained apprentice,* revealing his basic skill in workmanship. His workspace is free of clutter, reducing any distractions from his work.

His labors are regular and repetitive, making this a *fixed* card.

Prime elements at work in this card

Number:	Eight. Routine, endless repetition, penance, practice, training. Even
Suit:	Coins. Basic employment, apprenticeship, artisans, construction. A Mint
Direction:	Northeast. Job security, financial sector work, factory. Mid-morning
Element:	Earth. Economic growth (public), arts and crafts, small business

Traditional meaning: *"Work, work, work."* This card can mean many things. At first blush, it reveals an apprentice, or one whose level of skill is worthy of employment, but not such that they are an *artiste,* or a master, capable of opening up their own shop. That leads this card to be an indicator of a *job,* or simple gainful employment, even if that job lasts twenty years. The card also indicates an *artisan,* or craftsman who specializes in a certain area of service or manufacture. In this case, the card shows us a physical artist, a true artisan, or a skilled specialist in physical matters (e.g., construction, auto mechanic, engineer, etc.). Finally, the alternate aspect of the apprentice is one who studies, meaning a student of a vocational school, or the act of attending "adult education" to better oneself. Look to aspecting cards *first*.

Traditional reversed meaning: Sloth, laziness, inattentiveness at school, not applying oneself, being late for work, unreliable, *unemployment.*

Personal Notes:

Now it's your turn

__Please note:__ You can fill this in later if nothing comes to mind right away. It is far more important to get a good feel for this card than it is to write something in right away.

What is your interpretation? What does this card say to you?

_____

_____

_____

What does it say to you when it is *reversed*?

_____

_____

_____

If you saw this card as an "end result," what would you say to your client?

_____

_____

_____

How would you use this card as an "affirmation helper"? Keep in mind that each card is extremely valuable as an assistant in your *"Laws of Attraction and Repulsion"* exercises. Any time you *desire* something intensely, **or** find yourself in a situation *you want out of,* you can use the imagery of your chosen card (or recommend this to your clients) to enhance your visualizations and "speed up" your results. Of course, much, much more of this is covered in depth in our *Advanced Tarot Secrets* course and workbook if you choose to learn even more about the Tarot.

_____

_____

_____

What other feelings, impressions, or uses do you want to note about this card?

_____

_____

_____

Nine of Coins

(Fixed Earth)

Description: A finely dressed woman lounges in the vineyard of her estate, surrounded by ripe, succulent fruits, more wealth than she can even care about, and her pet falcon. She wants for *nothing*. Wealth to her is nothing more than an assumed way of life. There is no other existence she can imagine, so she doesn't waste her valuable time dreaming up the impossible, or the nonsensical. She has her passions *(falconing)* and her bountiful garden of grapes that is the envy of everyone she knows. What else could anyone ever ask for, or need from life?

Her decadence is unquestionable, and her lifestyle is *fixed*.

Prime elements at work in this card

Number:	Nine. Fruition of goals, retirement, "end of the rainbow." Odd
Suit:	Coins. Financial independence, "kept (man or) woman," farm or vineyard
Direction:	Northeast. Luxury, sensualism, nature, passions, beauty. Mid-morning
Element:	Earth. Self-made people, druids, estate lands, easy life, *hedonism*

Traditional meaning: This is a *kept woman*. Of course, this card is applicable to either gender, and people of any age, as long as they are among the idle rich, or merely serenely content with the wealth they *do* possess, their passions, and their ease of life. This extremely fortunate card betokens material success to the point of leisurely inactivity. But this is more than simply *having money*. This card is about <u>enjoying your passions</u> in life, and having an ease of existence so that you can chase your dreams, and not have to put up with the drudgery of everyday life that the rest of the population of Earth has to contend with, no matter how wealthy they are. This is life as a permanent vacation, no matter what your status otherwise.

Traditional reversed meaning: When this card is *reversed*, it shows what we are missing out on. "All work and no play . . ." leads to a life of work, and possibly wealth and power, but to what end?

Personal Notes:

Now it's your turn

__Please note:__ You can fill this in later if nothing comes to mind right away. It is far more important to get a good feel for this card than it is to write something in right away.

What is your interpretation? What does this card say to you?

_____

_____

_____

What does it say to you when it is *reversed*?

_____

_____

_____

If you saw this card as an "end result," what would you say to your client?

_____

_____

_____

How would you use this card as an "affirmation helper"? Keep in mind that each card is extremely valuable as an assistant in your *"Laws of Attraction and Repulsion"* exercises. Any time you *desire* something intensely, **or** find yourself in a situation *you want out of,* you can use the imagery of your chosen card (or recommend this to your clients) to enhance your visualizations and "speed up" your results. Of course, much, much more of this is covered in depth in our *Advanced Tarot Secrets* course and workbook if you choose to learn even more about the Tarot.

_____

_____

_____

What other feelings, impressions, or uses do you want to note about this card?

_____

_____

_____

COINS

Ten of Coins

(Cardinal Earth)

Description: An old man lounges in the garden of his estate in a large village. His greyhounds attend him, even as a playful young girl grabs at one's tail. Her mother chats happily with a young man armed with a spear in a wide stone arch which is, in turn, decorated with shields emblazoned with the Coats of Arms of powerful families, and a massive tapestry illustrated with a skillfully woven scene of a mountainous fortress. Life is easy, gay, and relaxed here.

This is the card of *generations* of wealth compiled, and power consolidated into one strong, large family of absolute luxury. And it is a *cardinal* family.

Prime elements at work in this card

Number:	Ten. End results, system reset, sum total. Total market dominance. Even
Suit:	Coins. Generational wealth, powerful *families,* empire(s), Camelot
Direction:	South. Authority, autonomy, influence, ruling class, executives. Midnight
Element:	Earth. Opulence, born into wealth, retirement, inheritance, corporations

Traditional meaning: Old money. This is the *estate card*. This is not indicative of winning the lottery, or doing well at your job. This card means wealth and power that most people never *visit,* much less possess. The ease and comfort with wealth and power shown in this card come only from being raised in wealth, or adapting to it so completely that it becomes like a second skin. Thus, this card best reflects a *very healthy* pension or a retirement in style (and then some) after a lifetime of investing one's time and energy toward this end goal. As a location, or an *entity,* this can indicate any powerful family (industrial, political, or royalty), a museum, a wealthy investor for your project, or a large and luxurious house. As a *result,* it can be a bank loan or other big-project financial action. If you wanted to play this card loose and fast, it could conceivably indicate "moving back in with mom and dad" if this interpretation was supported by *aspecting cards*.

Traditional reversed meaning: Loss of economic stability, the fall of a great house of power, infighting among insiders (in a family or business) that threatens to tear an empire apart. Living so far beyond one's means to keep up appearances that one's foundation is shaky.

Personal Notes:

Now it's your turn

Please note: You can fill this in later if nothing comes to mind right away. It is far more important to get a good feel for this card than it is to write something in right away.

What is your interpretation? What does this card say to you?

_____

_____

_____

What does it say to you when it is *reversed*?

_____

_____

_____

If you saw this card as an "end result," what would you say to your client?

_____

_____

_____

How would you use this card as an "affirmation helper"? Keep in mind that each card is extremely valuable as an assistant in your *"Laws of Attraction and Repulsion"* exercises. Any time you *desire* something intensely, **or** find yourself in a situation *you want out of,* you can use the imagery of your chosen card (or recommend this to your clients) to enhance your visualizations and "speed up" your results. Of course, much, much more of this is covered in depth in our *Advanced Tarot Secrets* course and workbook if you choose to learn even more about the Tarot.

_____

_____

What other feelings, impressions, or uses do you want to note about this card?

_____

_____

_____

COINS

Page of Coins

(Weak Cardinal Earth)

Description: A young squire stands in a lush, green meadow overlooking carefully worked farm lands. The fertile soil is rich, moist, and capable of providing *generations of* various crops if tended with care. From all accounts, that is the course of action. The squire here represents the newest generation of estate lords who are custodians of this area, and his poetic stance and worshipful gaze at the coin he holds with absolute reverence indicate his fascination with his lot in life. His reverence for his trade creates a spiritual resonance in him that will one day translate into the work he applies to these lands.

Prime elements at work in this card

Status: Page. Apprentice, assistant, student, youth, messenger
Suit: Coins. Contract, promotion, raise, new job, financial plan
Direction: South. School tuition, loans, grants (etc.), thrift, ability to budget. Midnight
Element: Earth. Good news financially, small budgets or profits, "nest egg"

Traditional meaning: *Pages* are meant to illustrate many things. As a person, it can show a young boy or girl of the *Earth* signs (*Taurus, Virgo,* or *Capricorn*). It can also show someone one who is deeply in love with money and luxuries. As a message, it bears small tidings of money, usually news of a raise, a bonus, a gift, or a refund. But it can also indicate the act of study (or economics, accounting, banking, or any of the financial sciences), or even tuition money for school, as *Pages* can represent *students* learning their trade. Compare this card directly to the question at hand, and look for *aspecting* cards to indicate exactly what the message is here, as *all of the Page cards are highly dependent on other cards to give them clarity of meaning.*

Traditional reversed meaning: (Minor) bad news financially or small loss of income or savings. One who spends far too easily with no appreciation for the efforts required to *earn* money. Not getting *paid*.

Personal Notes:

Now it's your turn

__Please note:__ You can fill this in later if nothing comes to mind right away. It is far more important to get a good feel for this card than it is to write something in right away.

What is your interpretation? What does this card say to you?

_____

_____

_____

What does it <u>say to you</u> when it is *reversed*?

_____

_____

_____

If you saw this card as an "end result," what would you say to your client?

_____

_____

_____

How would you use this card as an "affirmation helper"? Keep in mind that <u>each</u> <u>card</u> is extremely valuable as an assistant in your *"Laws of Attraction and Repulsion"* exercises. Any time you *desire* something intensely, **or** find yourself in a situation *you want out of,* you can use the imagery of your chosen card (or recommend this to your clients) to enhance your visualizations and "speed up" your results. Of course, much, much more of this is covered in depth in our *Advanced Tarot Secrets* course and workbook if you choose to learn even more about the Tarot.

_____

_____

_____

What other feelings, impressions, or uses do you want to note about this card?

_____

_____

_____

COINS

Knight of Coins

(Intense Fixed Earth)

Description: A young knight sits comfortably on his steed, scowling at something off in the distance. His mount's reins are pulled tightly, *holding his horse* in place with his left hand. His right holds up a coin, as if to show his possession of it to whomever or whatever he is glaring at disdainfully. *He is sending a strong message.* He is prepared to ride long distances and fight toe-to-toe for his cause, but by reining his horse in, refusing to advance a step, he is demanding his audience to approach him *on his terms*. This stoic "take it or leave it" attitude is fortified by <u>his</u> possession of the coin *("He who has the gold <u>makes</u> the rules")*.

Prime elements at work in this card

Status:	Knight. Youthful, warrior, bravado, manager, protector, commander
Suit:	Coins. Financial offer or assistance, business travel, loan officer
Direction:	Northeast. Reliability, practicality, sensuality, common sense. Mid-morning
Element:	Earth. Persistence, patience, waiting, ambition, duty, honor, resilience

Traditional meaning: Unlike other *Knights* whose testosterone levels *force them* to initiate action, this man's same biochemicals create a smugness and bravado that challenges others to *bend to his will by taking action* that he finds amusing, or acceptable. His confidence is rooted in his possessions, his inherent obstinance, and his readiness to wait out any situation until he finds circumstances to his liking. This card shows a stubbornness in people, or refusal to budge, or compromise that is both the hallmark of great leadership and the cause of many of society's ills. This card allows *no compromise*. When you see this card, the person it represents is saying, "Come and *get* it. I <u>dare</u> you." But the subtle inflection underneath is that things will progress at their comfort level, and only in the manner they desire.

Traditional reversed meaning: Complete *lack* of self-control. Weakness. Inability to stand up for oneself. Foolishness with money and resources.

Personal Notes:

Now it's your turn

__Please note:__ You can fill this in later if nothing comes to mind right away. It is far more important to get a good feel for this card than it is to write something in right away.

What is your interpretation? What does this card say to you?

_____

_____

_____

What does it <u>say to you</u> when it is *reversed?*

_____

_____

_____

If you saw this card as an "end result," what would you say to your client?

_____

_____

_____

How would you use this card as an "affirmation helper"? Keep in mind that <u>each</u> <u>card</u> is extremely valuable as an assistant in your *"Laws of Attraction and Repulsion"* exercises. Any time you *desire* something intensely, **or** find yourself in a situation *you want out of,* you can use the imagery of your chosen card (or recommend this to your clients) to enhance your visualizations and "speed up" your results. Of course, much, much more of this is covered in depth in our *Advanced Tarot Secrets* course and workbook if you choose to learn even more about the Tarot.

_____

_____

_____

What other feelings, impressions, or uses do you want to note about this card?

_____

_____

_____

Queen of Coins

(Fixed Earth)

Description: Our *Queen* sits comfortably on her elaborately carved throne, gazing down at her exceptionally large gold coin, enjoying the weight and feel of it. She is surrounded on all sides by lush flowers and vines; life explodes around her in full bloom, and even a rabbit *(symbol of fertility of womb and her land)* scampers by happily. For all of this, however, her communion with her coin is so powerfully hypnotic that she is lost to the rest of the world. Her entire essence is drinking in its virtues through all of her highly acute senses. She is at peace, and the world around her is at peace through that.

Prime elements at work in this card

Status: Queen. Mother, boss, nurturer, business woman, public figure, woman
Suit: Coins. Wealthy woman, manager, financier, matron, materialism
Direction: Northeast. Emotional stability, kindness, possessiveness. Morning
Element: Earth. Beltane, fertility, nursery (plants), nursery (children), maid

Traditional meaning: Folklore tells us that *the king and the land are one*. This is no less true of the ruling queen. The woman in this card is no dainty waif who happened upon a wealthy prince. She is the embodiment of the earth and the essence of fertility. This card can be used *astrologically (Taurus, Virgo, Capricorn)*, or it can represent a woman of patience and common sense, one who is attuned with nature, a florist or farmer, animal-rights activist, a warm, caring, maternal, authority figure, nurse, doctor, teacher, or any wealthy woman over 30.

Traditional reversed meaning: *As <u>character traits</u>*—Selfish woman, impatient and demanding, elitist; scornful of others, especially those she considers *inferiors*. Shamelessly materialistic. Evil boss. Gold digger. Alternately, *as an <u>effect or event</u>*: a loss of social or financial status, "falling from grace," feminine health issues *(see a doctor now)*, abandonment by husband, loss of stability, "having your world turned upside down."

Personal Notes:

Now it's your turn

Please note: You can fill this in later if nothing comes to mind right away. It is far more important to get a good feel for this card than it is to write something in right away.

What is your interpretation? What does this card say to you?

_____

_____

_____

What does it <u>say to you</u> when it is *reversed*?

_____

_____

_____

If you saw this card as an "end result," what would you say to your client?

_____

_____

_____

How would you use this card as an "affirmation helper"? Keep in mind that <u>each</u> <u>card</u> is extremely valuable as an assistant in your *"Laws of Attraction and Repulsion"* exercises. Any time you *desire* something intensely, **or** find yourself in a situation *you want out of,* you can use the imagery of your chosen card (or recommend this to your clients) to enhance your visualizations and "speed up" your results. Of course, much, much more of this is covered in depth in our *Advanced Tarot Secrets* course and workbook if you choose to learn even more about the Tarot.

_____

_____

What other feelings, impressions, or uses do you want to note about this card?

_____

_____

_____

King of Coins

(Intense Cardinal Earth)

Description: *"It's good to be the king!"* The smugness of the *Knight of Coins* is only outclassed by the man who *invented* smugness. Truly, the only thing better than being young, handsome, and wealthy (for a man) is to be young, handsome, wealthy, *and in charge.* The man before you has no problems with his wealth; no problems with how he got his money, and *no* problems with how he uses it to get what he wants. This card shows us that wealth and power may not be *everything* in life, but that they sure go a long way in the eyes of one who knows how to enjoy, and *enforce his will* through, them.

Prime elements at work in this card

Status: King. Boss, overlord, alpha male, landlord, tycoon, industrialist
Suit: Coins. King-maker, investor, corporate officer, banker, consultant
Direction: South. Yule, Oak king. Conservative, tradition. Midnight
Element: Earth. Prudence, predictability, patience, stability, fiscal responsibility

Traditional meaning: Any wealthy man. Also: Men of power, prestige, authority, confident, or stubborn, especially men associated with land and real estate. *Astrologically: Taurus, Virgo, Capricorn.* This card most often indicates corporate executives, businessmen, investors, kings, and men directly involved with finance and the details of funding projects. As an *effect* or a *result:* more than simple success in business, *absolute dominance* of your niche market. Wise counsel from experienced men who want to see you succeed. Patience is needed in matters of finance at this time. This also indicates the wheels of industry moving, but the wheels are large and elephantine, moving slowly due to the massive amount of resources and *human factors* that need to be brought in line.

Traditional reversed meaning: A wasteful, small-minded, arrogant man. "Small" man's syndrome. Petulance. Stubborn, rude, elitist, tyrannical, or bullying cretin. *Alternately:* loss of power, status, money, health.

Personal Notes:

Now it's your turn

__Please note:__ You can fill this in later if nothing comes to mind right away. It is far more important to get a good feel for this card than it is to write something in right away.

What is your interpretation? What does this card say to you?

_____

_____

_____

What does it say to you when it is *reversed*?

_____

_____

_____

If you saw this card as an "end result," what would you say to your client?

_____

_____

_____

How would you use this card as an "affirmation helper"? Keep in mind that each card is extremely valuable as an assistant in your *"Laws of Attraction and Repulsion"* exercises. Any time you *desire* something intensely, **or** find yourself in a situation *you want out of,* you can use the imagery of your chosen card (or recommend this to your clients) to enhance your visualizations and "speed up" your results. Of course, much, much more of this is covered in depth in our *Advanced Tarot Secrets* course and workbook if you choose to learn even more about the Tarot.

COINS

_____

_____

_____

What other feelings, impressions, or uses do you want to note about this card?

_____

_____

_____

Section Five

The "Major" Arcana

Here at last we examine the famed "major" Arcana, being the 22 cards that deal with some of the aspects of daily life that seem beyond "mortal control." We have saved the "major" Arcana for last, as the images are stagnant and "posed." There is less action and more *impression of concepts* at work here. These cards have always been designed to be intimidating, as they represent concepts that have vexed mastery by the masses over the centuries. Here is an easy way to avoid that trap: Simply remember that <u>all "major" Arcana cards</u> are *highly dependent on* "minor" Arcana cards to *define, shape,* and *clarify* them.

The "major" Arcana cards will show you overall concepts, large forces, institutions (e.g., hospitals, government agencies), "major" events (being ones that deeply impact your clients), priorities, and karmic paths; **but they will not usually show the means or the details.** This is why the two Arcana work seamlessly together, and why we wanted you to become comfortable and familiar with the "minor" Arcana first. Consider the "major" Arcana simply an extension of the "minor" Arcana for the purposes of *reading* for your clients.

If you decide someday to enroll in any mystery school, you will learn all sorts of interesting tidbits of esoteric wisdom; but for right now you need to know that you are not missing out on anything by *reading* the cards "as you see them." Have fun with your deck and develop your bond with them to make yourself an extremely talented prognosticator. Then worry about "additional information" as you like.

The Fool

Description: A gaily dressed young man traverses the heights of his world. His burden is light, the Sun is shining, and the rose in his hand still holds its scent. He literally is "on top of the world," lost in his own joyous meditations. His next step may be his last, or perhaps he may have mastered the ability to walk on air. Either way, he is simply too in love with whatever occupies his mind to pay attention to such trivialities. He has found optimal bliss. Even his fluffy white dog's happy barks do not call his attention away from his serenity.

Esoteric interpretation: *The Fool* sits outside of the fixed "reality box" of the numerical concepts of positive and negative numbers. The Tarot limits existential understanding to 21 hard-coded stages. *The Fool* laughs gleefully at them all. The essence of this card is the essence of "humanity." This card emphasizes the Buddha seed in all of us, the spark of creativity, the joy of unbridled freedom as we escape from the limitations of the "minor" Arcana (food, sleep, money, sex, love, etc.). We are free of these addictions in this card because this card represents that part in all of us where these needs are satiated or no longer a concern. This is the absolute freedom of choice, and it is that choice being acted upon "right now."

Traditional meaning: It is an interesting point that at the moment of chaos you are most truly free. It may not feel that way at the time, but once you lose everything, you gain even more. Without the burdens of luxuries or (self-imposed) responsibilities to tie you down, you can go *anywhere* you desire. Think on this for a moment. This is why the "chaos star" has eight arrows. This card represents that freedom. You do not have to "lose everything" to find this freedom in yourself. You simply need to click your heels together three . . . er, take a deep breath and just say "___ it!" (use your favorite term). You find joy in life by pursuing what is important to you, not your boss, or what your parents want you to do, or how your friends "think you should behave." Note how he is completely at peace with whatever befalls his next step. That is you when you stop caring what <u>other</u> <u>people</u> <u>want</u> <u>you</u> <u>to</u> <u>do</u> (so *they* can be happy).

This card can represent you enjoying any new beginnings, whether they are new ventures, freedom from restriction, new directions in life. This is your personal "get out of jail free card." When you see this card, see the opportunities ahead of you and the courage that comes naturally with pursuing what is most important to you. Whatever happens next is not as important as what you want it to be. One of the metaphysical secrets of this card is that it *is* a wish card. The future is <u>not</u> <u>set</u> (he has not stepped off of the cliff yet). Circumstances are *always* a result of people deciding how reality should be *and making it so*. The fact that everyone else simply shrugs and goes along with their vision is simply a matter of history. When this card shows up, it is time to take that leap of faith and spread your wings *(and flap like crazy!)*. Take this card and put it anywhere in the deck—and that is where you will be. *That* is the real power of this card.

Traditional reversed meaning: Missteps and fear brought about by overanalysis. Fear of the unknown. Self-limitation forces one to remain in whatever prison they have created for themselves. Inability to act decisively. Check *aspecting cards* to see who and what is helping create (or enforce) this limitation. *Open it up* to reveal how this can be overcome. Hesitance almost always means opportunities missed. Also: If *The Fool* steps halfway, trying to be both on the cliff and off, he will almost certainly fall. Don't do that.

Now it's your turn

Please note: You can fill this in later if nothing comes to mind right away. It is far more important to get a good feel for this card than it is to write something in right away.

What is your interpretation? What does this card say to you?

_____

_____

_____

What does it say to you when it is *reversed*?

_____

_____

_____

If you saw this card as an "end result," what would you say to your client?

_____

_____

_____

How would you use this card as an "affirmation helper"?

_____

_____

_____

_____

What other feelings, impressions, or uses do you want to note about this card?

_____

_____

_____

"MAJOR" ARCANA

The Magician

Description: A master practitioner holds his double-ended candle high and simultaneously points to the earth below him (multiple meanings, but the most obvious in Tarot teaching texts is "as above, so below" indicating the power of this man and the usage of this card; for more information ask your teacher or enroll in a mystery school). His tools lay before him on his work-table, being the sum of all worldly endeavors, and flowered vines and plants of all sorts surround him, reminding us that he is one with Nature. His belt is the encircling snake of "self-containment" and eternal regeneration, his halo of infinity, white robes of purity of intent, white headband of purity of thought, red overcloak of action and purpose incarnate.

Esoteric interpretation: Our friend *The Magician* is primarily representative of the jewel of the achievement of humanity: the force of the human will. "I AM!" A statement so simple yet profound simply by the speaker's ability to make it. As the (alleged) "dominant" life form, we enjoy the ability to shape and control our planet and everything contained on it with ever more daring and skill. This is a skill reserved to *homo sapiens* among known primates, and it is the power over all of "existence" (as existence is merely a concept of awareness). The amount of layers and symbolism one can draw from all of this has been catalogued by various books and secret texts, and we will not go into all of that here. For your current use, know that this is not a force to be played with like a toy. This is the root base of *the Laws of Attraction and Repulsion,* and it is a tool capable of harnessing the full power of *the Mystic and Complete Law of Cause and Effect.* This is inside you even now. Advanced training can help you draw it out more clearly, but this natural part of you is why you exist and how you get what you want (and need: *hint*) from life. Meditate on this for further clarity.

Traditional meaning: This card has a lot in common with the *Ace of Wands.* It is the act of, and power to, manifest "something from nothing" (which is an esoteric misnomer we use only for the sake of convenience in teaching). This is the card of *purposeful* creation and destruction, not some random act of the gods or circumstance. This card represents *the act of commitment.* Pair this up with a "minor" Arcana card to see what is being "decided and acted upon." This card also shows the autonomy of self-governance and the reliability of assumed responsibility. There is no hesitation in this card. It is not a card of *action* per se, but the force behind action or the command presence to instill action to follow along a prescribed path. When you see this card, see decisions, initiations (the commencement of activities), a revelation of the power of whatever this card points at, the will and the confidence to act decisively, and the ability to utilize resources at hand. This is a supreme *Alpha* card. It represents initiative combined with action, and is not for the timid or the weak. As a person: these are the qualities of this person *(male or female).* This card is genderless. As advice: do these things. *Take* action, *make* decisions, *be* confident, *use* what you have now, and *stop* whining or procrastinating. This card offers no excuses and allows for none in turn. This is not the outward authority of status or position (Emperor, Hierophant . . .). This is inherent in *everyone* and must be tapped into to actuate. This is the channeling of the energies accessible to anyone towards a set goal or problem.

Traditional reversed meaning: Unskilled labor. Indecisive person or action. *Weak will.* Sacrifice without reward. Cowardly behavior. When *reversed* this card indicates an untrained, or incompletely trained "expert," a "false-prophet" if you will. Bad advice from a fool (not *"The Fool"*). It is sacrilege and anathema to the wisdom and knowledge *that come from* careful and patient study and practice. It unearths shoddy workmanship and even scandal brought about by laziness pressed into authority. This is a very disturbing card reversed as it shows not just merely a lack of potential or of effort, it denotes a willful disregard for the values of patient and persistent training of a needed skill.

Now it's your turn

Please note: *You can fill this in later if nothing comes to mind right away. It is far more important to get a good feel for this card than it is to write something in right away.*

What is your interpretation? What does this card say to you?

_____

_____

_____

What does it say to you when it is *reversed*?

_____

_____

_____

If you saw this card as an "end result," what would you say to your client?

_____

_____

_____

How would you use this card as an "affirmation helper"?

_____

_____

_____

_____

What other feelings, impressions, or uses do you want to note about this card?

_____

_____

_____

"MAJOR" ARCANA

The High Priestess

Description: Pomegranates. Our lady of mystery sits on a simple throne which is little more than a block, with pillars left and right supporting the weave of pomegranates behind her, masking off the evening sea of her domain. Some argue the crown she wears is that of the triple goddess. It is, in fact, a pearl (see below), as the moon is already indicated at her feet, aswim in her flowing tresses of watery imagination. The equilateral cross (or its later Christian adaptation) marks her purity as certainly as her white tunic/robe. The Torah in her lap shows her to be a student of mysteries and spirituality, rather than a "woman of the world," further indicating her great storehouse of knowledge.

Esoteric interpretation: First the pomegranates. Pomegranates are so woven into mythos by so many ancient cultures, with so many variations that you can simply *pick* which interpretation you want to personally believe. That being said, the most appropriate one for the Tarot *Priestess* in use is that of Persephone [Per-sef-uh-nee], daughter of Demeter and Zeus, sometimes wife of Hades, and always "Queen of the Dead." This reinforces the notion that *The High Priestess* card *is power beyond* the subconscious, along with the sea behind her, the crescent moon of intuitive insight is at her feet, and the twin pillars of light and dark. Her crown can be interpreted as you like, but consider the pearl is the sea's most precious and rare jewel. It has always been found only rarely in oysters that "swallowed" a grain of sand and built the pearl as a response (this ignores modern artificial culturing). Pearls are another statement of insight and purity, as well as representations of the moon. All miscellaneous aspects aside, the importance of *The High Priestess* is her representation of duality.

A *sine wave* arches "positive" and then "negative" as stimulus is offered and withdrawn. We see this as a polarity, most often in terms of male/female, day/night, "good/bad," up/down, "heaven/hell," right/left, "God/devil," and so on, ad infinitum. She represents psychological dualism (the *"this or that"* paradigm that is all too common in bilaterally symmetrical life-forms). As *The Magician* is the act of will pressed outward upon the world (phallus), she is the <u>receptive</u> organ of creation (you can guess where this is going). She is "imagination," which is not to be underestimated simply because the act of will is so *obvious*. *The High Priestess* is a full half of the creation process, as she is the gateway to the ether. Neither she nor *The Magician* is more important nor more powerful than its counterpart. They are a team on a Tantric level of awareness few magical practitioners can even grasp, much less actually aspire to achieving.

Traditional meaning: Intuition, imagination, dreams, creative spark or inspiration. She brings new understandings of situations through *listening*, not *acting*. She is communion, prayer, knowing when to seek guidance and doing so. As *The Magician* is <u>active psychic power</u> channeled outward, she is receptive information gained, as well as <u>active psychic power</u> of *calling in assistance*. As forceful and direct as *The Magician* is, his partner is just as oblique. She "uncovers, or reveals" where he "takes action." Her abilities lie in everyone. They exist *at all times* in our subconscious minds and are our direct connection to whatever we individually call "God." This card shows or advises reflection, quiet listening, intuitive work, seeking out expert knowledge and assistance (both on a "higher plane" and physically). Pair this up with a "minor" Arcana card to see what she is alluding to.

Traditional reversed meaning: As a mental state or physical condition—confusion, alcoholism and drug abuse/overdose, paranoia and superstition. Disillusion (especially with *6 of Swords, 7 of Coins*, etc.) spiritual weakness, clouded judgment, false spirituality (look at aspecting cards), psychosis, fanaticism and extremism, not doing one's research or homework, abduction, buried treasures, and bad pomegranates.

Now it's your turn

Please note: You can fill this in later if nothing comes to mind right away. It is far more important to get a good feel for this card than it is to write something in right away.

What is <u>your</u> interpretation? What does this card say to you?

_____

_____

_____

What does it <u>say to you</u> when it is *reversed*?

_____

_____

_____

If you saw this card as an "end result," what would you say to your client?

_____

_____

_____

How would you use this card as an "affirmation helper"?

_____

_____

_____

_____

What other feelings, impressions, or uses do you want to note about this card?

_____

_____

_____

_____

The Empress

Description: Our celestial lady sits comfortably on a cushioned throne. In case you were wondering, this is what "Mother Nature" looks like *(at least according to one P.C. Smith)*. The goddess symbolism of this card is unmistakable, from her Venusian throne (with extra-cushy pillows!) to the wheat (sacred to Demeter, mother of Persephone; see *The High Priestess*), the crown of stars, <u>more</u> pomegranates . . . Her presence brings life to all. Trees are alive with leaves and fruits, water flows freely, and the sun shines brightly. We will politely ignore the inconsistency of separating her feet from the earth by setting her "throne" on a stone pillar and we ask that you do as well. Not all Tarot art is symbolically correct.

Esoteric interpretation: *Mom.* (aka mommy, mother, *"maaaa!"*, one who rears and occasionally scolds us, giver of life, and "she who loves you more than anyone—no matter what"). Yeah, *her*. This card is everyone's mom, in a celestial kind of way, and every mom has a bit of this card in her. This is more than simple *empress* (power), or *queen* (status). This is that squishy kind of unconditional love that nurtures the soul, warms up the coldest nights, and makes the worst times bearable. This card is the glue of the Tarot. As such, it is also its emotional backbone and support system. She is both womb and caregiver "after" birth is a distant memory (to all but her). Do *not* make this woman angry.

Traditional meaning: Pregnancy. "<u>Congratulations</u>!" Also indicative of mothers if associated with supporting "minor" Arcana cards. See this as the *concept of,* the *energy and actuality of* motherhood, rather than any one person in all but rare cases. Identify the person by finding aspecting cards or by *opening this card up.* As a *verb*, this card indicates applied compassion, caring, the act of nurturing, and caretaking. This could just as easily be nursing along a new business venture with great care and love as it could be the act of "taking in a stray." The emphasis here is the sincere care and attention given by the person behind these kind acts. As a quality in a person, it speaks most highly: that rare quality of genuine compassion, consideration, grace, beauty (inner and most likely outer, to some extent, as well). As a situation, it indicates a happy home life, a time of more than peace. Think more *renaissance,* where arts and luxuries abound as repression ends. Creativity, free thought, and the free expression of that thought are allowed to blossom. In every way this is truly a *happy* card. It is not a beginning (except in the case of a pregnancy), nor an ending. It is a state of being, or a state of affairs for a time, and those times are ripe with food, friends, emotional and physical security.

Addendum: Some (alleged) "experts" fear discussing matters such as birth (pregnancy) or death, as if by *avoiding* discussing these fundamental parts of life, they can somehow avoid them perpetually. We have a more pragmatic point of view: Your clients come to you for advice. If you fail them, you risk your credibility and you may actually injure them. If you see something, say it as politely as you feel you must. Sidestep and meander conversationally all you like, and even couch what you say in terms of "possibilities" or phraseology such as "perhaps it would be better if you considered *this* instead" if you feel the need. But do <u>not</u> ever believe that you can attain immortality simply by refusing to see reality exactly as it is. The Tarot is not "politically correct." Death (card "13") and Birth (indicated in several cards) are two of the three "guarantees in life." If you suspect something "dire," *always* verify what you *think* you see before saying too much; but trouble known is trouble avoided. The Tarot shows possibilities, and sometimes that means it shows only *possibilities*. Don't fear "ghosts."

Traditional reversed meaning: <u>Lack of support</u>. Alienation, emotional despair, heartlessness, insecurity, *instability*. "Unpleasant" woman. False loyalties or lack of morals. Adultery or divorce *(verify this through aspecting cards)*. Environmental destruction. Miscarriage *(verify before saying <u>anything</u>)*.

Now it's your turn

Please note: *You can fill this in later if nothing comes to mind right away. It is far more important to get a good feel for this card than it is to write something in right away.*

What is <u>your</u> interpretation? What does this card say to you?

_____

_____

_____

What does it <u>say to you</u> when it is *reversed*?

_____

_____

_____

If you saw this card as an "end result," what would you say to your client?

_____

_____

_____

How would you use this card as an "affirmation helper"?

_____

_____

_____

_____

What other feelings, impressions, or uses do you want to note about this card?

_____

_____

_____

The Emperor

Description: Quick! What do *The Emperor* and *The Devil* have in common? (Hint: They are both allegories for authority figures and you have probably worked for both of them at one point.) Okay, so this guy is not "pleasant," but he is "the boss." He sits on his stone throne bearing the symbols of *Aries* (the astrological sign, not the god). He is the prime patriarch in the Tarot. His rule *supersedes* even the *Kings* of all of the suits because the emperor in any feudal "empire" is the <u>overlord</u>, not just the reigning monarch of a particular provence. *This is a man of action:* scarlet robes, burgundy sash, armor worn <u>on the throne</u>, and attentive posture that is poised to spring at any moment.

Esoteric interpretation: Patriarch. As *The Empress* is representational of the prime maternal energy and the matriarch of the Tarot, *The Emperor* is its father, grandfather, judge, jury, and executioner. This man's authority is <u>absolute</u>. The inclusions of kings and queens and emperors into the Tarot reminds us that it was created in a time long gone, one where kings and queens lorded over all of the other residents of an area, usually under the guise of "protection." This stigma continues to this day in multi-national corporate autocracies and *plutocracies,* where high-level executives have taken the place of their more transparent feudal counterparts. These systems of "government" survive *because they work*. As a group, such as "the general public" for instance, people *like* having someone in charge, someone they can rally to, or against, someone who will make the decisions that very few want to make on a regular basis. *Someone to blame when things don't work.* Thus, this outdated throwback to some political neolithic age will never go out of style. We will <u>always</u> need someone to tell us what to do and to complain to when someone does it (what we are "not supposed to do") to us.

Traditional meaning: Government. *Any male authority figure:* boss, judge, executive, decision maker, father, Cardinal (priest). This is the card of judgment or command (lawsuit, parking ticket being issued, summons, meeting with a "superior," etc.) *and also of* the person or authority behind that command or judgment (e.g., "the IRS"). In still other words: it is the act of being told what to do, and the person who tells you to do it. As harsh as this may seem at first, it is this very structural dominance that makes this the card representational of the person or authority you would go to when you seek grievances against oppression or abuse.

<u>As a quality in a person</u>, this card speaks of leadership ability, resoluteness of mind, capable use of logic and command-decision ability. This is not a person easily swayed by random emotions nor sob stories. A good manager, a reliable person of great character. <u>As an action</u>, this could be the issuing of a decree, or sagely advice. *The Emperor* implies the experience of age; and if this card is well aspected, then wisdom accompanies that experience.

Traditional reversed meaning: Tyrants, dictators, corrupt public officials, vastly overpaid bosses. Also overregulation of a situation, micro-management, abuse of power and authority.

Now it's your turn

Please note: You can fill this in later if nothing comes to mind right away. It is far more important to get a good feel for this card than it is to write something in right away.

What is your interpretation? What does this card say to you?

_____

_____

_____

What does it say to you when it is *reversed*?

_____

_____

_____

If you saw this card as an "end result," what would you say to your client?

_____

_____

_____

How would you use this card as an "affirmation helper"?

_____

_____

_____

_____

What other feelings, impressions, or uses do you want to note about this card?

_____

_____

_____

"MAJOR" ARCANA

The Hierophant

Description: The word hierophant comes to us from ancient Greece and our favorite mother-daughter team *(Demeter and Persephone—is there anything they can't accomplish?)* and the priests (female and male) who guided the faithful into the "parts holy." If you want the long version, you are just going to have to join the mystery school, so we will simply state here that *The Hierophant* has been "Christianized" (like so many of the Tarot concepts) to reflect the beliefs popular at the time of its creation. This card shows us a priest as an authority figure much like an emperor, rather than a guide to the divine. It shows religion as a state (system of government) rather than a path of philosophy. This is neither correct *nor incorrect*. It simply "is."

Esoteric interpretation: The original point of a hierophant was that while most members of the tribe toiled for the common good of their collective, a set few would spend their days and nights laboring in constant meditation, study, research, contemplation, questioning, debate, and sharing of their findings to the rest of the group *for the benefit of all.* The investment of one's life searching out the meanings and mysteries of life, magic, and deep philosophy may sound like fun on the surface, but it is intensely demanding both physically and mentally. Students are taxed to the very edge of sanity, which is often where they find their greatest revelations on daily life. This position was no "life of luxury" and was an integral part of any society as they learned, preserved, and shared the collected wisdom of the tribe (village, clan, family, hamlet, community . . .).

As time progressed and religion became more structured and regimented, the ranks of "the learned" became as orderly as any government. "Good ideas" (don't steal from your neighbor) became "laws" of society, and for all of the good this accomplished, it also entrenched religion into the very fabric of the governance of society and, therefore, religion came to be a *governing body*. This turned guides (priests) into overlords (priests), judges (also priests), and executioners *(see Malleus Maleficarum, the Inquisition, the burning times, the Crusades, etc.).* This means that the old concepts our card (above) once represented have been changed prior to the card's (above) creation, even though it carries the old name, symbolic of the teachings mystery schools to this day seek to espouse. This makes this card dualistic and variable in interpretation (depending on one's view of "organized religion"). We included the history lesson to remind the student that structure can be *load-bearing* (a good thing), or *imprisoning* (a bad thing) when it comes to spirituality. "Judge not, (this card) lest ye be judged" (or something like that). When this card comes up, take a deep breath and examine everything carefully.

Traditional meaning: Orthodoxy—doing things "by the book," *and only by the book.* Strict regimen. Morals and dogma. Social conservatism, conformity, institutionalism, obedience to tradition. Being preached to by someone either *in authority,* or by someone *who presumes authority.*

Conversely: Professors, lecturers, priests (male or female), guidance counselors, or the act of receiving advice from any of these qualified experts. Higher education (only if aspected by supporting cards).

Traditional reversed meaning: The act of following tradition unquestioningly. Fundamentalism. Rule-mongering, bureaucracy, proselytization, browbeating, *excommunication.*

Now it's your turn

Please note: You can fill this in later if nothing comes to mind right away. It is far more important to get a good feel for this card than it is to write something in right away.

What is your interpretation? What does this card say to you?

_____

_____

_____

What does it say to you when it is *reversed*?

_____

_____

_____

If you saw this card as an "end result," what would you say to your client?

_____

_____

_____

How would you use this card as an "affirmation helper"?

_____

_____

_____

_____

What other feelings, impressions, or uses do you want to note about this card?

_____

_____

_____

"MAJOR" ARCANA

The Lovers

Description: Here we have the prototypical "Adam and Eve." (Apparently they were both *blonde*—who knew?) Throw out any esoteric or occult meanings for this card; it is straight out of the Bible: burning bush (although Waite calls it "the tree of life"), snake, tree of knowledge, that "Raphael" guy, and naturally that nondescript mountain in the distant background, and sea below *("phallus and chalice")*. Really . . . Can you be ANY more blatantly obvious with your symbolism Pamela?

Just for fun . . . compare this card directly to *The Devil*. It's like one of those "before and after" scenes. Love *is* pain.

Esoteric interpretation: The imagery of this card has been altered over the centuries by various artists to the point where you will find any number of meanings for this extremely simple but powerful card. On some decks cupid replaces the angel; other times it is a priest. Some cards will show two women where the man has to choose lust *versus* family. That is an oppressive puritanical spin on the fact that love is lust, <u>and</u> it is friendship, sacrifice, pain, heaven, and the magic of continued breath. The problem with replacing one of the most important "major" Arcana cards with a question of values is that it removes the single most powerful force presently known to humanity from the Tarot; thus reducing the value of this as an esoteric learning tool (and it takes away all of the fun of divination). Besides: *You* try to explain to your client's puppy-dog, hope-filled eyes, that **"it doesn't mean what you think: it means <u>choice</u>!"** They will start calling you names <u>and</u> <u>throwing</u> <u>things</u> <u>at</u> <u>you</u>! We *strongly recommend* that you see "Love" when you see this card. This primal force is one of life's greatest mysteries and will probably always be, no matter what advances science makes along the way. No matter what your opinion on the psychological roller coaster that love is, it makes the world go around and <u>it is the very reason</u> we invented money (which also helps rotate the planet). This card is not simply about "choices"; it is about *partnership*. It is about bonding, and having your heart ripped up into tiny little pieces every time your boyfriend, husband (etc.) is away. It is about the bonding and sharing of ideals that changes a world of individualism into one of communalism. Without this gooey, sticky, and all-too-often bitter emotion, we would have no great monuments, no masterpieces of art, no drive to improve the world around us. This card forever changes "one" into "many," *and many into one*. <u>This</u> is the secret of *high magic*.

Traditional meaning: Partnership, bonding, love, marriage, soul mates, deep lasting friendships. When you see this card in a *reading*, see it as a *concept* and look to see how it ties into other cards. Occasionally this will show up as an *event*, but more often it will need one or more "minor" Arcana cards to help clarify <u>exactly</u> what is coming to pass. This card's energy is so vast and sweeping that it is best to interpret it through several other *clarifying cards*. When you are facing a client in a *reading* and this card comes up <u>anywhere</u>, **the first thing they will do is point directly at this card and ask you what it means.** What they are really asking, behind their hopeful expression, is "<u>when</u>?" This card represents the destiny that everyone seeks. Above all else we want to be admired, loved, worshiped, cared for, nurtured, and ultimately *accepted* by someone whose opinion we not only value but lust after. This card may often indicate a successful business partnership or the formation of a support group, but the imagery is so powerful that it will pull the all-consuming desires for *acceptance* and *exclusive attraction* from even your most stoic querents.

Traditional reversed meaning: Pain. Then more pain. In fact, so much pain . . . Okay, so it's not pretty. This shows <u>separations</u> (of all sorts): divorces, broken pacts, false friends, job loss; it is *the removal* of one from *the source* of life and happiness. Again, it needs to be *clarified* by other cards to find out the how and why.

Now it's your turn

<u>Please note</u>: You can fill this in later if nothing comes to mind right away. It is far more important to get a good feel for this card than it is to write something in right away.

What is <u>your</u> interpretation? What does this card say to you?

_____

_____

_____

What does it <u>say to you</u> when it is *reversed*?

_____

_____

_____

If you saw this card as an "end result," what would you say to your client?

_____

_____

_____

How would you use this card as an "affirmation helper"?

_____

_____

_____

_____

What other feelings, impressions, or uses do you want to note about this card?

_____

_____

_____

"MAJOR" ARCANA

The Chariot

Description: Okay, take a nice, slow, deep breath . . . Warrior-priests riding about freely dispensing (their idea of) "justice" is as arcane a concept in most parts of the world today as chariots. The man here is not royalty, not a military hero, nor is he a wealthy merchant. He is the archetypal "warrior-priest" and *"he is one with"* his chariot of stone (faith, solidity, resoluteness, strength) which is, unsurprisingly, drawn by mythical beasts, thereby strengthening his "righteousness." Forget the fact that the religious symbolism of this card is drawn from a dozen highly-incompatible religious beliefs. This man is *sacrosanct*. He is "the law" and the adjudicator of the law. *He can't fail* (an impossibility) because "God" (over a dozen actually) supports him.

Esoteric interpretation: (see above) Depending on the deck you look at, this card will be an emperor or prince on his "mobile fighting platform," a priest on (or as above "part of") a chariot, or a shiny red corvette. Thus, the subtle inferences change, but the basic meaning is clear to all. *This man wins*. This card shows us victory and power, but it does so in a style that equates being "right" (winning) with "being right" (as in "God" speaks through me—*not you*). It shows us an indignation that only *The Hierophant* (or the *Queen of Swords reversed*) can match. The danger of this message can be a "win-at-all-costs" mentality, or such a passionate, fervent belief in something that it blinds one into a mindset where the only option is the one that the ensorcelled mind perceives. This is the card of *zeal* and several Tarot authorities assign to it the qualities of the astrological sign of *Sagittarius*. Personally, we couldn't agree more. It has "politics" written all over it.

Traditional meaning: Victory, but more. Righteous victory without having to sacrifice one's morals or personal beliefs. This is a card of *strength*. You don't win because you "got lucky." You win because you are good at what you do, and/or you have powerful friends and resources. You succeed because you keep your animalistic rages under the control of your disciplined and highly-skilled mind. You harness the power of *masculine* and *feminine* (esoteric principles) and you are steadfast and resolute in your quest. Of course, sometimes this card can also simply mean "a brand new *car!*" or some long distance travel. In either case, however, it will be spelled out by clarifying "minor" Arcana.

Compare this to the *rune* "Fehu" which means: domestic cattle, *mobile* wealth, possessions won or earned, abundance, financial strength, success and happiness. Also: social success, vibrant energy, foresight. And interestingly enough when reversed, this *rune* matches *The Chariot* rather nicely as well: loss of personal property, esteem, failure. Cowardice, poverty, loss of freedom, and so on.

Traditional reversed meaning: Loss; almost always through a lack of skill, preparation, or a lack of "moral fiber." Defeat due to either weakness or weakness of character. Being "knocked off of your high horse" (or fine social standing) through treachery and deceit. This is often called "character assassination" (which is a deliberate manipulation of facts to present an unfavorable, and usually untrue, picture). Cowardice leading to downfall. The "fall from grace." The long and the short of this is that as a *concept card,* this indicates severe and sudden loss and needs to be clarified (like all "major" Arcana) to ensure clarity, and to prevent you from giving bad advice.

Reversed, this card can even indicate auto accidents. *(If you really suspect an accident, get all kinds of verification before you start spreading the news of impending doom, and even then be extremely careful what you say and how you say anything.)*

Now it's your turn

Please note: You can fill this in later if nothing comes to mind right away. It is far more important to get a good feel for this card than it is to write something in right away.

What is your interpretation? What does this card say to you?

___

___

___

What does it say to you when it is *reversed*?

___

___

___

If you saw this card as an "end result," what would you say to your client?

___

___

___

How would you use this card as an "affirmation helper"?

___

___

___

___

What other feelings, impressions, or uses do you want to note about this card?

___

___

___

"MAJOR" ARCANA

Strength

Description: *(Note: In some decks this may be card 11, in others it is card 8. Either way it is still valid.)* The image of a young woman calmly restraining a lion is a classic medieval image. It is a timeless allegory of one of the earliest "secrets" known to (wo)man. <u>Femininity</u>, seemingly harmless and needing of protection from the harsh realities of daily life by the strong protectorate of masculine rage, can (and has throughout time, too many times to count really) *destroy* the strongest man with a smile. This woman is *in tune* with her innate powers and prowess as a woman as symbolized by her garlands and the infinity symbol floating above her head. She *owns* this kitty.

Esoteric interpretation: Strength in all its forms—physical, mental, emotional, *comes from will*. Deep inside every giant and every miracle worker is a fierce determination to a cause. That determination can be a quiet one, or it can be loud, and fueled by rage. It can be ignited by a spark, or it can be an ongoing passion that is as much a part of life as is the breath we draw. It is fed by purpose, by the feeling of being supported by others who mean something to us. It can be gained from a belief we hold, song we hear in passing, or a single phrase we read in a book. Desire is a great motivator to create this determination, and *need* is the most powerful motivator of all. Think carefully on this, for below all of our plans and dreams lie these subtle impetuses. These are destiny makers, and this is the root of all magic. Therefore, this card is *the root* of all magic. This is the conveniently hidden tool of *The Magician*, and it is <u>how</u> he makes his candle(s) burn at both ends simultaneously, even to the chagrin of gravity. This is the shaping of the *Laws of Attraction and Repulsion,* and the conjuring up the powers of the other mysterious laws of might and magic.

Traditional meaning: Perseverance is called for. This doesn't mean "wait." It means use a gentle hand *(one with an iron grip if you happen to have one handy)*. You don't "snap" a lion's jaws shut. You keep applying pressure until like any other cat he gets tired of fighting you and tries it your way for a moment. The trick is not closing a cat's mouth, it is keeping the cat from squirming and clawing you to shreds while you are doing this. And that is what the *Strength* card is all about.

Take your time. Stay with this. Do not give up, not now. Not *ever*. Surrender is defeat. When you *see* this card, it is a warning, an omen, a command of patient application of inner strength. But always remember that strength does not mean stupidity. If you are in a bad relationship and the *Strength* card shows up in a *card position* of "advice," this card is not telling you to "grin and bear it." It is telling you to draw on your inner strength, draw from the source (from friends, from your deity, from your inner desires, etc.) and take whatever actions that are indicated by the other cards. Do so from a position of strength, even if that means "running away." Sometimes it takes more courage to leave than it does to stay in a bad situation. There is the devil you know versus the devil you don't.

If this card shows up as a character quality in a person, it is a good indicator that you can rely on that person. In a job it lends itself to stability and tenure, and the ability to make decisions with enough autonomy to be truly effective in that job rather than just another corporate placeholder in line. In almost every case, the querent is "the woman" and not "the lion."

Traditional reversed meaning: Except here . . . now you get to be "Mr. Lion." Occasionally this card *reversed* will show being dominated (we hear that some people are actually into that), but not just by a "woman." This could be an alcohol, food, sex, or drug addiction (look for *Cups* and *Swords* obviously). Other times it will show weakness, fear, hesitancy, or running away from issues.

Now it's your turn

Please note: *You can fill this in later if nothing comes to mind right away. It is far more important to get a good feel for this card than it is to write something in right away.*

What is your interpretation? What does this card say to you?

___

___

___

What does it say to you when it is *reversed*?

___

___

___

If you saw this card as an "end result," what would you say to your client?

___

___

___

How would you use this card as an "affirmation helper"?

___

___

___

___

What other feelings, impressions, or uses do you want to note about this card?

___

___

___

"MAJOR" ARCANA

The Hermit

Description: An old guy stands "atop the mountain" (some say the edge of a cliff) and holds up a light. He is old. Really, really old. That's about it. Of course, it is entirely possible to look at the "contained" (captured, harnessed, stolen) "light of God" (and won't he be happy to find out *that's* missing!). It's that six-pointed star thingy inside his otherwise empty lantern (no candle, no fuel or wick . . .). So this stolen "light of God" he has "mastered the knowledge and use of" allows him to penetrate the veil of mysteries that mere mortals *(basically anyone sensible enough to stay home in a nice comfy warm bed on a snowy night)* cannot see. Therefore, he is "better" than us. That is until "God" finds out he stole his pointy star and put it in a lamp.

Esoteric interpretation: A long, long time ago, Prometheus, one of humanity's best friends, stole fire (back) from the gods and gave it (back) to humans, and saved us all from certain destruction. Zeus did not like this one bit. In fact, he disliked this thwarting of his will (ego) so much that he chained our hero to a rock where a vulture (some say an eagle) ate his liver—daily. For *years*. In fact it took Hercules (another friend of humanity) to kill the bird (it was an "evil" bird) and free our (other) hero. The moral of this story? Wisdom equals *pain*. Moreover: <u>There is no magic without sacrifice</u> (sorry). Esoterically, Prometheus' theft of fire has a metaphysical meaning in addition to the obvious physical connotation of survival. Fire is the element of creativity, it is the "spark of life," and the mastery of it is one of the fundamental points of humanity—that which separates us from every other (known) species.

Similarly: One does not gain "the light of God" without faith, practice, and study (*lots* of study). Our friend (the creepy old guy in the picture) looks down on us, shining his light both to help him deepen his own knowledge as well as provide a beacon for those of us who prefer to witness "the light of God" through a nearby window from our comfy warm beds on a snowy night. The pursuit of wisdom is not for everyone. Some of us just want to have a comfortable life, make babies, and die happy and popular. This is why we need creepy old guys with funny lanterns lighting the way for us, so that it is easier to achieve these lofty goals while avoiding the various potholes along our individual paths.

Traditional meaning: As a person—a college professor, any teacher, therapist, consultant, researcher, or priest (male or female—and not necessarily "old" nor creepy); one who seeks "truth" or provides advice. There aren't a lot of prophets running around these days, so it could easily be any elder who has wise counsel, a (reliable and *wise*) religious leader, or even a sherpa should you be in the Himalayas at the time of the *reading*. Otherwise, it is usually an institution (vocational school, junior college, university, or any of the teachers said to inhabit such locales). This card is usually too "big" to simply imply a person who gives you advice, so *open it up* or look for aspecting cards to determine the full extent of the meaning behind this card.

As an action or an event it can indicate deep, intense study, or enrolling in any of the schools above. Conversely, <u>it has a secondary meaning</u>: that of withdrawing from society. If you suspect this at all, you should *definitely open it up*, as this withdrawal could be the reaction to depression, drug use, a loss of friends, or running away from any other unpleasantness. The act of withdrawing is not in and of itself bad. Try to determine the *motivation* for this act and see if the *response* is equitable (called for).

Traditional reversed meaning: Sometimes we can run away from problems by being hyper-social. <u>Instead of quiet reflection</u>, we do everything we can to hide from "the voices in our head" (the good ones). This can also indicate *not* listening to advice, *not* spending time learning necessary information, bad advice, or false professionals (scams, cult leaders, pop-messiahs), refusing to rest and recuperate.

Now it's your turn

__Please note__: You can fill this in later if nothing comes to mind right away. It is far more important to get a good feel for this card than it is to write something in right away.

What is <u>your</u> interpretation? What does this card say to you?

_____

_____

_____

What does it <u>say to you</u> when it is *reversed*?

_____

_____

_____

If you saw this card as an "end result," what would you say to your client?

_____

_____

_____

How would you use this card as an "affirmation helper"?

_____

_____

_____

_____

_____

What other feelings, impressions, or uses do you want to note about this card?

_____

_____

_____

_____

"MAJOR" ARCANA

Wheel of Fortune

Description: This is a fun card (be sure to see the "funny captions" section). A giant orange wheel emblazoned with various letters spins randomly as three mythological creatures take their turn "on the wheel" while others record the events of the day. The whole of it takes place in some similarly mythological location (in the clouds). Note that these clouds provide our little group privacy and comfy platforms on which to recline, but not a hint of rain or lightning.

Esoteric interpretation: "*. . .and the wheels of the bus go 'round and 'round.*" For all we plot, do, and hide from, the whole of everything keeps moving along with us along for the ride, and when we are gone, it just keeps going. Such is the way . . . Part of being *human* is to personalize our experiences here, to see the world around us as <u>we exist in</u>, rather than a whole of which we are a part (an important one), and that means that we all too often take things *very* personally. This is important in so many ways, as it is the catalyst for inspiration and invention. It is the stimulation of artistic endeavor which reveals itself in incalculable ways. But "taking things personally" is also the cause of more human suffering than any other core psychological reaction—*ever*.

Thus the beauty of this card is that it is simultaneously impersonal and *intensely* personal. "Stuff" doesn't just happen. "Stuff" happens to <u>you</u>. Other "stuff" happens to people you will never meet, *and you never know they are any worse the wear* for what has transpired, so really it is not your problem to even think about. The trick (on the surface) appears to be to stay "on top" of the wheel at all times, thereby avoiding the "ups and downs" of life; but really that just makes you a hamster on a wheel, always investing all of your attention and energy trying to avoid pain and inconvenience. <u>The wheel never stops</u>. The lesson here is to enjoy the good times while they last, and when you can no longer avoid "being on the down side," minimize your exposure and ride through the cycle safely. This card teaches us to <u>stop taking things so personally</u>, and to look at the greater scheme of things rather than obsessively focusing on the instant gratification of daily *distractions*.

Traditional meaning: It's really hard to overstate the "face value" if it is facing up; it really is a *very* good card. Things go your way, plans come together. In essence, you are *swimming downstream* in the great flow of the universe (the current pushes you along, so you end up going faster and further with less effort). Some authorities like to compare this card to the notion of one's karma; but really, what is *karma* without *dharma* anyway? You can't earn any *karma* unless you have some personal *dharma* to start with. In non-gibberish terms: You are *you*. **Be you.** Don't run around trying to be something you are not. *Yes, yes, yes!! Develop yourself!* <u>But do so</u> along your lines of purpose and innate strengths and deepest desires. The trivialities of "popularity" and "success" *will come* to those who are so true to themselves that they create real (and often unique) values to society. "Play to your strengths" and you will do well. This card shows us that everything has cycles, and that the only thing we truly own are our *character* traits. When we *prepare* for life's "ups and downs" by developing our own individual strengths and qualities, our passions, and our inner resources, we will find others who support us both when we are "up" and when we are "down" instead of simply on the day we are popular.

Traditional reversed meaning: Well, it's been fun, but . . . Okay, so if this card is *reversed*, it's definitely time to limit your exposure, take nothing for granted, plan carefully, save your pennies, and <u>get new friends</u>. This indicates challenges (*yaay!*) and opportunities coming from work (*ugh!*) and sacrifice.

Now it's your turn

__Please note:__ You can fill this in later if nothing comes to mind right away. It is far more important to get a good feel for this card than it is to write something in right away.

What is <u>your</u> interpretation? What does this card say to you?

_____

_____

_____

What does it <u>say to you</u> when it is *reversed*?

_____

_____

_____

If you saw this card as an "end result," what would you say to your client?

_____

_____

_____

How would you use this card as an "affirmation helper"?

_____

_____

_____

_____

What other feelings, impressions, or uses do you want to note about this card?

_____

_____

_____

Justice

Description: *(Note: In some decks this may be card 8, in others it is card 11. Either way it is still valid.)* "Our lady of justice" sits on her throne between the twin pillars the Tarot uses to illustrate authority, a bland drape behind her. A sword is raised high in her right hand, scales in her left, and the obligatory crown on her head also indicating the supremacy of her authority, *for Justice can do no wrong* (a purely metaphysical concept). What is interesting is her solid red robe of *action*. She "only looks" like a judge sitting (er . . . in judgment). Her robes and slightly extended "leading foot" belie her otherwise passive stance. She is judge, jury, *and* executioner (we have seen this before in two other Tarot cards). But she is the force behind other power. She *is* pure.

Esoteric interpretation: The esoteric concept of justice implies a natural order to the universe, a baseline or rudimentary set of laws that govern the resulting chaos of so many individual forces acting upon each other. This is a highly popular notion, one at the very core of all but a handful of the world's religions, and the foundation of scientific research. This card is representational of one of the greatest of all "secret" laws, that being *the Manifold and Mystic Law of Cause and Effect*. It is both "manifold" and "mystic" because there are just too many variables to account for everything (see also "chaos theory"). You can't have a reliable "effect" if the bedrock of science or philosophy is as fluid as water. Hers is the hand that turns *The Wheel*. But please remember that Lao Tzu correctly admonished us that *"Nature is not human-hearted."* We keep inventing new ways to contain human aggression, but in so doing only create more human oppression. True justice is inherently personal. It comes from within, or it is merely the punishment of animals.

Traditional meaning: This card is *institutional* when physical and *conceptual* when esoteric. First, the physical meanings: This card can indicate actual *locations*, such as city halls, courtrooms, law offices, prisons (eek!), and political establishments. It is imperative to *open this card up* or find *aspecting* and *clarifying cards* to enhance your correct interpretation of this rather vague card. On an *esoteric* level, this card denotes "justice" (as in payback, vengeance, or "karma") and applied social moral values. Once again, *clarify* the meaning before attempting interpretation. As an *event*, this card can indicate a successful resolution, restitution, or settlement in your favor. Of course, this is mildly infringing on *Judgment's* divinatory turf, but as these two cards are so densely intertwined it should not come as a surprise if they show up in a *spread* complementing each other. But back to this chaos thing. Chaos theory states something about butterflies and hurricanes, and what they are really saying is that sometimes the most seemingly inconsequential thing can be the tipping point in the direction of which way a huge decision falls or process ends up. *Justice* says "you may not see all of the reasons for this decision, but it will make sense," so it's best not to take things *too personally* if you don't get everything you wanted from the situation.

One last thing, just for fun: For those of you who really need a little extra pain to get through the day, here is a cute little metaphysical mind-bender—*Justice* is the card you would use for *dharma*, or *correct causality* in your magical workings to effect your *"Laws of Attraction and Repulsion,"* whereas *The Wheel* represents the resultant *karma* or *effect*.

Traditional reversed meaning: Sometimes the bad guys win. Someone is conspiring in the background. Sycophants, "yes-men," office politics, *drama*, unfavorable treatment, and possibly being on the losing side of any large battle (*clarify* everything through *aspecting cards* before deciding meaning). If this card comes up *reversed* in the present or the future, continue *reading* to find out who is doing what to whom, and then toss out the *Roundabout spread* to find out how to undo or avoid these nefarious cretins.

Now it's your turn

Please note: *You can fill this in later if nothing comes to mind right away. It is far more important to get a good feel for this card than it is to write something in right away.*

What is <u>your</u> interpretation? What does this card say to you?

_____

_____

_____

What does it <u>say to you</u> when it is *reversed*?

_____

_____

_____

If you saw this card as an "end result," what would you say to your client?

_____

_____

_____

How would you use this card as an "affirmation helper"?

_____

_____

_____

_____

What other feelings, impressions, or uses do you want to note about this card?

_____

_____

_____

The Hanged Man *(or "Hanging Man")*

Description: Before you do anything else, stop and turn this card around so that *the card* is upside down. Now look at him. Squint your eyes if you have to, but use those amazing powers of visualization you are developing to see him on the deck of a ship. He is now (when *the card* is upside down) in the classic pose of a sailor dancing a jig. *Why, why, why?* The other masters have inferred the associations with the element of water but they never bothered to tell anyone (except maybe *their* students) about this part. They really should retitle the card once and for all as *The Hanging Man,* instead of *The Hanged Man.* The current card title has caused far too much confusion for far too many years—most in the name of "secrecy," so don't tell anyone we told you.

Esoteric interpretation: So why is he dancing upside down? Sailors placed their hands behind their backs when they danced for a number of reasons: it kept them from flailing about in an undignified manner, and it certainly kept them from slapping into things (like people, and lines [ropes], masts, and other boat "stuff"). It also was a rather controlled ("manly") placement. The pose here (when *the card* is upside down) shows our friend mid-leap, with the classical "pointed toe" of a ballet dancer, and the kicked up heel (as in to "kick up your heels") mid-leap. Dancing has always been the primal and even ultimate celebration of life. We didn't always have televisions to waste our lives in front of, so when we finished the chores of the day, we rested a bit, gathered with our friends, drank lots of alcohol, *and danced*. This is the way it has always been, in almost every society throughout time, but especially in the European ones that spawned the whole "mystery school" paradigm. Dancing is the celebration of life. Dancing *is* life, in a "daily life" kind of way, just the same as crappy jobs are (another constant for the masses of society). Dancing is the *fun* part of life. In most dances men and women were allowed to touch each other. *(Oooh!)* Try touching some random stranger you find attractive the next time you are in public, see where *that* gets you (be sure to have "bail money" in your pocket)! Thus, our friend above, the dancing man, is really **"the non-dancing man."** The reason for his pose is to show his willful exit from society (and the touching of women). Then there is the halo. Are you seeing the pattern here? "Godliness" coming from abstinence. Sacrifice for a greater goal (and as they say . . . "What is greater than . . .?"). The legs are the "active" body part here. (Notice the heavy use of red? *Waite was soooo predictable.*) So there you have it. He is not "hanged," or "hung." He is stepping away from the joys of life to invest his time (his most valuable asset) in search of deeper meaning. He is looking for answers, but the halo in the image shows us that he is finding them, thus indicating that his time of waiting is already nearing an end. By the time this card shows up, the hardest part is over. Stay with it.

Traditional meaning: Turning your back on routine and searching out answers. This could be a style of problem solving that is used by the person the card relates to (seeing things differently). Sacrifice for a greater goal. Missing out on "life," but usually because one is preoccupied with something important. However, if this card shows up with, say, the *9 of Swords,* and/or the *4 of Coins* (you get the idea), you may be seeing someone who is afraid to live, or afraid of spending their money, time, youth, or some other valuable commodity. They are hiding from life. This happens quite a bit really, but like any other "major" Arcana card, you really need to tie it in to "minor" Arcana cards to give it definition. *This card also shows* a time of waiting, inaction, deep thought, passive magical exercises (meditation, prayer, "attraction" here as "seduction").

Traditional reversed meaning: Ahh, the joys of life—of being young and alive and free, without a care in the world! This is how those celebrity "billionaire babies" must feel every day, running from party to party, laughing mercilessly at all of "the little people" who actually have to *work* for a living. *Oops! I used the "w" word. Silly me!* This shows an abandonment of responsibility, study, effort, or bothering to care.

Now it's your turn

__Please note__: You can fill this in later if nothing comes to mind right away. It is far more important to get a good feel for this card than it is to write something in right away.

What is <u>your</u> interpretation? What does this card say to you?

_____

_____

_____

What does it <u>say to you</u> when it is *reversed*?

_____

_____

_____

If you saw this card as an "end result," what would you say to your client?

_____

_____

_____

How would you use this card as an "affirmation helper"?

_____

_____

_____

_____

What other feelings, impressions, or uses do you want to note about this card?

_____

_____

_____

Death

Description: Death rides a pale horse into town at sunset. Sunset, by the way, was the official ending of one day and the beginning of the next in Druidic calendars, which are the basis for much of modern paganism. Today's calendars start each day at midnight (the daily equivalent of Yule), even though the sun rising every day is synonymous with spring, and "the time of waking," both physically and metaphysically. Here a priest of some high rank begs for mercy, a king lies dead, a young girl falls over ill, and a very young girl looks at the pretty horsie. Perspective bequeaths reality. The king *dies* from his knowledge of nature, the priest begs because of his understanding of nature, the girl on the right falls victim to *expectation,* and the little girl sees wonder.

Esoteric interpretation: *"To everything there is a season . . ."* The one constant in a universe of endless change is that everything that is born by definition dies at some point. "Death and taxes" are the two great equalizers (at least in theory). What is more important than worrying about death is actually *living* life so that by the time Death rides in on his horsie you are "so over it" and yelling at the poor guy that "he is late!" Note how *Death* is the thirteenth card. When the Tarot was devised, and through most of its major changes, the number 13 was feared. Before you laugh at the thought of anyone being afraid of a number (like say . . . one, two, *oh my god! Three's coming up!*), the official term for this superstition is "Triskaidekaphobia." To this day a good many high-rise buildings politely exclude the thirteenth floor, going conveniently from twelve to fourteen (like the gods can be fooled that easily). Being afraid of a unit of math* (a number) is as silly as being afraid of *this card*. But people like their superstitions, so if your client freaks out because this card comes up in *their reading*, simply tell them that this card means "they will be getting a pony soon."

Traditional meaning: Death. But not usually. You see, there are only 78 cards, so the chance of any one card showing up is 1 in 78, which aren't bad odds at all. Now in a *multi-card spread* like the *Celtic Cross*, the chances for any one card showing up (even before you start *opening up cards, or the reading itself*) drop to 1 in 7-point-something, depending on whether you use a significator (or two), or not. The chances of most people dying in the next 30–60 days is hardly "1 in 7." Thus, each card has to pull "double duty." This doesn't mean that the *Death* card will really start to mean that it's "new pony time," but it will *also* show things like endings and beginnings. Please remember that **every "major" Arcana card is an allegory that must be deciphered**.

For example: If someone walked up to you and said in a sagely voice, "There is no spoon," you might think (and rightly so) that they are both intrusive *and* insane. But if they explained (before you had a chance to run away from the crazy person) that the line they just used on you was a quote from the movie *The Matrix* and explained that a small child was explaining to the confused and very frustrated neo-messiah of the future that the whole of reality was just a figment of our imaginations (hmm . . . where have we heard that before?), all of a sudden it would make sense. You still may not like random strangers using oblique pick-up lines on you, but you would understand what they meant by, "There is no spoon." That is why you want to *open up* or *associate* "major" Arcana cards with "minor" Arcana cards instead of allowing your clients to get the heebie-jeebies every time a card comes up they don't *understand,* and *don't* like. **Death means change**. Big change. But where? Life? Divorce? Job? Is this part of a move? *Death* comes along and "shakes things up" (much like *The Tower*), but *Death* is intimately personal, whereas *The Tower* is impersonal and external. When you see this card, find out what changes your client is going through internally and help them with *that*.

Traditional reversed meaning: Stagnation; *refusal to let go*. Holding on to outdated ideas. A boring life.

* *Conversely: Being afraid of math itself is the sign of a healthy mind—one free from the desire to torture itself needlessly. Which is why "God" invented calculators.*

Now it's your turn

Please note: *You can fill this in later if nothing comes to mind right away. It is far more important to get a good feel for this card than it is to write something in right away.*

What is <u>your</u> interpretation? What does this card say to you?

_____

_____

_____

What does it <u>say to you</u> when it is *reversed*?

_____

_____

_____

If you saw this card as an "end result," what would you say to your client?

_____

_____

_____

How would you use this card as an "affirmation helper"?

_____

_____

_____

_____

What other feelings, impressions, or uses do you want to note about this card?

_____

_____

_____

Temperance

Description: "So we were like, at this rockin' party last night, and get this—*Arch*-angel Mike was totally pouring these wicked jello shots . . ."

Actually the angel is a woman* by most accounts, and in many of the most *symbologically correct* decks, it is a woman (angel or not). But that is less important than the fact that the image on the left tries to repeat a concept endlessly: two wings spread wide "balancing" just off of the ground, but also visually illustrating the concept of "balance," pouring *from* one cup *to* another, standing both on the earth (lightly) and in the water, and the sacred (angel) visiting the profane (earth).

Esoteric interpretation: (see above) "Temperance" is one of the four *cardinal virtues* in ancient Greece, and thus through Rome became one of the four *cardinal virtues* central to the Catholic Church (and thus the Tarot). Even Buddhists admire it, claiming it as one of their five precepts. But it is far older than any of that. Here it is in "secret mystery school lingo." Ready?

Nothing too much

"Nothing too much" is a potent yet delicate, *feminine* (as in the power of feminine persuasion—which is obviously not all about "sex") expression of a harsher "moderation in all things" commandment. You see, even the phraseology of it expresses, *breathes* the essence of the wisdom. It neither offends nor does it withhold. It is as powerful as a rock thrown at one's head, but as gentle as the caress of a feather. This is the reason we have "mystery schools": to teach life's lessons in ways they can be easily assimilated and *acted upon* by not just the student-seeker but by the general populace as well. If only a handful of society's citizens were applying the methods and precepts of civilization, that collective of humans would dissolve into barbarism within a generation. This is the essence of the *Temperance* card. It shows the need for <u>the application of</u> divine inspiration and virtuous existence. By stating it so softly the voice may go unheard to many; but it is still far more effective than shouting, where it will only gain resistance among those who do not understand the message. *(Try shouting at the next person who doesn't understand you, just for fun.)*

So where did this delicate phrase make its appearance in history *and influence empires* and the world's great religions? This message appeared on the right pillar at Delphi (the left read something to the effect of *"Know Thyself." Please* see our secret mystery school text *Aphrodite's Book of Secrets* for more on this). The message is timeless, but the expression is best when whispered rather than shouted, phrased gently but firmly rather than weakly, or worse, with pointed words. This card shows us the value of the alchemical process of <u>combination</u> and of enjoying <u>right</u> <u>up</u> <u>to</u> <u>the</u> <u>limit</u> <u>of</u> "excess"; thus being able to find everything we *want* in life without the hassles of *punishment* or *lack*.

Traditional meaning: Teamwork *works*. None of us is as smart *as all of us*. Properly <u>blended</u> <u>energies</u> make "magic cookies." Success is a recipe. Failure comes from any number of deviations in that recipe (too much salt, not enough baking time . . .). Draw together your resources and use them to reach your success. Do all of the above until exhausted and then rest. Start again when you are refreshed. If time is short, split your team into separate groups so that activity is ongoing but no one is overtaxed. Note this card blends two major meanings into one overarching message: *do* <u>correctly</u>.

Traditional reversed meaning: Imbalance, bad planning, poor execution, lack of wisdom, rushing anything. *Too much of this, not enough of that.* Too much at once. Selfishness, prima donnas, lack of understanding.

*An oxymoron that never appears in traditional Christian mythology. God created woman from Adam, not before.

Now it's your turn

Please note: You can fill this in later if nothing comes to mind right away. It is far more important to get a good feel for this card than it is to write something in right away.

What is your interpretation? What does this card say to you?

_____

_____

_____

What does it say to you when it is *reversed*?

_____

_____

_____

If you saw this card as an "end result," what would you say to your client?

_____

_____

_____

_____

How would you use this card as an "affirmation helper"?

_____

_____

_____

_____

_____

What other feelings, impressions, or uses do you want to note about this card?

_____

_____

_____

"MAJOR" ARCANA

The Devil

Description: This is another fun card, one your clients will no doubt enjoy seeing in *their spread*. *Señor Diablo* is waving at the crowd for the publicity shots in hell. (They were going for an image makeover that never really caught on). It's not so much that he is trying to hide his torch as it is that he lit the man's tail on fire *for effect*. Leave aside all of the endless arguments of "Christian devil *versus* Eliphas Lévi's* pagan horned-god rendition" and just call this guy the Devil and be done with it. He perches on his throne and Adam and Eve get to rot in hell for all eternity (until you turn the card upside down of course).

(*his cool nom de plume)

Esoteric interpretation: This card really is a mish-mash of religious symbolism that would give Jung nightmares in its inconsistency. It is the ultimate bondage card, but it is also a *"get-out-of-jail-free!"* card, a warning of the excesses of enjoying life, too much responsibility, the effects of tyranny, complacency, bad partnerships, lack of foresight, and the dangers of playing with matches. The (Christian) devil allegedly promises fun but in the end only brings pain. Whether that is true or not (we haven't met the guy so we are not 100% certain of this fact), the emphasis of this meaning is the loss of "life" that folly brings. This goes back to *The Hanging Man* (or *The Hanged Man* to the uninitiated). This is the esoteric state of the dancing to exhaustion, the hangover after an "all-nighter," the drudgery of endless routine, or the seemingly endless contractual obligations after one has committed to a quest.

Traditional meaning: When this card shows up in a *reading*, it usually indicates physical incapacitation. "You are stuck—here." This could be a bad marriage, a boring job (with the obligatory evil boss), an extended hospital stay, waiting—endless waiting for other people to fulfill *their* obligations so you can move on, or any other slow systematic torture that seems well beyond the control of your client to change or eliminate. As such, it needs to be *opened up* to find the root cause of this, and then *re-opened* to find the "way out." This is obviously a concept card and almost never directly relates to an individual or a single event, unless it is speaking as a purely visual example of your client's emotional experience (*"That 'mandatory office Christmas party' was four hours of hell while I was hit on by every upper-management troglodyte over 50!"*).

Occasionally this card will (like the devil) play tricks on you and show up as variations of its central theme. This is why we avoid hard, fast meanings in the Tarot. For one client of yours this card may be the ruination brought on by some action or lifestyle (*"Hi, I lost my job, my wife, my great life to the evils of alcohol . . ."*) and thirty minutes later another one of your male corporate executive clients comes in who is being sued by his dominatrix and he is afraid that *his wife* will find out and divorce him (this is a poetic interpretation by the Tarot, combining the meanings of oppression, bondage, and a sense of hopelessness). This card is the embodiment of evil in a philosophical sense and in a very real "so and so did/is doing this to me" kind of way. It is *far* more important to understand how to tease answers from this card than it is to memorize any set interpretations.

Traditional reversed meaning: This is where the *"get-out-of-jail-free!"* part comes in. When *reversed*, *The Devil* indicates a release or an escape from oppression. Again, this can be on a number of levels. It's like squeezing a giant pimple. It's not very pretty, but the release of pressure that has been nagging at you for what seems like forever feels good in an almost "guilty pleasure" sense. Unlike *Death*, where things are usually pretty cut-and-dry, *The Devil* oozes along, leaving a trail of odor that lingers for a while. While this indicates that the worst is over (leaving that bad job, abusive relationship, beating cancer, etc.) there is still both stigma and consequence that has to be *cleansed* before things can be "totally normal" again.

Now it's your turn

***Please note:** You can fill this in later if nothing comes to mind right away. It is far more important to get a good feel for this card than it is to write something in right away.*

What is <u>your</u> interpretation? What does this card say to you?

_____

_____

_____

What does it <u>say to you</u> when it is *reversed*?

_____

_____

_____

If you saw this card as an "end result," what would you say to your client?

_____

_____

_____

How would you use this card as an "affirmation helper"?

_____

_____

_____

_____

What other feelings, impressions, or uses do you want to note about this card?

_____

_____

_____

The Tower

Description: "God" is not happy. Lightning strikes at (the Tower of Babel in this version) and the "crowning achievement" of mankind is torn asunder while both architect (designer of this masterpiece) and emperor (facilitator and caretaker of this enterprise) are thrown from its heights. Fiery *yods* accompany our unlucky victim's free-fall descent. For added effect, fire escapes from the windows showing that even stone can burn; and, of course, the ground to which our erstwhile geniuses are falling is rocky and jagged. Just in case we miss any of the "added" symbolism and thereby fail to realize how unhappy of a situation this is, it also happens *during the dead of night*.

Esoteric interpretation: *"There is nothing the hand of man can create that the hand of God cannot destroy."* This is a simple "ego-check" for all who aspire to power, most notably the domination of humanity to the point of challenging the gods themselves. The tower in *The Tower* represents the raw collective power of humanity's ability to band together in physical, mental, and emotional congruency to harness resources and create physical and psychological monuments of function and form, and ultimately how empty those achievements are if the soil they are rooted in is devoid of the nutrients of divinity. *The Tower* warns those in power not to hold themselves too highly lest greater powers than they control come along and destroy both achievement, creator, and possessor. This relates back to the old axiom that "history is written by the victors" (of war). History is littered with great accomplishments that have been destroyed and even written out of history (forgotten forever) because the creators or inheritors of said monument, system of belief, or accomplishment lacked the humility to either the divine or to the people they served. In short, someone or something slew the indestructible giant. The unwritten message in this overtly Christian card is that "God works in mysterious ways," meaning that the destruction wreaked may not be the flashy and dramatic lightning bolt, but a poorly cemented stone that allows the tower to fall in on itself, or a janitor who leaves the door open for thieves, or even the earth giving way under all of the weight of "authority."

Traditional meaning: "*And stay out!*" Okay, let's look at change in the "major" Arcana. We have *Death* ("Poof! Be gone!"), *The Devil*, reversed, ("Quick! The guard's not looking! Let's get OUT of here!"), and now *The Tower*. This is the very earth shaking the house down to the foundations. *Death* is a highly personal experience (usually internal) that can affect many, whereas *The Devil* is almost always an external experience involving people or situations close by. *The Tower* can be either of these, or it can be monumental in scale or meaning.

The Tower is most often external change relating to job, residence, paradigm, or "traditional authority." It is a direct challenge to our perceptions and beliefs. It can be the first shot in the revolution or it can speak for the revolt itself. It is not necessarily unpleasant, but it is sudden and it is a *major* change. This card can just as easily point to a divorce or an auto accident as it could quitting your cushy job and retiring to Spain to grow wine grapes. It is a spooky card, but only to those who are afraid of losing what they have in exchange for something "new and different." Once you have tracked down exactly what this card represents and when it will come to pass, be sure to look beyond it and see what is on the other side, and how large the fallout will be. This will help you advise your client better.

Traditional reversed meaning: Many traditionalists still see this as a "bad" card. We have found in our experience that this card indicates a time of *rebuilding*. Obviously, rebuilding can only come after a period of disruption and chaos, and that is *an awful lot of stone* to move, so this does not indicate an "easy," or overly "joyous" time, but it does indicate second chances, and time to learn from one's mistakes.

Now it's your turn

Please note: *You can fill this in later if nothing comes to mind right away. It is far more important to get a good feel for this card than it is to write something in right away.*

What is <u>your</u> interpretation? What does this card say to you?

_____

_____

_____

What does it <u>say to you</u> when it is *reversed*?

_____

_____

_____

If you saw this card as an "end result," what would you say to your client?

_____

_____

_____

How would you use this card as an "affirmation helper"?

_____

_____

_____

_____

_____

What other feelings, impressions, or uses do you want to note about this card?

_____

_____

_____

_____

"MAJOR" ARCANA

The Star

Description: A giant star dominates this picture (this holds true for various artist's renditions of this card—not just this particular deck). This star is, in turn, supported by other, smaller stars. A naked woman pours water from two pitchers; one into a small pool, the other onto the ground, where it splits into five rivulets. She kneels on the earth *and* the water for support showing us that she bridges the barriers between the two. The surrounding land is lush and fertile. A bird watches in the background. Some say this is an Ibis. In other variations of this card it is a butterfly. It is important to note that all of this takes place at night (naturally).

Esoteric interpretation: This is the single most misunderstood card of the Tarot. Most authorities attribute this card to the astrological sign *Aquarius,* and give the simple interpretation of "hope," as if that is all you need to know. Generally, when you see *The Star* you can have hope; good things will come to pass. Well, that's all fine and nice; but let's really look inside and see why everyone seems to accept this vague meaning of happiness. First: the name of the card is *The Star,* not *"The Naked Lady Who Pours Water Onto the Ground."* The single most important visual stimulus here is the star, not all five, seven, eight, or fifteen stars (various decks have various numbers of minor stars, so assigning any value such as chakras, physical senses, (etc.) to the actual number of stars is ludicrous). The woman pictured is the personification of the main star in the image, which, in turn, is "*The* Star." She is naked because she is divine, pure, and a "star." Her human form is nothing more than a visual representation of energy or purpose that has been used throughout history in mythology, magic, and religion. See her as "the star," not "the naked lady." See her as "she who bridges the realms."

Okay, so now that we have successfully belabored that point, here is what it all means: A star shines or *radiates* light, which becomes one hundred times more important at night (in the "dark times" than during the day when everything is happy and sunshiny). She is "radiating" her energy (pouring from containers) into the pool (the measurable ether, or what we know of the spiritual realm), and simultaneously on the earth. This essence "fills" the spirit realm and *nourishes* the earth. Star's energies penetrate (they "see all" from far above) and so her energy seeps into every (humanly) measurable "thing." She is *the source* of the nourishment of life, and the source of the energy which "magic" manipulates into form and function. This is why the card represents "hope." It is a visual representation of Hekate, the "goddess of magic." (This is really a *savage* understatement.) Hekate is one of the most powerful goddesses of mystery school traditions, for it was she who assisted Demeter to find her lost daughter when every other god and goddess turned their backs against her (and thus humanity), fearing the wrath of Hades, or being too self-obsessed to care. This card is a clear visual representation of Hekate freely giving her assistance both in the earth and the ether *(the "spiritual realm," "the underworld," etc.).* Therefore, this card is representational of "assistance from the gods." Use it to mean the flow of magic happening to make your dreams come true. Use it to represent any goddess you are calling upon, or if you prefer your own "godhead" or "superconscious mind" simultaneously reaching into the ether and the physical world to create a spiritual resonance ("P.M.E."*).

Traditional meaning: Hope. Faith. Magic. More to the point: When this card comes up, it shows a need to, or the action of, reaching out to the gods for assistance. It is "divine assistance" coming to play. If you are *already* praying, this is a positive response. If you haven't started praying, this card asks what you are waiting for. It is situations getting better through divine intervention (so you know who to thank).

Traditional reversed meaning: *Just turn the card around.* Or: hopelessness, despair, lack of spiritual connection.

* See *Aphrodite's Book of Secrets*

Now it's your turn

Please note: You can fill this in later if nothing comes to mind right away. It is far more important to get a good feel for this card than it is to write something in right away.

What is <u>your</u> interpretation? What does this card say to you?

_____
_____
_____

What does it <u>say to you</u> when it is *reversed*?

_____
_____
_____

If you saw this card as an "end result," what would you say to your client?

_____
_____
_____

How would you use this card as an "affirmation helper"?

_____
_____
_____
_____

What other feelings, impressions, or uses do you want to note about this card?

_____
_____
_____

"MAJOR" ARCANA

The Moon

Description: A combination moon (both crescent and full) looks down on a wolf, a dog, and a lobster ("*So a wolf, a dog, and a lobster walk into a bar . . .*") with two fortress towers standing guard over the path that leads straight from "Mr. Lobster" to the distant mountains. Moonlight *yods* fall to the ground, symbolizing the rain of ethereal moonlight energy.

It is more important to "get to know" your *Moon* card and decide exactly what it means to you on a regular basis than it is to keep looking for answers from other authors. This card is not necessarily negative, but many authors believe it so. Decide for yourself how you feel about *The Moon*.

Esoteric interpretation: The moon really got a bad rap in the Tarot. When the Tarot was invented, and during its major revisions over the centuries, the moon ("luna") was "known," by scientific minds at of the time, to cause mental illness; hence the long-standing association of the moon with lunacy (insanity in all its forms). You can blissfully ignore all of this if you want to use *The Moon* in your magical or meditative workings to illustrate the moon (the one in the sky).

If, however, you want to harness the handy stockpile of *thought-energy* (the galvanic psychic battery of long-standing collective belief) this card represents, then look at the moon (the one in the sky) as "reflected sunlight" of various quality—amount and filtration, such as clouds, pollution, depth of atmosphere, *that being your current altitude*—and, therefore, an imitation of the source: unpure, diluted, and deceptive. If you really want to have fun with this, do all of your magical work left-handed (sinister) and walk backwards if you can do so without falling over or bumping into stuff.

Traditional meaning: *(mostly negative, really)* Confusion. Deception (see above), hidden enemies, lies, illusions, alcoholism, drug use, addiction of any kind, hysteria (specifically), indigestion and/or heartburn. Rumors: watch your back at work or in close-knit social circles. Is someone you know talking behind your back? It is especially important to verify this (through *aspecting cards*) before you start making accusations. Also: mysteries, paranoia, unfounded accusations. **Denial.**

Less overtly negative associations: menstruation, psychic powers, detective work, occult powers, secret organizations, seafood (yes, really—especially shellfish), issues associated with the breast or stomach, maternity (look for verification of pregnancy, or pregnancy issues in related cards and/or in *aspecting* and *clarifying cards*). This card can also portend romance if it is positively *aspected* by a positive *Cups* card, and possibly *Coins* as well. Also: poetry, creative inspiration, romantic locations and activities. This is another card of the "subconscious mind," whereas *The Sun* is the "conscious."

Traditional reversed meaning: Deception revealed. Light is shined on the denizens of the darkness *(and don't expect them to be happy about it!)*. It's not so much a time of "Truth" as much as it is the end of a time of deception and trouble. Someone very bad for you leaves your life. You leave a crappy job. This also could indicate kicking bad habits, ending (or strongly minimizing—and thus controlling) harmful addictions.

These (above) all assume a negative *Moon* card association. If your standard *Moon* card association is a positive one, then *reversed* this card would be an ending or a removal of/separation from something positive in your life, most likely a gentle, nurturing source of security, romance, love, and quiet support. (In a man's chart this might indicate the divorce of a good wife. The entire *spread* would have to point to this—but this is an example for consideration.)

Now it's your turn

Please note: You can fill this in later if nothing comes to mind right away. It is far more important to get a good feel for this card than it is to write something in right away.

What is your interpretation? What does this card say to you?

_____

_____

_____

What does it say to you when it is *reversed*?

_____

_____

_____

If you saw this card as an "end result," what would you say to your client?

_____

_____

_____

How would you use this card as an "affirmation helper"?

_____

_____

_____

_____

What other feelings, impressions, or uses do you want to note about this card?

_____

_____

_____

"MAJOR" ARCANA

The Sun

Description: A baby (blonde *naturally,* he's probably a *Leo* anyway) rides a white horse while the Sun looks on. Sunflowers tower overhead and the baby miraculously holds high a flowing red banner of relatively gigantic proportions. Note the Sun's rays spread in all directions, the straight lines indicating the spread of *light,* while the wavy lines indicate the radiance of *heat.* This shows the Sun in its "infinite glory," unobscured by those pesky *clouds* or eclipsed by the nascent moon. "Nothing can stop the power (and joy) of the Sun!" . . . until it sets (leaves you for some distant land), or you walk behind a tree, small hill, building . . . Still, all in all a happy card if you are into tan lines.

Esoteric interpretation: This is the Sun *über alles* (before or above all others). Everyone knows the raw power of the Sun. It officially gives earth life. **Haud sol solis , haud vita.** (No Sun, no life.) In fact, the Sun is the single most worshiped object *ever.* In all parts of the world the Sun is equated with the local deities, mostly male, but occasionally female. The Sun is everywhere and is always welcome, although in the most harsh of desert climates it is often seen as a harsh master rather than a benevolent "god." Kind of like a military drill instructor (". . . *hup, two, three, four! Get in line soldier! Did I give you permission to bleed? Walk it off mister!*"). Face it: the Sun is a monster. It is big, <u>really *big*</u>: as in it's over 100 times as big as us (Earth). It never sleeps (which is rather creepy when you think about it). It is always shining at us no matter which way we (the Earth) turn, and if you look at it for more than a few seconds at a time, you will lose your eyesight *very* fast. The Sun is so hot that you could not even stand on it. In fact you can't get close enough to stand on it, you would crisp up like a french fry a few million miles away from *Herr-Sonne.* We take the Sun for granted because it is always there, and by our standards "it always will be." None of this changes the fact that it is big and powerful and it affects us in psychological and chemical ways we have yet to completely understand. This card represents all of that power in one overly simple scene.

Unlike the energy of *The Star,* however, *The Sun* is cyclical. The Sun rises and sets, whereas the stars always shine, only blocked by the closest of them all (our all-encompassing Sun). When the Sun is "here" (during the day), nothing else matters. Rain, wind, and snow can block out the Sun for periods of time; but unlike night, we know that on the other side of those pesky clouds our giant ball of fire still shines for us, <u>eating away at the barriers from the other side</u>. *(Are you getting this?)* This gives us insight into the meaning of such a card. When *The Sun* is present, it feeds us life-giving energy. It gives us light *and* heat. It can also be overpowering in its delivery. It is so pervasive that we don't even need to look at it to know that it is there, as its effects are everywhere. When *The Sun* is not present in *a reading,* we still know that it exists somewhere, shining on some distant land, and that the secondary effects still aid us, and we can draw off of them, even in the darkest of times, *if we only learn how.* We can block the great expanse of energy *The Sun* lends us (and as humans we often do) just as we can avoid sunlight by ducking under a tree, going inside a building, or even just closing our eyes to the light all around us. The Sun provides, but we have to accept. *The Sun* is no different. *In order to win,* <u>you must be present</u>.

Traditional meaning: Success, usually after struggle. More specifically: energy and intent is being offered to you from various sources. This can be "divine intervention," creative inspiration, physical assistance from others, loans of any sort, sound advice, etc. You are in the spotlight. People and "things" are looking to help you at this time, but you must be alert to opportunity and aid if you are to accept the goodies in store for you. Destiny is an *opportunity*—<u>not</u> a guarantee. Never forget that.

Traditional reversed meaning: Closing off from help; depression, paralyzing fear, *lack* of support.

Now it's your turn

Please note: You can fill this in later if nothing comes to mind right away. It is far more important to get a good feel for this card than it is to write something in right away.

What is your interpretation? What does this card say to you?

_____

_____

_____

What does it say to you when it is *reversed*?

_____

_____

_____

If you saw this card as an "end result," what would you say to your client?

_____

_____

_____

How would you use this card as an "affirmation helper"?

_____

_____

_____

_____

What other feelings, impressions, or uses do you want to note about this card?

_____

_____

_____

"MAJOR" ARCANA

Judgement

Description: An angel toots his horn signifying the mythical day when everyone will be judged, and a select few will get toys and candy, and the rest will burn in hell forever, and ever, and ever. *Amen!*

Esoteric interpretation: This is the end of the line. *"The test is over. Please close your books and turn in your papers. You got about as far as you are going to get, and any of you who 'finished early' and have been waiting for the rest of the class can finally leave. Have a great summer everyone! See you next year!"*

This card actually draws from a number of religious beliefs from Christianity to Hinduism, Egyptian, and so on . . . No matter what belief you subscribe to (including the "non-belief"), this card is highly useful to call it "the end of the day" and move on. Whenever you want a card that means "I have had enough of this. I want it over *now!*" this is your card. Whatever you were doing, you are done with it now. This card has a lot in common with *Death,* or *The Tower,* but this is not simply a change of state alchemically, it is a change of state with a chemical reaction. (This is also why we have "mystery schools" to explain all of this esoteric mumbo-jumbo, but just go with us on this.) *Judgement* gives us "a say in the matter." Some situations end and you just feel empty (*Death*), or like you have been cheated (*The Tower*), but *Judgement* is all about having your voice heard ("*. . . and another thing! . . .*") before the curtain falls. It also indicates reports on *your* "progress" (being a double-edged sword). In legal matters, say small-claims, or divorce for example, this card shows you getting "your day in court," where no matter what happens, you officially get redress. You are vindicated in some way, with the *aspecting cards* showing how much so and what happens as a result. In religious terms of "life and death," it can mean just about whatever you want it to: resurrection, the final day when an angel comes along and collects everyone all at once (Imagine *that* line! What if you have to go pee? Do you lose your place in line?).

Traditional meaning: Zombies. Well, they look like zombies to us (gray skin, rising from the dead . . .). This card indicates (as noted above) the end of something, but not necessarily the beginning of something else. It is both a "progress report" and a respite from action; a *pause* if you will. In the most simple cases it *does* indicate lawsuits or judgments in lawsuits, report cards, school graduations, breaking up after a loud shouting match. It simply represents the end of something and a marker stone placed in the Akashic Records that says "this happened and as a result . . ." Now it is time for something else, but what that is will be left up to you, and that old devil *circumstance.*

Traditional reversed meaning: "*. . . and so there I was at the party, trapped in the corner by this really creepy old guy who just kept going on and on about how he owned this company and that, and how much money and power he had, and . . .*" Back in days when music was recorded onto vinyl, the circular disk had a long spiral that the "record player" needle sat in and responded to all of the little bumps, in turn, translating that into sound. But sometimes the "record" was scratched, and the needle would jump the groove and play the same section over, and over, and over . . . The effect was very annoying. This is "just like that." You go around, *and around,* and look for a way out of this mess, but you can't seem to find one. Perhaps it is time for a clean break—even if you have to make sacrifices to get off of this ride.

Now it's your turn

__Please note__: You can fill this in later if nothing comes to mind right away. It is far more important to get a good feel for this card than it is to write something in right away.

What is your interpretation? What does this card say to you?

_____
_____
_____

What does it say to you when it is *reversed*?

_____
_____
_____

If you saw this card as an "end result," what would you say to your client?

_____
_____
_____

How would you use this card as an "affirmation helper"?

_____
_____
_____
_____

What other feelings, impressions, or uses do you want to note about this card?

_____
_____
_____

"MAJOR" ARCANA

The World

Description: A celestial woman (goddess) dances in the air with her twin wand-candles *(see The Magician)*, which she is the undisputed master of, not merely the possessor *(also see The Magician)*. This is reinforced by her purple sash. She is surrounded by a laurel of victory that is also a portal to her home dimension, or a gateway *to* her. Four guardians sit in attendance: angel, eagle, lion, bull, representing various character qualities as well as the elements of awareness and existence. This "audience of mythical beings" is an ancient allegory used by various religions to illustrate the value and power of the central figure at the gathering. She is obviously "above and beyond" the limitations of all earthly influence (including gravity it seems).

Esoteric interpretation: Tranquility, enlightenment, evolution. If the Buddha were a female (and one made a special guest appearance in the *Lotus Sutra*), this would be her. She is both source and seed, being the physical manifestation of and the spiritual essence of purity through experience and awareness. She has completed "the circuit" and passed all judgments, tests, and has moved well beyond such mundane concepts as "testing and progress." She simply *is*. This is an existence far beyond the toils of the field or the wealth of nations. This is an existence of awareness embodied in human form, free of need or desire. She is a celebration of life unchained by any restrictions.

Some have said that *"the universe will not end with a bang, but with a whimper,"* suggesting that life will simply die out slowly as (measurable, or 'light') matter is stretched too thin to support itself. Suns will consume themselves and planets will simply be rare floating cosmic debris. One of the many things they have failed to consider by use of this prognosis is that *energy can neither be created nor destroyed.* In the very same way that "one man's food is another's poison," the energy of the universe will evolve and metamorphose into something else eventually. Leaves bud, grow, drink in the light of the sun, *breathe in* carbon dioxide and *breathe out* oxygen, and eventually wither and die, falling to the ground, a seemingly empty husk of their glory. But to the tree who watches generations of its leaves die and fall away at its calling, these very same expressions of itself become future food for its own roots and that of its children. Nature may be rather cannibalistic, but it never "wastes." This card represents the endless series of cycles of completion and renewal with each twirl of her double-ended candle wands. Her dance continues joyously even as the world turns, dies, and becomes something else entirely.

Traditional meaning: This is a very happy card on the physical level. At its most basic it represents the pampered and *the idle rich;* those wonderfully happy people born into generational wealth (see *10 of Coins*) who have nothing better (or worse) to do than to play all day and wonder how they will play all night as well. It truly is "the world at your feet." The key to this card is that it is *evolution* on so many levels of meaning that it can easily apply to any situation. It is extremely ambiguous and all but *demands clarification* by accompanying "minor" Arcana cards to give it <u>focus</u>. This is another <u>completion</u> card, but as noted it is a card of evolution from one state to another. The alchemical correspondence is that of transmuting lead *into* gold. The base chemical composition is almost identical, but the elemental change is eclipsed by the perceived value change. In the same way, you stay "who you are" but become something much more valuable through this card. This is the ultimate "happily ever after" card (compare to the *10 of Cups*).

Traditional reversed meaning: *"Leftovers <u>again</u>?"* (or) *"If I have to go back to that horrible job one more day . . ."* Endless, meaningless, repetitive, redundant existence—*"Every day the same thing: Breathe, breathe, breathe."* You really need a vacation right now. You are missing out on all of the fun in life. Go <u>dancing</u>!

Now it's your turn

Please note: *You can fill this in later if nothing comes to mind right away. It is far more important to get a good feel for this card than it is to write something in right away.*

What is <u>your</u> interpretation? What does this card say to you?

_____

_____

_____

What does it <u>say to you</u> when it is *reversed*?

_____

_____

_____

If you saw this card as an "end result," what would you say to your client?

_____

_____

_____

How would you use this card as an "affirmation helper"?

_____

_____

_____

_____

What other feelings, impressions, or uses do you want to note about this card?

_____

_____

_____

"MAJOR" ARCANA

Section Six

"Okay, so what do I do now? . . ."

If this is your first time reading through the text, and you have yet to actually get started, now is a great time to do so. Putting things off is a reliable recipe for them not getting done—*ever*. If you have worked your way through the book, and you have practiced each exercise, filled in the worksheets (either in the book or in a *Tarot journal*), and you have read through our suggested meaning of each of the cards, augmenting those with your on impressions of what each card <u>says to you</u>, then it is time for you to get out there and start reading for friends, family, and even strangers, if you can find anyone interested in a student reading.

We hope that you have already registered at our *EasyTarotLessons.com* website, and asked questions or helped out other students (and pestered the experienced members of the "secret societies" with endless questions in the forums). On the next few pages are the 60- and 90-day study guides. These are only suggested study schedules and we *always* encourage you to take guidance from your teacher first and foremost. Our goal is to help you develop a lifetime skill quickly and easily, whether you decide to take your abilities to a professional level *(because the world will always need <u>skilled</u> readers)*, or if you just want to have fun at parties, and generally making new friends.

We encourage you to keep up your practice for as long as you can. Certainly at some point most of you will spend less and less time with your cards, but this moment in time, *right now,* is crucial to your education and your future. You have the ability to solidify your understanding of the Tarot, and to build a bond with your deck, a skill that will lead you to the next level of understanding. The next level is your ability to manifest your dreams and desires, using the *"Laws of Attraction and Repulsion"* to get what you really want in life—quickly and easily. Don't worry though; if you do end up in our *Advanced Tarot Secrets* class, we will teach you the real names of the secret laws, not the dreamed up public faces they have. You will have a lot of fun working with these forces of nature that are all around you, without all of the authoritarian dogma the public is spoon-fed.

Remember, at our site we have Tarot blogs, and podcasts, and games, and contests, and other fun things appearing over time to keep you amused and interested in your studies. You can also follow our *TarotSecrets* <u>Twitter</u> should you want short daily mini-lessons on Tarot cards and Tarot magic. Find us at *http://twitter.com/TarotSecrets*

Keep playing with your Tarot cards, and **keep them handy so they are not forgotten,** or set aside, <u>because they can help you improve the quality of your life dramatically</u> in as little as 30 days. As always, we are here to help. Oh! And be sure to look for our next fun and educational title in this series, **The Easiest Way to Learn Astrology—EVER!!** Thanks for reading. Now go have some fun!

Easy Study Guides
(part 2)

Over the <u>next</u> 30 days . . .

If you need more than 30 days to accomplish all of the exercises go ahead and add a few days and don't feel guilty about it, but try to do all of them over a period of 45 days or less, or you will end up avoiding learning the Tarot. <u>Life has a habit of throwing things at us when we are unfocused</u>. Being as you only have to learn the Tarot *once*, it is more than worth it to do it now while it is still fresh and exciting.

Over the <u>next</u> 30 days, we would like you to keep up with your daily practice if at all possible; *but if it is absolutely not possible,* try to get in at least 30 minutes a day three to four times a week. This is time you need to be spending bonding with your cards, not memorizing meanings from a book (ugh!). The more you do these basic exercises, the more comfortable you will be when you are "on stage" giving *readings*. You will see patterns you recognize; and when you are *casting* actual *spreads,* you will have "real questions" cards relate to rather than an abstract notion of what the cards "might mean." You will find answers come to you easily and your confidence in yourself and your deck will rise quickly.

So . . . stay with exercises 1 through 11. If you are feeling a bit randy, try out some of the *advanced exercises* we have provided in the book <u>and then</u> look to find various ways you could describe these scenarios with cards. Also fill in **the first set** of quick and easy "Cheat Sheets" *(be sure to do both the "major" and "minor" Arcana tables, but not necessarily in one sitting).* Do these <u>without</u> looking at Sections Four and Five (or any other book, or online, or . . .). Skip over any of the cards that are giving you trouble at the moment. <u>Just fill out what you know</u> "right now." Of course, we recommend you use a pencil or a light-colored pen in case you want to write over your answer a few minutes later. Once you have filled in all of the cards you are confident about, take a look at the overall feel of the table and make any adjustments or corrections that nag at you. *Then* look at the "holes" in the table, cards you may have skipped over or feel can use a bit more "depth," and fill them in. Now, you can look in the back of the book, ask your teacher, or go online if you need. Refer back to this "Cheat Sheet" as often as possible over the next 60 days to see how you feel about these meanings and "key words."

Also start giving practice *readings* to any of your close friends who have been nagging you to "do them" or give yourself a *reading* about the next 30 days, or your future job, or give your cat a *reading*, or even a complete stranger if you get the chance (and find a willing stranger who will humor you). Once again, take anything you see in the *reading* as an interesting pastime, serious enough to pay attention to, but not so serious that you believe it <u>until</u> <u>you</u> <u>see it</u>. This is your primary practice and experimentation time. By now you should be reasonably comfortable with the mechanics of *casting* a *spread,* or *throwing* out a few cards to answer simple questions. It is more important right now to get practice shuffling, cutting, and *spreading* your cards than it is to worry about what they say. You will start to develop certain *preferences* during this time that will eventually become the basis of your personal *style* of *casting spreads* over the years to come. Try shuffling and cutting your cards in many different ways and make the decision now about how you feel about other people *touching* your cards.

The next 30 days . . . (roughly 60–90 days from now)

Now the fun really begins! Keep doing your exercises (all of them). Practice with your *one-, two-,* and *three-card spreads, open up* cards and *spreads,* use *clarifying* and *aspecting* cards, and do as many *Celtic Cross,* and *Roundabout spreads* as you can for as many people as you can, reminding each one of them (repeatedly if you have to) that this is "just for fun" even though you will do your best, and that they should take anything they see or you say as "fun advice" and just see what happens. Tell them that if you end up being right, *they can come back later* and buy you a coffee or tea. Now you should decide how you like to shuffle, cut, and turn your cards, and whether you will be *reading* cards *reversed* or not (at least in the near future—you can always change your mind later). Also develop your "yes or no" *spread*. These 30 days will be where you find out which of the basic *spreads* you like to work with the most, but make sure that you keep using a variety of *spreads* so that you don't end up limiting yourself. It's still a bit early to start reading every book on the Tarot you can get your hands on or trying out esoteric *spreads,* so don't rush too much. You have years and years to more thoroughly develop your skills and *styles* of working with your deck(s); so take it slow now, and after a month or two of continual practice, start expanding on your repertoire.

At the end of this 30 days (around 90 days from now if you keep working with your cards regularly), **go through the second set** of "Cheat Sheets" and write in your new answers (without looking at your old answers first). Make sure you fill in *all* of the cards (which should be no problem by now). *Then* sit back and compare them to each other. Now spend some time over the next few days with your cards coming up with funny captions of your own. Sit quietly with them and ask yourself what the people in the cards are saying or doing. Don't worry if captions don't come very quickly for all of the cards. We were *reading* for *many* years before we scribbled our first captions on our own cards. At this point, we do *not* recommend writing captions on your deck, unless you have the extra funds to purchase a special deck just for this exercise. Just think them up in your head, or go on to our website, and somewhere in the forums we will probably have a section where people can post their favorite captions for any card.

The point of all of this is to help you expand your awareness of what each card can mean in various situations, rather than just knowing some sacrosanct *"traditional meaning"* of any card. Remember that life *breathes*. Experience is a new thing daily, but the cards remain the same. Your cards have to reflect the variance of daily activities with only 78 pictures to work with, so they will need to stretch and contort their basic meanings occasionally to correctly answer your questions. This is why you are learning to *listen* rather than to *memorize*. **You are not a parrot!** You will even see your intuitive abilities develop before your eyes and you will be amazed at how your understanding of the Tarot coupled with your heightened psychic awareness and ability to physically spot relationships between objects will sharpen your abilities to solve problems and "predict events" on a purely material level. These are your first steps at using the Tarot to develop your psychic abilities. (Enroll in any credible mystery school—including ours, *when* we are accepting students—to learn more on how to do this.)

Here are the first steps: *Get a pen and paper* (not right now, but during the 60-90 day "from now" period) *and write down five things you want within the next 30 days*. Then prioritize them by writing the numbers 1 through 5 next to them. Now carefully think about these things until you come up with *one card* to represent each one of these things you want. (This is where it is good to have a second or third deck to work with.) Tape those cards up in order of priority somewhere where you will see them every day, preferably several times a day, but where they won't get wet, torn, or damaged. As to *tape,* we have successfully used that "magic" invisible Scotch™ tape to gently affix cards to walls, mirrors, etc.

Use your best judgment. If you personally have *any doubts* as to as to whether the tape will damage your cards, don't use it. But put the cards up where you will see them several times a day. Take a *quick* moment and focus on one card every time you pass by them. Think of what it means and what you are *attracting*. Then see how these results work for you. For more information, please see either our *Advanced Tarot Secrets* course or our *Aphrodite's Book of Secrets*.

Also, use your cards to solve problems. Think of some dilemma you face and pull out the smallest number of cards you need to directly and adequately illustrate the "problem at hand." Now dig through your deck and come up with *three-card* solutions. If you need to use five cards, that's okay too if it is a complex issue, but don't *just go* for the obvious answer. <u>Start</u> with the obvious answer to get your mind working on the issue <u>and</u> <u>then</u> look for alternative possibilities. For future reference, jot down the cards you use for both the problem and various solutions.

These various exercises and activities will sharpen your intuition, your *reading* abilities, and your problem solving capabilities as well. You will also find that your visualization skills will increase significantly, both in the quality of your images *and the results you get*. Over time you will find your bond with your Tarot cards bringing you many interesting benefits both esoterically and tangibly in the physical world, whether you attend "advanced training" or not. The Tarot, after all, is simply a visual stimulus to assist the development of innate mental skills you have not been fully trained by other means. The magic is within you, waiting to be released. Thank you for sharing your time with us.

Remember to stop in often at

EasyTarotLessons.com

We are always adding new information to help you learn and master the Tarot, and we welcome your voice in helping future students as well. Once you have completed this course and feel comfortable with the Tarot, it is time to turn your abilities with the Tarot into practical magic, using your cards to help you build a better, adventurous, and <u>more fun</u> life for yourself!

Join us for your continuing education and our

Advanced Tarot Secrets
course!

Appendix A:

TROUBLESHOOTING
(what to do when . . .)

Tarot *reading* is obviously not an exact science. In fact, it's not a science at all; it is an *art*. That means sometimes things will go horribly astray (especially when you are first starting out) and you may get frustrated with your cards, or your*self*. We have listed a few of the most common concerns among new students. If you need further assistance, please visit us online at **EasyTarotLessons.com**.

Problem: You *cast your spread* and (Surprise!) it tells you what you already know, or what you and your client just talked about, sometimes *word for word* (only in pictures). Times like these make you want to scream at your deck.

Recommended solution to try: Smile. Better yet, laugh and pat yourself on the back for being such an *amazing reader!* Out of the infinite possible number of combinations the cards *could have* come out, you picked one of the few that matches up with what you already know. In fact, this verifies everything you know or have been talking about. That's a pretty impressive trick that you were able to do that. (If you are sitting across from your client, make sure *they know* how special you are too.)

Okay, this is actually a *very* good sign. Your deck has revealed what exists, and now you have all of those cards to use as one giant *significator*, or as individual *significators* to *open up*. First look to see if the cards reveal anything you *don't* know. Usually in cases like this you will see 90 percent of what you know, and one or two cards will be pointing at something you have to clarify. People often go through life understanding a majority of their situation and "what they need to do" to make things better for themselves, *but it's that little part they don't know* that is the difference between stress and success. Look for that "extra information" in the existing *spread*. Once you have either found it or you have decided that it doesn't exist, look to see if any cards need to be *opened up*. What is the motivation behind those cards? For example: Your client is asking about her boyfriend, and he shows up in her *spread* as the *King of Coins*. You can *open him up* to see what his motivations are, or what he is feeling or doing (that affects your client), what he is not revealing. You can *open up* any card in the *spread,* or you can proceed directly to the next step: Thank your deck (this is really a rhetorical thing, but it sets you in the right mental space) and then ask a simple question and do a *one-, two-,* or *three-card spread* <u>on</u> <u>top</u> <u>of</u> the existing *spread,* and continue asking exploratory " . . . and then?" questions without *tearing down the spread* until you have your questions answered, or you run low on cards and have to shuffle and *re-cast*. This is called "extending the *spread*."

Problem: You just don't feel like *reading* for someone, or you are in the middle of a *reading* and you "lose it"—suddenly your mind goes blank, or you (temporarily) lose contact with that part of your mind that is "in tune" with the cosmos. Now you are looking at a pile of cards with funny looking pictures on them.

Recommended solution to try: If you just don't feel like *reading* for someone—tell them, **without hesitation.** Try to be polite of course, as people will often get offended if you won't *read* for them, as if you are personally insulting them. On the outside it looks like all you have to do is throw down some cards and explain what "they say" *(as if they "always mean the same thing")*. Successful Tarot *reading* is like professional massage. It "looks easy," like you are just rubbing your hands on someone. *Why should anyone pay for that?!* You know differently of course, but it's not something you can simply explain and have people come to your way of thinking. This is why you have to be polite but firm. Ask them if you can take a rain check, or "reschedule them" <u>then</u> <u>and</u> <u>there</u> for some other day. This is far better than giving a bad *reading* and resenting them for imposing on you. Now, when you are <u>in the middle of a *reading*</u> and you "just lose it," your mind goes blank, or your client distracts you and you can't get yourself back in the right frame of mind (don't worry, it happens to everyone at some point), here's what you do:

Go do something else. Even if you can only take a few minutes to clear your head, get away from the *reading*. Take "a smoke break" (public service announcement: *"smoking is bad"*) or stretch, change the music you are listening to or grab your iPod, a CD, or even the radio and play a song you like to reset your mindset. If you can, take a short walk with your client around the block and talk to them in generalities about anything *related to* the issue but peripheral, not central. This will help restimulate you gradually so that you will be in the right state when you "get back to your cards" without dragging you so far from their issue that you lose your connection completely and have no "connection" to your cards when you return.

Problem: Your client (paying or not) is abusive.

Recommended solution to try: *Refuse to read for them.* No one deserves to be abused by idiots, most especially someone like you who is generous enough with your time to give someone something so personal and intimate as your impressions of their future or solutions to their problems. Tarot *reading* is intensely personal (never forget that part). You are looking into parts of people's lives they won't share with their friends, their doctors, husband or wife, mom and dad . . . Often you will find stuff they wish you did not see—and they will let you know, usually obliquely (by lying to you, or getting suddenly angry, and so on). If and when this *does* happen, you should be polite (it's never a good idea to argue with "crazy" people) and simply fold up your cards and inform them that you have "lost your connection," or that the vibe is all wrong. Telling them that you don't feel comfortable *reading* <u>for them</u> will only encourage them to validate their egos to anyone who will listen by making up stories about how horrible of a person you are. Don't do that to yourself. Fortunately, the rude or abusive client is a rare creature. Most people who ask you for a *reading appreciate* your service.

Appendix B:

A Tarot F.A.Q.

Okay, so there are a thousand questions students have about the Tarot when they are first starting out. We will not address them all here, but we will cover a few of the most popular ones. You can read through or skip over this part completely, or even make up your own answers that best suit your individual personality. <u>All that matters is that when a client seeks your help in a *reading* that they are so impressed</u> with your "amazing abilities" that they recommend their friends, their mother, their dog, and everyone else they know to you. **Use what <u>works</u> for you.** What follows is merely a guide to help you get started. Remember to practice with your cards a lot. That is more important than any other one thing you can do or know.

There are so many Tarot decks!
Which deck is right for me? Do they all mean the same thing?

Various artists want to place their stamp on history, or apply their vision to the Tarot. Others want to change various cards to suit their personal interpretations. Some decks (like *The Halloween Tarot*) retain accuracy with the Tarot, while others either change the meanings of the cards or are so ambiguous that they require you (the *reader*) to have your own set opinion firmly in place about the card and its meaning before you set about a *reading*. Over time you will probably have a few decks. In fact, you should "try out" as many as you comfortably can. The illustrations on the cards are important, *but <u>they have to work for you</u>*.

The Tarot versus "other decks." What's the difference?
Why are there so many divination systems? Are they Tarot decks too?

Several styles of divination decks have gained popularity over recent years. The Tarot is simply the most popular, and the most enduring so far. Only the Tarot is "The Tarot," but this does not make any other deck or divination system (astrology, dowsing, runes, entrails, scrying) any less valid *(although entrails are positively messy, especially at dinner parties)*.

The Tarot versus "regular playing cards."
What's the difference? Can I read with either (or both at once)?

The Tarot is like a "super deck" of "regular playing cards." It has exactly the same cards as a normal deck but it also has 4 *Pages* (one per suit) and the 22 "major" Arcana cards as well. Once you know the meanings of the cards (or have a handy Tarot book in a pinch), you can *read* "regular playing cards" just like a Tarot deck, except that you won't have any "major" Arcana cards to help out. Some *readers actually prefer* to *read* with "regular playing cards." Just remember that *Wands* = Clubs, *Cups* = Hearts, *Swords* = Spades, and *Coins* = Diamonds. It's all pretty easy to remember, once you do it a few times. The hard part is trying to match the picture of the Tarot card to the "regular playing card" you are holding at the moment. As for doing simultaneous *readings*, we do recommend that you get some practice *reading* one *spread* at a time first. One *reading* at a time will keep you focused on pulling out the maximum amount of information from each *spread*.

Various Tarot spreads:
Which ones work? Which ones are better than others?

We have included several *spreads* in this book that we would like you to practice and master. They will all serve you well. Your teacher may have additional *spreads* for you as well. In time, you may even design your own *spreads*. For now, please stick with the basics. These spreads <u>will</u> <u>work</u> <u>well</u> <u>for</u> <u>you</u>. All that matters right now is that you get reliable answers, and that you develop a comfortable and solid rapport with your deck. <u>The best *spread*</u> is the one that is most appropriate to the situation at hand: one that addresses the question being asked, and the way the question is phrased. Before *throwing your cards*, take a moment to consider what it is that your client wants to know. Find out what are they really asking.

Too many times people will ask you for a *reading* (especially if it is free) and they will not know what they are asking about. They will say, "just tell me anything you see," and will expect you to knowingly pick out some interesting and important detail of their life as it affects them now, or is going to affect them soon, and give them sagely advice on how to handle situations, often before they arise. This can be incredibly frustrating, and it is a waste of your talents and time. Unless your client has an urgent question they need answered in the next 30 seconds, it is far better to simply sit and talk for a few minutes with your client and develop a bit of a psychic bond through the shared emotions common in good conversation. This opens up your channels and helps your client's subconscious rummage around the recesses of their mind for questions they "really want answers to." This is a good time to shuffle your cards thoroughly while focusing your energy into your cards.

You will be surprised at how easily a few minutes of chatting pleasantly will get just about anyone to suddenly vomit questions at you (quite mercilessly). Pay attention to <u>what they are asking and how they phrase their questions</u>. Will a *"yes/no" spread* be appropriate to start with? Perhaps a *"one week forecast"* or a *"this or that" option spread* will help you uncover answers quickly and easily. *Spreads* like the *Celtic Cross* are good "general *spreads*" that can be useful for a look at a situation where your client is completely confused or where you are dealing with limited amounts of information and you need to establish a set of facts before making any predictions. In this case, you would use the base cards to verify the accuracy of the *spread* before committing to believing the resulting answer cards. The first few cards should accurately portray the situation at hand; if not, *tear down the spread* and reshuffle, focusing on a particular point of information. Then *recast the spread* with a clear mind. Preparation for *casting* is more important than which *spread you cast*. **Think of your spread as a map to a distant location.** The map will show you routes and obstacles. The map reveals the terrain along the path you will follow, <u>but it will not tell you where to go</u>. Knowing where you want to end up makes reading a map (any map) infinitely easier.

How do I hold the cards? How do I shuffle? How do I cut?
"Do I hold the cards or set them on the table and draw them from there?"

Hold the cards in a manner that is comfortable for you. Tarot cards come in "standard sizes" and most of the decks are roughly the same size (being a bit too big for most people to be comfortable with at first). U.S. Games makes "tiny" decks and even jumbo decks, so try to get as many decks in your hands as possible early on and play with the feel of each of them. Also, remember that a new deck will always be slippery and frustrating to handle. As your cards get worn in over time they will be much easier to work with (they won't slide around in your hands so much). If you feel comfortable holding them in one hand and drawing cards with the other, *so be it*. If you need to set them on the table because they keep "flying around" or you have small hands, that is a time-honored practice as well. There is no "right" or "wrong" method as long as you are not damaging your cards in the process of holding or shuffling them.

As to shuffling your deck: This will be tricky at first, even if you play cards a lot. Most Tarot decks are much larger than a standard playing card deck (and there are 26 more cards as well), so shuffling will need a bit of personal experimentation. Some people use the "rifle shuffle": set the deck on the table and "cut off" the top half, slide it next to the bottom half and bend the corners up and merge them together. This is the way professional dealers shuffle in Las Vegas. You could also shuffle them sideways (the standard card shuffle, only shuffle the *sides* together instead of the *ends*), or even a "normal" card shuffle if your hands are big enough.

Some *readers* simply cut the deck into itself again and again (and again . . .) and alternate that with what was at one time called "the French cut" where you pull the middle third of the deck out between your thumb and one of your fingers and you "slap" it on top of the deck (repeatedly). Still others simply swirl the cards around in a pile gently but thoroughly while they are deeply considering the question at hand, and then carefully scoop the cards together. This *reverses* cards however, so it is not advised if you do not *read* cards "*reversed*."

Cutting your deck runs along the same lines. Cut as you like, but because shuffling and cutting are as much a part of the *reading* as any *spread* you may choose to *cast*, it is imperative that you shuffle thoroughly and completely, stopping only when you feel it proper. Some *readers* shuffle a few times, others shuffle for a few *minutes*. If your cards aren't cooperating with you, it is probably because you don't shuffle enough or you cut too much (or not enough). This is where practice comes in.

How do I draw cards from the deck? How do I turn the cards? Do I turn them sideways or flip them over vertically?

This is one of the most important things to consider when developing your habits as a *reader*. It's best to develop this by feel rather than analyzing it to death, but we want to address it here so that it doesn't become an issue later. Assuming that your cards are facing lengthwise (either in your hands or on the table in front of you), your options are to "flip" a card (lengthwise), turn a card (sideways), or grab one at random from the middle of the deck. "Flipping" a card generally entails taking it off of the deck by its top edge and turning it lengthwise so that it reverses itself. If the top edge of the card was facing you when you were holding it, it is "right side up" when you lay it down on the table in front of you.

This matters if you *read reversed*, as that means you would technically be holding the deck itself *reversed* and then *reversing* them when you flip them over. Whether the cards came up *reversed* or not from there would be a natural part of the *reading*. Or you can "turn" the card (pulling it from the side edge) and rotate it left or right (so that it is now face up). The end result is that one method *reverses* each card as you draw them, the other does not. Neither is preferable, but once you get in the habit of a certain style, <u>stick with it</u> at least throughout the *reading*. If you "flip" some cards and "turn" others in a single *reading*, you will alter the meaning of the *spread*.

If you prefer to not *read* cards *reversed*, then you can ignore all of this and simply rotate the cards to face "up" no matter how they come up. Find a style of handling the cards you like <u>and stay with that</u> during each *reading*. This is what practice is for. Practice is your private time to play around with new ideas and sharpen your skills without other people judging you.

Hey! Quit touching my Tarot! Do I <u>really</u> need to let other people put their grubby hands all over <u>my</u> Tarot cards? Should they shuffle my cards, or even cut them? Can I smack someone for touching my cards? Do I have to let other people <u>touch</u> my cards?

Absolutely not! People have "germs" and residual psychic residue from all of the weird thoughts they have been thinking, and food crumbs . . . Some *readers* like other people to shuffle their deck, or even just "cut them three times" after the psychic has shuffled. This is perfectly acceptable, and don't worry about our rants of germs and residual emotions. Practice with what works for you. A lot of it depends on how you feel about your client and their question. Always remember: They are *your* cards, and <u>you</u> must have a bond with them. If you are into sharing, then *great!* But the decision of whether you want to psychically infuse your client's question into your cards or have them hold your deck is entirely personal. If you ever *read* for a psychic hotline or do *readings* online, your clients will not be able to touch your cards, so you should be comfortable drawing the question from them and infusing it into your cards, even if you have to ask them for specific details to use as a foundation to start the *reading*. On an unrelated, but essential, side note: **Never, ever, <u>ever</u> allow a client to bully you.**

Hey! My cat keeps sitting on my Tarot cards whenever I try to do a spread. Is it considered good luck if my cat sits on them?

What is it with cats and Tarot cards? Ever since the pharaohs adopted them, cats seem to have developed this innate sense of knowing when you are concentrating on something (especially psychically) and they <u>have to</u> jump up on the table and walk all over whatever it is that you are working on. This is *especially* true of your Tarot *spreads*. It seems there has never been a more comfortable "cat couch" than the *Celtic Cross spread*. However, until your cat learns to speak English, you may have to brush up on your ailuromancy skills (divination by observing your cat's movements—especially which cards its tail knocks off of the table).

Should I sleep with my Tarot cards (on the first date)? Tarot under your pillow, wrapped in silk, in a lead box, in a wooden box, carrying it wherever you go.

This goes back to what to keep your Tarot cards in. Some people like to sleep with their deck under their pillow. We recommend this habit as long as your deck doesn't get lost behind the headboard, or create a lump in your pillow that keeps you awake at night. As to what to put it in: *something protective.*

How often can I read my Tarot cards? How often <u>should</u> I read my Tarot cards? Can I read for myself?

Let's see . . . Every day, as often as you like, and yes, wait . . . no . . . er . . . yes!! Like everything else Tarot, whether you can (or should) *read* for yourself is debatable. We say "yes." The problem is that you may not be objective enough to get any reliable results. See a bad *spread*? *Simply toss it away!* (Sounds like a late-night TV commercial, actually.) The good part about *reading* your own cards is that you get a lot of practice, and no one knows <u>you</u> like you do. You can ask about anything and not lie to yourself. Of course, the bad part about *reading* for yourself is the temptation to lie to yourself. That, and exaggerating what you see (good or bad), and driving yourself crazy in the end (not sanitarium crazy, but "extremely frustrated and stressed out" crazy). So, when you *read* for yourself, stick to fun trivialities at first, and take everything with a grain of salt. If you are really worried about something, go to a professional, but don't explain what "you think" the cards mean. This brings up an important point that is simply not covered enough in most Tarot literature. Your *spread* speaks to <u>you</u>. If we looked over your shoulder and told you what *we* thought *your spread* meant, we would be <u>wrong</u>. You *threw* your *spread* and the cards that came out did so in response to your understanding of them. Other people can observe your *spreads* and offer their opinions, but only you can say with all certainty exactly what each card means in <u>*your* spread(s)</u>.

What if I don't want to read cards reversed?

Then don't. All Tarot decks are designed to give you thorough and complete answers whether you choose to use the additional information accessible through *reversed* cards or not. If you want to ignore any *reversals* and simply "turn the card around," then please do and don't let anyone ever make you feel like less of a *reader* for doing so. Tarot is highly personal: Your job is to develop your skills, not to listen to a bunch of "rule mongerers" *(including us!)*.

Oh yeah? Well, what if my teacher <u>disagrees</u> with you?

<u>Do what your teacher says</u>. Try it out for yourself and see whether that works for you. This is why you have a teacher: to help guide you along while you are developing your skills and practicing. *You can always come back later* (if you feel the need) and try it "our way" at any time; <u>but if you have a live teacher in front of you</u> who you can ask questions and get help from, definitely use that resource. That is an invaluable aid to your learning that you should take full advantage of whenever possible.

Can I get a job reading Tarot?
What should I expect?
How much will I get p-a-i-d?

The whole purpose of this book is to train and prepare you so that you <u>could</u> (if you want to at some point) become a professional *reader*. Yes, the world needs *talented—and—<u>skillful</u> readers*. The first thing we would like you to do is to perfect your skills *reading* (know <u>your</u> deck—whether or not you have memorized any of the various alleged "official" histories of the Tarot). We would like you to have a solid grasp of each card (without having to look at any book) *and* have given *readings* to at least 300 clients before you start officially charging any money (friends, family, parties, or your local coffeehouse), and at least 1,000 *readings* before you step foot into a metaphysical shop looking for a job. Your teacher may be a bit more lenient than we are.

A great place to get a *lot* of practice *reading* for a *lot* of people is on a psychic hotline. You should have *read* for a minimum of 200-300 clients before you call up one and ask for a job. But if you do "the psychic hotline thing," you can expect to give several *readings* a day to people you will never see in person. This is extremely challenging and rather high pressure, as people want answers to their questions quickly so they can get off of the phone before their bill runs too high. This quickly becomes frustrating as you try to help them in the least amount of time as humanly possible. But "speed" and "accuracy" have a hard time coexisting peacefully when it comes to Tarot card *readings*; so if you are "working the lines," you will need to develop thick skin very fast. Some of the joys you can expect from working a psychic hotline are the freedom to "work at home," with all of its distractions, and the ability to set your own hours (some where no one calls, others where you can't get a break to go pee).

<u>You will be your own boss</u>, so when that phone rings (you will need two phone lines), you need to stop everything and "get to work" with a smile. **As to clients:** Expect lots of people wanting to know their "lucky lottery numbers." I have hit the lottery (various amounts, <u>some</u> <u>very</u> <u>small</u>) over a dozen times for my clients, and not one of them offered me a bonus. A lot of clients will want to know about their love lives. Worst of all, most of your "phone clients" will expect you to have some kind of magical abilities to read minds (know what they are calling for without them telling you) and/or the ability to work some voodoo to get their boyfriend to do this or that, or their wife to have more sex with them. Once in a blue moon you will get a call straight out of "The Twilight Zone."

You have to understand that these are real people with real needs. They would not be calling you unless they really needed help that they are praying you can actually give them. This means you have to deeply care for their well-being and do the best you can for them (quickly). If all of this sounds like your idea of a good time, then you should look for the "customer service" numbers of the various psychic hotlines and call around offering your services—*once you feel you have met the minimum requirements above.* It's not an easy job, but it will teach you more about human nature in six months than you would learn in five years in a boring retail job.

When it comes to pay: 30 to 50 cents per minute is pretty average. Don't get suckered into working for any less than that, as people will be paying $3-$5 *per minute* for your advice. Before you get all excited about the prospect of making $18 to $30 an hour "yapping on the phone in your jammies," keep in mind that you will be lucky to average 30 minutes per hour on average, and that this job will occasionally make you very depressed (people with real problems are calling you endlessly expecting you to work miracles for them). It makes a great part-time job if you have lots of time and are writing a book, or creating art, or any other endeavor you can set down for a moment to "take a call."

As far as "psychic fairs," "Tarot parties," or working your local coffeehouse are concerned—if you have *read* for several hundred people already and have a small crowd of happy clients who have come back and told you how wonderful you are (which always feels nice), you might approach your local independent coffeehouse (if you hang out at one frequently) or ask around at your local metaphysical shops for psychic fair organizers and get your name on the list of psychics who "have a table" at the event. Usually there will be a registration fee or "table rent" (this goes to the organizer, who will probably have a booth to *read* and/or sell things as well). Expect to see astrologers, Tarot card readers, aura photographers, and palmists at any decent size psychic fair. Rune masters, phrenologists, tea readers, and dowsers will be extremely rare to see, so if you find one, be sure to corner them for valuable information. UFOs are huge at psychic fairs. People who attend psychic fairs just love our little extraterrestrial friends. So, if you have a cuddly little stuffed alien to plop on the side of your table, be sure to bring it along as a conversation starter.

Readings at psychic fairs generally go anywhere from $10 to $30 on average. Smaller psychic fairs, especially in less densely populated areas will charge a bit less, and places like Sedona will fetch higher rates. Also, the more intensive and exotic the *reading* ("*I draw your spirit animal hovering over you in all of the colors of your aura, in charcoal*"), the more you can get away with. Visit a few psychic fairs in your area to see how they are laid out and be sure to <u>make friends with everyone possible</u>. Psychics who are on the psychic fair circuit *know* the psychic fair circuit. Get the business card of the psychic fair organizer and ask if they have other fairs, how much a table (for you) would be, and if they have any special needs that you might be able to fill *(for example: astrology, Tarot, aura photography, or anything you may be skilled at—that they may need).*

At some point you may want to *read* at a local metaphysical shop or even open up your own *"Readings by Zelda!"* one-psychic shop like you see in various neighborhoods. **You can do this.** Just make sure that you have a <u>lot</u> of practice first. We recommend *at least* 500 clients (and at least 100 of those "paying clients" *and another 50 or more* have had the decency to buy you coffee for your trouble). Pop into your favorite meta-store and say hello to the owner. Get on the standby list in case they "ever need a *reader*" (in six months or so . . .) and be sure to participate in their community events, and refer clients to their store if and when you can. In and of itself this won't get you a job, but it is important to become known as a part of the community.

What about parties?
How do I politely say "no" when I am tired of giving readings?

Okay, so you are at this rockin' party and you are having a blast dishing out *readings* left and right, and you are just feeling the love *and* "the power!" flowing through you. Then suddenly it stops, or you get a headache, or someone wants a *reading* but they are so filled with negative energy at this moment that you physically *feel* yourself soaking it in. Quick! What can you do?

<u>Take a break</u>. Even if you are in the middle of a *reading* at the moment, get some space to clear your mind if you can't breathe psychically. If you are with a client and you want to finish *reading* for them, you may want to simply go to the bathroom and wash your hands, taking those few moments to regain your sense of balance. Make it clear that you need a break by your posture, the arrangement of your "stuff" (whatever you have on hand), or even a little sign if you have one that says "back in a few minutes." Anything you can physically do to give a clear, polite indication that you "have taxed your psychic muscles and just need some time to unwind and enjoy the party" or (if you are "working the party" on a psychic-for-hire job) you just need a few minutes to get some "punch" (fresh air, a smoke, some sushi, whatever . . .), *just do it.*

Do it <u>and</u> <u>don't</u> <u>apologize</u>. Take the time you need to re-center yourself and prepare for whatever comes next (including scooping your "stuff" up as quickly as possible and running for the door if you have to). No matter what excuse you need, never feel bad for walking away when you have had enough. Stay "sane" by keeping this fun. It will be "work" sometimes, and it will be challenging and even frustrating occasionally, but never push yourself so hard that you end up resenting your abilities, your clients, or your deck.

How do I make my own Tarot deck? Will it work just as well?
Will it be better? Do I have to study for a hundred years
before I can make my own deck? Where do I get the blank cards?
What if I just want to color in my personal deck?

At some point in the future you may get the urge to design your own deck either professionally (you plan on selling it) or personally (you plan on <u>using</u> it). Your deck will work just as well as, if not better than, any deck you can buy once you know, understand, and can interpret the various layers of symbolism of your *working decks* (the ones you "work with" on a regular basis) in any situation you are faced with. This means a <u>lot</u> of *readings* for actual clients. Figure on several years of Tarot study and practice before you endeavor to do something like this. Otherwise, your personal deck will be somewhat bland and devoid of interpretational value when you need answers the most.

Blank cards can be found at any office supply store. Look for blank "flash cards" in their education section. Of course, you can always go to an art store for art supplies. You may want to hand paint your personal deck using oils, watercolors, or even colored pens. Alternatively, the B.O.T.A. (and other mystery schools) provide their students with their own decks to color, and the *Hello Kitty Tarot* is another example of a pre-printed deck available to color in if you like.

What are these "mystery schools" you keep yapping about?
Why are they so <u>secretive</u>? Are they a scam?
Can't I just go online and find all this stuff out for free?

Mystery schools have been essential in the preservation of esoteric knowledge since the dawn of civilization. For every empire there seems to be some religious nut who wants to keep the general public ignorant, because uneducated people are <u>much</u> <u>easier</u> to scare into submission. Mystery schools guard knowledge that has been laboriously gathered over generations, and pass it carefully into the hands of those truth-seekers who prove over time their own commitment to preserve the sacred knowledge of philosophy and magic that actually works. This educational exclusivity is necessary to prevent the perversion of knowledge, but it is also the basis for much confusion and suspicion among those who stand outside the gates of the sanctuary.

The process of creating "miracles" is far more complex than simply "attracting" something by wishing really, really hard for it. Magic is an ongoing process of personal enlightenment and commune with the divine. It is not some parlor trick one can learn and master in a few hours. You can study and see results fairly quickly, but to measurably raise the fundamental quality of your life takes time and personal commitment to a better life and a better self. You have at your disposal all sorts of tools and helpers, including the Tarot, astrology, psychic magnetism, meditation, and the forces inherent in nature. Herbs, water, wine, and the chemistry of Nature all want to help you along your path. Many thousands of people have invested their entire lives ferreting out these secrets over the generations before you. This information is closely guarded by those who have spent this lifetime understanding it. You can learn any of this sacred knowledge from us, at the rate you desire to make it a part of your life. You progress at your own pace, learning hand-in-hand with those who wish to share the beauty of this knowledge with you.

The purpose of the great mystery schools is to organize the vast storehouse of information that has been collected over the past few thousand years. If you had to guess on your own whether to learn astrology <u>before</u> herbalism, or the Tarot <u>versus</u> numerology, the Kabbalah, Buddhism, or various meditation techniques, the whole of it would be overwhelming and even depressing at the sheer vastness of it all. Many roads lead to your destination. Knowledge is the central path and dogma is the handrail that keeps people balanced. Different schools will teach you different avenues based on their preferred view of the world. Eastern wisdom holds different views than Western thought, yet both worlds exist and create magnificent wonders. The point is to learn, and the school that is best for you is the one that <u>inspires</u> you to keep learning. When you find the right teacher, learning becomes effortless. It becomes a passion for knowledge that chases away all distractions.

We have listed several credible mystery schools in Appendix F. The B.O.T.A., Rosicrucians, Masons, Golden Dawn, O.T.O., and other places will all teach you various esoteric secrets; some will include <u>their</u> <u>version</u> of the Tarot. If you are interested in this, see our list in Appendix F. In addition, we will have links to these and other esoteric schools at our website **EasyTarotLessons.com.** Finally, at any time of your personal spiritual progress, should you wish information on our mystery academy, please visit us at **www.EnlightenedSisterhood.net**. We are always happy to help students along the path to their own mastery of magic.

Appendix C:

A BRIEF HISTORY OF THE TAROT

My metaphysical training began as a toddler, well before I was aware of exactly what it was that I was being taught. I didn't learn Pythagorean formulae, or Byzantine chants, or even the difference between mugwort and a blade of grass. I was taught to recognize and organize patterns, just like we all were. I was taught how to attract what I wanted (point, ask, whimper, then scream, and finally cry if that did not work) and how to repel (reverse the preceding order) what I did not. Sciences like herbalism and astrology were years away, but manifestation 101 started with Napoleon Hill's sagely advice (which I did not read until over a decade later), "Desire something more than life itself," and "Whatever you can dream up, you can conjure up!" In both instances I have paraphrased, but the message remains intact.

So it is with the Tarot. A scholarly knowledge of the Tarot can help you become a more knowledgeable reader, which in itself is extremely useful, but it will always remain a distant second to your ability to understand the Tarot, being your deck, the one you are *reading* with right now, not some deck that served someone 500 years ago, someone with a completely different view of the world. Five hundred years ago it was "common knowledge" that the world was flat. Everyone knew that! We also "knew" that people could not fly like birds, demons caused sickness, and no one had ever heard of "germs." The very notion that the Earth revolved around the sun was "blasphemy unto God" and it was just that sort of talk that got people burned at the stake. Religion and government conspired to control the masses both in life and in death. Ahh, the best things in life never really change, do they? Five hundred years ago the common person had a good grasp on gravity, or at least the effects of it, even if not by name as per se. In short: We were right about a lot of things, and like today, we were completely off the mark on many we held sacrosanct and inviolate.

Keep this in mind as you study the history of the Tarot. The Tarot has changed several times throughout the centuries to "fit" the beliefs of different times and different locales. Eastern Europe Tarot designers put their cards in a different order than Southern or Western European designers of the same era. Names and numbers of cards have been changed time and again, and undoubtedly caused no end of arguing over "the correct" order and titles. This is all fun to read and fascinating history, but what you must take away from any study of Tarot history is that the past is p-a-s-t. **Whatever happened to bring you here to this point is secondary to the fact that you are here now** and you are facing issues that need to be dealt with now. The fact that you had a sandwich last week is extremely important, as it kept you from starving then, but last week's sandwich does not stop you from being hungry now. In the same way, your deck is more important than its origins. What your cards say to you in a *reading* today is far more important than what some deck "originally meant" several centuries ago. So, please do have fun finding out where the cards originated, but remember that this is all just backstory. That being said, here's what we know today:

The Tarot originated in or around Milan between 1420 and 1440 CE, give or take a few years, depending on whose history you subscribe to. By its very nature, it had to be designed by educated gentlemen with a fair amount of time on their hands, which ruled out the peasantry. That leaves the court or the church. Evidence points toward the court, as the church was not a place to design questionable games for idle hands. The notion of cards and card games was not new, having arrived from Islamic society, most likely through Spain as an entry point to Europe. Playing cards can be traced back to the late 1370s in various European cities. Early cards had suits of polo sticks, cups, swords, and coins. These suits still appear in various Spanish and Italian playing cards.

The Tarot, as a game, had the base cards of 1 through 10, dominated by Kings, Queens, and their offspring, but added a dimension of archetypes and forces of nature. The game included trumps and a separate fool card (think court jester: entertainer, adviser, wise man/fool), and in many ways it was similar to the modern card game Bridge. The Tarot survived local and international politics, wars, and passing fancy thanks in many ways to the era it was born in. The Renaissance was a time of learning, of questioning, exploring, and leisure. People needed new shiny things to keep their attention, and this crazy new game was an instant hit among the nobility, who had *lots* of time to party.

Famous in Italy led to famous in France, Germany, and other countries throughout Europe. In each country subtle variations crept into the Tarot based largely on local beliefs and the whims of the artists who were consigned to interpret the images they were given to work from. Cards changed numbers and appearance dramatically, even names and colors, all to match their new homeland wherever they ended up. When especially skilled artists placed their stamp on the Tarot by designing a particularly popular deck, their deck became the de facto official deck of the land, the must have among the "haves." No one cared about the "have nots," so let's not spoil our little elitist tea party worrying about them for the moment. Pictures on cards meant that you could instantly know the meanings of each card even if your literacy level was a bit sub-par, so anyone who was anyone could easily play, even with foreign decks.

One of the most entrancing aspects of art is that it is ever so much more fun to draw and view fanciful scenes than still life (bowls of fruit for example). Legends of lions with wings and heads of birds, scaly dragons, and other imaginative creatures abound through all of time and every civilization. Gods and mythological beasts have always been favorites among artists (and the masses), and what better illustrations to adorn your cards with than vibrantly colored virtues and vices, heroes and celestial forces? The only entities more powerful than the rulers of the age were those of nature, of the divine, and of ancient mysterious legends. These were the psychological counter-balance to the absolute command of all of life and death that the nobility exercised in the days of feudalism. A game of chance needed titanic forces to be controlled and dispatched to keep the attentions of people who had everything money and power could buy. These *trumps* were representational of forces normally outside of the control of the most powerful in society, but just like a modern video game, one could hold unbelievable power in their hands, and lie in wait for their enemies to learn the true meaning of pain. This is what makes a good game exciting, the suspense of whether you will be the victim or the dealer of wrath. It's not about winning; it is about the excitement building to a frenzy, *and then* winning.

As with any other societal invention (color TV, the calculator, CDs, cell phones, etc.), cards became available to more and more people as they went from exclusive hand-painted decks to mass-produced decks. The commoners of society were allowed to experience the rush of adrenaline card games brought, and the Tarot was a part of that wave of "trickle-down culture." The symbolism of the Tarot *trumps* were the basis for much speculation of meaning, and in time people sought out to lay a sense of order onto the whole of it, rearranging the order of the cards, changing the images to suit their personal views of the world, and inventing their own stories about how the Tarot came to be. Occultists gravitated to the Tarot for obvious reasons. Tarot cards were clean, organized into tidy suits and hierarchies, and extremely portable. Symbolism was applied to meaning, and that gave a solid structure for a system of prognostication.

The word *Tarocchi* first appears around 1530 in Italy, and eventually becomes Tarot in French. It is argued that this is a brand name, created to distinguish the Tarot deck from other decks that one could play the game of trumps with. Much like a Big Mac™ is a hamburger, but a hamburger is not a Big Mac™, the Tarot is a deck of cards, but not all decks are the Tarot. Ask ten different experts what the word *Tarocchi* means and you will get a variety of answers. What matters is that since no one knows with certainty, it is an empty label. It can mean whatever you like it to; but all in all, at this time in history it is now a pretty word whose origin is lost in time much like the runes.

In 1909, Arthur Waite (A.E. Waite) asked Pamela Coleman Smith to illustrate a Tarot deck to his specifications. He was an important member of the Golden Dawn at the time and wanted a "public deck" that could be used by people outside of the mystery schools and secret societies, but remained true to the symbolism he held sacred. This deck became the basis for most modern Tarot decks, even the infamous *Thoth* deck later designed by Aleister Crowley as "an improvement" on the *Waite* deck.

This is what happens when master occultists (with vast resources) disagree on something as pivotal as the Tarot. Thanks to this vehement disagreement we have two distinct schools of thought on the Tarot that serve to better illustrate the most important aspect of the Tarot: It means what you want it to, so long as your meaning is consistent, encompassing of the relevant facts at hand, and repeatable. If your system of *reading* works for you on a regular basis, then your system of *reading* is more "correct" than anything you will ever read in a book. Card meanings have been handed down to us based upon what Tarot students have experimented with and found to work for them. Therefore, they are not easily dismissed, but they are more guides than absolute facts.

In the twentieth century, the Tarot exploded with popularity, with artists from all walks of life doodling out their own versions, some professionally published, others not; but all were valid expressions of meaning from the point of view of their creators. The *Golden Dawn* and the *O.T.O.* have had massive influence over modern Tarot decks, and even though new decks often diverge from the straight and narrow path of Tarot symbolism, they owe their core principles to the Tarot, and most often to these two institutions of higher (or lower) learning. If you would like to spend hours and days studying various theories of the history of the Tarot, we have listed some highly informative texts below.

Recommended reading:

A History of the Occult Tarot, by Michael Dummett

The Game of Tarot, by Michael Dummett

The Encyclopedia of Tarot, in four volumes, by Stuart Kaplan

The Tarot: History, Mystery, and Lore, by Cynthia Giles

Recommended websites:

www.waite-smith.com

www.tarothistory.com

www.pre-gebelin.com

Appendix D:

How to be a hit at parties

Tarot cards were simply made for social gatherings. Not only can you play fun games with them, but it seems that once your cards come out, *everyone* (except for a few fuddy-duddies) will want you to answer a few questions for them, especially if you look like you know what you are doing. You don't have to be witty and funny, making jokes about everything you see to be the life of the party, nor do you have to be *"Miss Serious."* All you have to do is take your *readings* seriously enough to answer any questions you have agreed to *cast a spread* on, but not so serious that you bring the energy of the party down. People go to parties to have fun, but people usually want a *reading* when they have a problem. This is one of life's crazy little factoids that can really drag a party down fast; so if you do whip out your deck at a party or one of your friends drags you off to the side to "find out what so and so is thinking, doing, or where they are . . ." it's *your job* to keep the tone upbeat and (at least reasonably) fun and refuse to answer anything too deep or serious ("Let's get to that *tomorrow*").

The most important thing to remember about *reading* at parties is simply to have fun and not be too obvious or pushy about *reading*. When you think about it, it comes down to simply not making senseless mistakes (or "party fouls") rather than *doing* anything "mystical" or special. If someone asks you for a *reading* or it comes up in conversation, look for a reasonably quiet spot and have at it; but make sure that you have a clean surface area that is not going to suddenly have drinks placed on it. If the lighting, noise level, or amount of space is not to your liking, it is *far better* to save the cards for another occasion than it is to try to change the atmosphere or complain. Also, while these may seem a bit obvious, please don't make these common mistakes: **Do *not* share *any* personal information about *any* of your clients.** Your clients are anyone you *read* for, whether they paid you or not, bought you coffee, or stiffed you. Think of yourself like a priest(ess) at a confessional. Whatever is said stays between you and your client. In fact, if you can get in the habit of conveniently forgetting their problems and any advice you gave them about their problems, you will find your life *blissfully* easy (even if they get their feelings hurt later that you don't remember all of their personal drama). If you talk about someone about who *did this or that to you,* or *had this or that problem,* you are just inviting people to think that you will share *their* secrets with the world. In some cases it is okay to speak in general terms ("a lot of my clients think . . .") or in reference to one long past who is impossible to identify, but even so be careful about this. It's best to forget old questions, problems, and advice if you can.

Next: **No making jokes about your client!** When you are *reading* for your one of your friends, it is extremely tempting to point out something in the cards and make fun of it. If you think they will appreciate your joke even more than you will *(for being so clever naturally),* then proceed at your own risk, but other than that be very careful about what you joke about in a *reading* and how you phrase it. Once again, while *reading* should be fun, it is too easy to cross a line and strike a nerve in your client if you get too chummy; so please just be careful and avoid silly (and avoidable) mistakes. Okay, so assuming that you do all of that well, the *readings* should take care of themselves. Start *reading* for one person and others will stop by and look over your shoulder, ask questions, or give you subtle hints that they would like a (free) *reading* too. As long as you are not dragging people away from the rest of the fun, your host should be okay with you sharing some of your insight, and if you see a line forming (or people ask "to be next"), try to keep your *readings* light and short (no longer than five or ten minutes each). Don't try to turn people into paying clients at a party, but it is okay to give them your card and offer to "meet them over coffee" sometime if you want.

Appendix E:

FUN PARTY GAMES

If you have more than one deck (and you really should, once you start *reading* on a semi-regular basis), **make sure that you have a "basic deck" that you reserve for parties** and other occasions where you don't mind if people want to paw through them. Sometimes you can even find a *used* deck at an independent bookstore, swap meet, or garage sale. These are great for party games as you don't have to worry about "keeping the psychic influences" affecting them "clear and pure."

Tarot cards are perfect for magic tricks if you know any, they make solitaire much more fun than plain old "regular" cards, and you can even play variations of other "regular" card games with them, like "Go fish!" In this variation of "Go fish!" the rules change only slightly. It works best for three or four players (although you might be able to include up to five or six <u>quick</u> and <u>witty</u> players in a pinch, at least for a short game). You start with seven cards each (use the whole deck) and you describe a simple situation, and the other player has to use *one* or *two* cards to illustrate your scenario. If they can, they get *one* to *three* points (at your discretion) based on how *apropos* their cards are. (How close are they?) If they can't, they have to draw a card and try again. If they <u>still</u> can't, then the next person gets to go. The trick to making this game fun is to keep the whole thing fast and light by keeping your scenarios easy and simple. The idea is not to get rid of your cards, but rather to get the most points by being able to use your cards to *correctly* illustrate the most situations.

<u>Here's an example</u>: It's your friend's turn. They say, "You get a flat tire on the way to work." Nice and easy, not too complicated (although if they said, *"You get a flat tire on the way to work <u>and</u> it's raining <u>and</u> you are an accountant,"* it's in the rules that you can dump your Pepsi all over them). So, you have eight cards at the moment: five of them are completely useless for this question, but you have the *Knight of Swords, The Chariot,* and *The Tower.* All of these are "helpful" but none seem to jump out at you, so you take the opportunity to draw a card and you get the *Ace of Swords.* <u>That's it</u>! You announce your brilliance and show *The Chariot* and proclaim that you were happily driving on your way to work, and that you were going to be <u>early</u> (since you are such a considerate and happy worker—one who deserves a raise by the way) when all of a sudden *"Pow!"* you get a <u>flat</u>! (and you slap the *Ace of Swords REVERSED* on top of *The Chariot* like a giant spike). Then stand up and take a bow, and when you get three points you do your little victory dance and annoy everyone (who wishes they were as clever as you).

Another variation of a popular "regular" card game is Spades, but with Tarot cards. Let's call it *"Swords."* Take the "major" Arcana out of the deck for now and put them away safely and you play just like you would play Spades, but the suit of *Swords* is now the trump, and the evil queen (the "bitch") is now the *Queen of Swords.* Hmmm . . . didn't see *that one* coming, did you? You can also play a variation of Crazy 8's (it's like UNO™ but with a "regular" deck of cards). In fact, you can even play poker, but leave *The Fool* in for that added chaos factor.

You can also play "The never-ending story" or other specific Tarot games you know as long as the other players are quick-thinking, creative, or are at least reasonably familiar with the Tarot.

Appendix F:

"Secret societies" and mystery schools

You may want to join

"Mystery schools" are an *ancient* tradition. Modern mystery schools vary in quality and age (like most things, it seems) and while we cannot list them all (some of them are so secret that they don't even want other people to know they exist), here are a few of the more popular ones that are said to be credible. We cannot *guarantee* any school (other than our own) only because we have no direct control over the quality. Rest assured, however, that any of the schools or organizations below have been around for a length of time to reach "maturity" and have a wealth of information that is worth investigating. As to our school, write to us for details (email address is at the beginning of this book). In the meantime, here are some of our favorites you may want to look into. <u>We have set aside vast amounts of space at our website</u> *EasyTarotLessons.com* <u>to provide you with voluminous amounts of additional information on each of the listings below</u>, including how to apply for membership (when they are accepting new members).

The Golden Dawn or ***The Hermetic Order of the Golden Dawn®***

Camelot. A long time ago brave, heroic, compassionate knights gathered at a "round" table that was designed so that (at least in theory) *"no one could sit closer to the king (and have 'his ear'), and that every knight would have an equal voice."* Then one of them had to sleep with the queen and the whole thing went to pot. Well, that's the version we heard. The point is that Camelot was a refuge of free thought, great ideals, and an icon of purity and the betterment of humanity. *Thus was the Golden Dawn.* Crowley came from the Dawn, as did Waite, Mathers, Westcott (co-founder), Yeats, and the list just keeps going! In "the day" this was the place to be. The Golden Dawn has had its ups and downs and currently there are a few organizations that claim the title. We are not "taking sides" in that mess! But, the tradition and knowledge still continues. If you would like to be a member of what once was truly a magnificent society of secrecy and study *(And maybe it will be once again if you join now that you know so much about the Tarot! In fact, you may in fact go on to become a great adept and resurrect the great schools of the past!),* you might want to check out **www.golden-dawn.com.** Of course, <u>do</u> know that *there are other organizations* that also claim authority, so please do diligent research to make sure that you choose the group that is right <u>for you</u>.

The following addendum is directly from the Hermetic Order of the Golden Dawn, so please take special note of it as well:

> "The Hermetic Order of the Golden Dawn, founded in 1888, created an eclectic magical system combining various streams of magic together Hermetic Qabalah, astrology, and tarot. The symbolism of the Tarot of the Golden Dawn reflects this synthesis as there are both Qabalistic and astrological attributions to be found in the cards of both the major and minor arcanas. The influence of the Golden Dawn and its successor, the Alpha et Omega, on the tarot has been ENORMOUS. The two most popular tarot decks today, the Rider-Waite and the Crowley decks derive their symbolism directly from the Golden Dawn, although Waite further pictorially embellishes the symbolism of the minor arcana. Yet a third modern tarot deck directly engendered by the Golden Dawn and its offshoots was that created by former Alpha et Omega member, Paul Foster Case, who later founded the Builders of the Adytum."

O.T.O. or *Ordo Templi Orientis*

This is "Uncle Al's" group. Crowley didn't *found* the O.T.O., but he is by far one of its most famous members (and rightfully so). This is serious stuff here: High magic, heavy usage of symbolism, and serious personal commitment and study are part and parcel to membership. They accept "newbies" but they prefer that you actually have a deep desire to learn *and practice* rather than "a passing or casual interest" in philosophical/magical/religious studies. Some of the best minds have passed through these doors, but you would probably never know it. They are into the whole "privacy thing," so if you ever wanted to be a part of a spooky secret organization *where your membership in said organization is not public knowledge* (kinda like the Illuminati), this is it. If you like the *Thoth* deck, you owe it to yourself to look into membership. You can find their website at ***www.oto-usa.org***

AMORC or *Ancient and Mystical Order Rosae Crucis*

Okay, so who doesn't like the Rosicrucians? The AMORC rocks! They have *great* parties, they share their knowledge freely, and they have that cool Egyptian temple in San Jose. The Rosie's *(don't call them that)* are sincerely interested in helping you understand "the whole metaphysical thing" from philosophy to developing your personal psychic abilities. They are not a religion, so their members come from all walks of life; and, as you can guess, these guys have been around for a long, long time. They are pretty pragmatic about you joining. They ask that you look around, read anything you like (that they have to offer "to the public"), and make your choice(s) *at your leisure*. Look: There are several "Rosicrucian" groups, and we can't speak for them (good *or* ill), but this is one you certainly want to be a part of if you are at all serious about enhancing your abilities and perceptions. Find them (or their members) in North America, or all over the world. Find them online at ***www.rosicrucian.org***

B.O.T.A. *(Builders of the Adytum)*

Now this is a modern "mystery school." The word "Adytum" means *inner shrine* or "Holy of Holies" (although we personally prefer the term *sanctum sanctorum*). Nonetheless, if you want to learn more about the esoteric side of the Tarot and are into the whole "hermetic Qabalah thing" (some people are, and some people are into *other* "things," and it's all good), then you really need to check these guys out. They are also non-religious, so you can be a Buddhist and study their Qabalistic Tarot teachings, or just about any other religion as long as your particular religion does not specifically *prohibit* studying hermetic teachings. Their Tarot is a bit different from the Golden Dawn (*Waite*), or the Rider (also *Waite* interestingly enough . . .) but similar. But they are so much more than a few Tarot lessons. Every month they send their members meta-philo-psychological lessons of ever-increasing intensity, but all firmly rooted in the Qabalah. They also have gatherings on a regular basis and are truly nice people. Remember that they are of the Western mystery school tradition, so they are vehemently *mono*-theistic versus the classical Eleusian (which we are forbidden to tell you about—sorry!), so know this before you jump in thinking that our fav goddesses will be showing up. Still, very much *worth investigating* if it fits your personal view of the world. Check them out at their website. It has more than enough information to help you see if they are for you. ("We like 'em!") ***www.bota.org***

The Masons: *The International Masonic Research Society, Scottish Rite, Shriners, Eastern Star, DeMolay International, Job's Daughter's, International Order of Rainbow for Girls and the Tall Cedars of Lebanon* ("If you need to ask . . .")

Masons are *tres cool*. If you believe the gossip, they built the pyramids, they are friends of the aliens, have secret connections to the Knights Templar, and they run the world; and they do all of these things every morning before breakfast. Even if they don't accomplish *half* of that before lunch, Masons are highly respected members of society and their "known membership" consists of **some of the greatest minds of recent history.** Ben Franklin was a "Grand Master" Mason (how cool is *that?*); John Hancock (the guy who signed his name really big on the Declaration of Independence, *aka "his own death warrant"*); George Washington was a Mason (unfortunately *so was that Judas* Benedict Arnold). So, "known" Masons run the gamut among society. If you choose to "join the club," you will find yourself in good company. By technical definition, the official word of modern Masonry is that they are *not* a "Secret Society," but that doesn't mean you won't learn a few things along the way. Either way, you can find one of their primary (public) websites at ***www.freemasonry.org***

The Philosophical Research Society *(The PRS)*:

This is Manley P. Hall's group. Nice people. Headquartered in Silverlake, CA (a few minutes east of Hollywood, just south of Griffith Park). They host a wickedly-cool library of rare and hard-to-find esoteric works you can sit down and enjoy in a quiet setting. Parking is almost non-existent, so plan ahead for that. They were founded in 1934 "for the purpose of providing thoughtful persons rare access to the depth and breadth of the world's wisdom literature." This place is *100 percent dogma free*. It's about philosophy, not mind control or religious dominance. These are very cool people. If you come, be nice. You come here to study and absorb the quiet esoteric wisdom of the place, not to brag about what you know. The compound itself is tiny by most standards, and easily missed, but their university is a serious graduate-level distance learning university, nationally accredited by the DETC (Distance Education and Training Council). You can obtain your Masters Degree in Consciousness Studies or Transformational Psychology if you like, which is not too shabby. Imagine relaxing on the beach in Bali while studying deep mind sciences from an institution thought to be one of the leading centers of philosophical thought in the modern world. So, what are you waiting for? Here's their contact info. Make sure you told them we sent you. Website: ***www.prs.org***

Physical location:

PHILOSOPHICAL RESEARCH SOCIETY
3910 Los Feliz Blvd
Los Angeles, CA 90027

phone   (323) 663-2167
fax   (323) 663-9443

email   *info@prs.org*

The Illuminati:

Unfortunately the toll-free number we use to reach our friends at the Illuminati headquarters seems to be disconnected as of the publication date of this book. We apologize that we are not able to find a working number. Of course, we are sworn to secrecy as to the *exact location* of their headquarters, and their website keeps redirecting us to several of the largest global corporation "front" pages. So we can only assume that they are in one of their "reorganization phases" again. Be sure to stop in at our website occasionally and see if we have been able to publicly update any contact info. Sorry for the inconvenience. We hope to have this fixed soon. In the meantime, please keep *consuming!*

Appendix G:

WHAT TO DO NEXT:

This may sound a bit self-serving, but your next step in Tarot mastery needs to be reading and practicing all of the new games, exercises, and techniques in *Advanced Tarot Secrets*. There simply is no other book like it ever written. Not only does it come with more free tarot lessons (from us) but it teaches you some of the most jealously guarded secrets of divination and manifestation, in a fun, relaxed way that has you doing the exact steps you will do as a professional. This book will take you from where The Easiest Way to Learn the Tarot—*EVER!!* leaves off.

You can find *Advanced Tarot Secrets* on Amazon, B&N.com, and BookDepository.com ships it free all over the world. Also, if haven't already signed up for our course, invest a few dollar a week in your future and get the best (*and last expensive!*) Tarot education anywhere on the planet. You will learn NO DOGMA or outdated superstitious rigamarole. All we care about is your ability to read the future and then master it through dowsing, manifestation, problem solving and brainstorming. We teach all skill levels, from beginner to professionals, and we can help you.

Try us out for a dollar. We will give you your first full month's instruction for one dollar, with absolutely no commitment on your part to keep paying or studying. We will get you started learning and doing, and let you decide from there if you want to continue mastering the tarot. You can quit at any time, but since most of our students don't, the few who do are quickly eclipsed in skill and popularity. Let us help you. Stop on by at *EasyTarotLessons.com* and see for yourself.

Glossary

Akashic Records

The *really, really, really* short version: The universal library. Everything that ever HAS happened, WILL happen, and is happening right now, is stored there. Some say it is the source of the four primary elements, others' say it is the substrata of the collective unconscious (which is a pretty big thing in itself). The (cosmic) library is always open if you need to access information, and information is often shared simultaneously with several people, even if they do not consciously ask for it. Think of it like a leaky roof in the library—several people can get wet at once.

Air *(See Elements)*

Aspect/aspected/aspecting cards

Every card in a *spread* is connected in some way to other cards in that same *spread*, but not necessarily directly. Sometimes a card will *lean on* another for clarification, or *lead to,* or point at, some other card. When one card shapes or defines another, the card DOING the shaping or defining (of the other card) is the *aspecting card* (or "clarifying card" if it is used to give expanded meaning to the target card). The card being affected is the *aspected card*.

Astrological signs, houses, planets

Astrology and the Tarot don't match up as well as some "experts" would like us to believe. However, the four suits of the "minor" Arcana easily lend themselves to the *elements* of *fire, earth, air, and water,* which are all present in the science of astrology. It wasn't planned out this way—it just sort of evolved, and as the whole notion caught on people started adding more and more "meaning" to help develop a system of interpretation. It all works as long as you don't try to force too much meaning into different systems of symbolism that simply don't entirely match up (*square* peg, *round* hole). However, in this course we have taken the astrological correspondence further than anyone else ever has in the interpretation of the Tarot by assigning correlating astrological energy to each "minor" Arcana card to help clarify its energy. For reasons revealed in our *"Advanced Tarot Secrets"* course, we have not assigned any astrological correspondences to the "major" Arcana, although it is possible to find various labels assigned to them online or in any number of books should you like. You can choose to assign astrological values to cards or ignore them altogether as you choose and still give good *readings*. Also, feel free to use our suggested astrological meanings for each card, or simply ignore them and use what works for you.

Burning Times, The

Dark time in history when the Catholic Church decided that tens of thousands of people should be executed, often by burning them at the stake after severe torture and cutting out their tongues. Usually referring to the specific period of religious domination occurring about 1480 to 1700 CE and involved religious massacres, genocide, and wars over whose god had the bigger staff.

Card Position

Card position (or simply *position*, or even "slot") simply means a pre-ordained location with a set meaning for a card to be placed. The "spot" (or "slot") where a random card will be placed in a *spread* is like an *astrological house*. **That meaning never changes.** The card that is placed there clarifies what is happening, will happen, has happened, or what it all means. For example: a *card position* in a *spread* could represent "the Past" and the *King of Wands* plops down in that "spot." This shows "a man from the past," whereas if the *8 of Coins* was placed there it could indicate "an old job you had." In *spreads*, card *positions* are empty placeholders or "reserved seats" awaiting the cards that will be placed in them. The purpose is to systemize *readings* so that when a card shows up, you know where its energy fits in to your client's question. One more time: the *The Devil* flies out of the deck while you are shuffling. What does it mean? Where does it fit? Who can say? So you put it back in the deck (in this example) and when you *cast* the *spread*, it shows up in the "job" slot (or "card position" meaning "job"). Now it makes sense: you hate your job. *Who doesn't?*

Cardinal/Cardinal energy

Astrological reference: The three primary *qualities of energy*, using the astrological system of categorization, are: *Cardinal* (beginning, pioneering, instigating, combative, etc.), *Fixed* (maintaining, stubborn, immovable, reliable, structurally sound, solid, unchanging, etc.), and *Mutable* (liquid, flexible, ever-changing, chaotic, dissolving, releasing, transitioning, etc.). *Cardinal* energy is restless, volatile, and struggles for freedom and change. Its main purpose is to enact change, to lead without question (and tolerate even less). *Cardinal* and *Fixed* energies are akin to sword and shield, and they could battle forever, but *Mutable* energy seeps in and dissolves all resistance like a solvent. It rots the shield and rusts the blade, so none are truly superior. *(See also Qualities)*

Chaos Theory

An attempt to measure and classify absolute chaos into any form of relative order. Similarly, an attempt to explain that in every controlled environment there is at least one tiny spark of chaos that can start a chain reaction of events that skews the results of your experiment. **Simply stated:** you can attempt to control everything around you and still the fickle fingers of destiny will slip you a random element every once in a while, just for fun (usually their fun, not yours). Surely the gods laugh at us all.

Clarification cards *(also Aspecting cards)*

Clarification cards are cards that you draw specifically to help decipher another card (see *opening up a card* and also Exercise Seven). The process is simple really: ask your deck (or your guides, your god(s), etc.) to "explain" any particular card and draw one, two, or three cards *(decide how many before you draw though)*. *Aspecting cards* are cards that affect another card and are found in the *spread*, not "drawn afterwards." They can clarify, change, or shape the meaning of any other card. Any card can aspect any other card, and *aspecting cards* can even affect each other.

Completion card

Any card that by design indicates an end of one situation and the beginning of something else. Main completion cards are: *Death, Judgement,* and *The World*. Other cards that are usually, but not necessarily, completion cards: *10 of Swords, The Tower,* and the *10 of Cups*. These interpretations are subject to YOUR understanding at the time of the *reading*.

Crusades, The

Proof that state-organized/sanctioned religion and peace are natural enemies. Holy wars undertaken with papal sanction. Any of the military expeditions undertaken by European Christians in the eleventh, twelfth, and thirteenth centuries against Muslims, pagans, Jews, various Orthodox Christians, Mongols, and political enemies of the popes. *(See also Burning Times)*

Damocles

Damocles was a weak-willed coward of a man who constantly complained about his lot in life. He was one of mythology's great sycophants who had his head handed to him (philosophically speaking) after he had pushed his luck by overspeaking. *(See also Sword of Damocles)*

Delphi

Coolest place on Earth. One of the most powerful ancient psychic vortexes on record. Home of the omphalos stone (sacred "navel" stone that focused rising gasses like a funnel) and thought to be the center of the known universe. **Location of the Oracle before later Apollonian desecration** and domination. Center of the Elysian Mysteries, Vestal priestesses, and divinatory legend. *"Before Apollo, there was Gaea."* —from the Temple of Persephone.

Demeter

Mother of *Persephone* (with help from *Zeus*), goddess of many secrets. Publicly: grain and harvest goddess (theorized by some that she took humanity from hunter-gatherers to agriculturally based societies, and thus founded modern civilization), central figure of the Elysian Mysteries. It is arguable that she is older than Zeus and the Olympians, but we will save that for another time. Quite possibly the most powerful and influential goddess—EVER!! Not wise to upset this woman.

Dowsing

(aka divining, water witching) Practice of locating hidden or lost objects with a pendulum or forked branch. In modern times metal rods have been employed. The most common use of dowsing has always been the search for fresh (drinkable) water, either underground, or by use of maps. Other objects commonly searched for using this method are buried metals, gemstones, and even oil. Easy to learn, difficult to master. Like the Tarot, the skill (and magic) is in the practitioner, not the tool, although as in carpentry and masonry the tool selected and the quality of the tool will greatly affect the outcome. Dowsing has fallen out of favor with the public but remains practiced by rational people with triple-digit IQs the world over. Efficacy is questionable, but the amazing results obtained are often otherwise inexplicable. It seems entirely possible to scientifically dismiss this as superstitious hoodoo once and for all, until some dowser (once again) performs the impossible.

Dominant Card

The dominant, or primary card in any reading is *the card* that is central to the meaning of the *spread*. This card is, in turn, *aspected* by other cards, which color or shape it, clarifying its meaning. Not all *spreads* have *dominant cards*, so don't drive yourself crazy looking for them. However, when they do appear, they are usually easy to spot with a little practice. "Major" Arcana cards can be dominated by "minor" Arcana cards if the "minor" Arcana card is more specific to your querent or the reading. Don't fall into the trap of seeing "major" Arcana cards as more powerful or more important than "minor" ones.

Earth *(See Elements)*

Elements

Metaphysically and esoterically the four "classic elements" are *Fire, Earth, Air,* and *Water;* being what the ancients thought everything was basically made of. Now science is up around 120 elements. Be that as it may, the (European) *four classic elements* correspond to four "sets of qualities" that govern existential awareness. Fire (as a "thing" you can see, and touch) is hot. It burns, it dances, it consumes. *Fire* (as a metaphysical "element") is vibrant, competitive, ambitious, energetic, and is a metaphor for those energies in magic, philosophy, or personality characteristics. *Earth* by contrast would be people or energy that is solid, slow, reliable, patient, stable, and so on. *Air* is worse than *fire*: it is changeable, fickle, ethereal, invisible, harsh, gentle, swift, and unpredictable. *Water* is similarly changeable but the psychological focus is on liquidity, so it is variable, gooey, clingy, and leaves stains. In the Tarot, these *elements* relate directly to each suit of the *"minor"* Arcana to help establish meaning quickly and easily. It gives each suit a theme, which makes interpretation much easier, especially among students.

Esoteric

"Knowledge known to the few," versus exoteric knowledge ("public knowledge"). Secrets; but almost always meaning valuable mystic knowledge dealing with psychic power and the laws of nature that can be tapped. Any real esoteric knowledge is jealously guarded by organizations or by church, and by state (depending on which group possesses that specific "esoterica"). Simply put: Any secret (valuable) body of knowledge that is shared over time with students as they progress in their ability to process it intellectually, use it wisely, and effect changes in reality through it.

Expansion cards

Expansion cards are added to your *spread* after it is completely *cast,* and you are in the process of *reading*. Your *spread* will have a set number of slots to fill, and so anything added to it after the fact is an expansion or clarification card. *Expansion cards* are very useful for asking, ". . . and then?" questions, and ferreting out additional information without having to break the structure of the *reading* by *tearing down the spread.* When you *tear down a spread,* you risk breaking the psychic resonance you have built up and might have to start clean, from scratch. *Expansion cards* save you from that hassle.

Fire *(See Elements)*

Fixed/Fixed energy

Astrological reference: The three primary *qualities of energy,* using the astrological system of categorization, are: *Cardinal* (beginning, pioneering, instigating, combative, etc.), *Fixed* (maintaining, stubborn, immovable, reliable, structurally sound, solid, unchanging, etc.), and *Mutable* (liquid, flexible, ever-changing, chaotic, dissolving, releasing, transitioning, etc.). *Fixed* energy is favorable for establishing permanence, but not very good for actually getting much done. Think "management," or "maintenance," but not "creation." *Fixed* energy resists change with an iron will, which is why mutable energy is called for (eventually). *Cardinal* and *Fixed* energies are akin to sword and shield, and they could battle forever, but *Mutable* energy seeps in and dissolves all resistance like a solvent. It rots the shield and rusts the blade, so none are truly superior. *(See also Qualities)*

Fixed nature

Possessing the qualities of Fixed energy. *(See Fixed Energy, above)*

Hermetic

The modern meaning of the world means to seal securely, as in an "airtight" seal. But the variant meaning that you will see when dealing with esoteric knowledge, such as the Tarot, refers to the teachings of one *Hermes Trismegistus,* the father of numerology and an extremely smart mathematician.

Modern mystery schools, much Western paganism, and many branches of occult science are heavily steeped in the theories of this particular genius. *This line of magical philosophy* is less Gaea centered (less faerie) and more masculine, or logic-centered, and tends to value organization and categorization (labels) as a method of understanding (mysteries), over the more ancient and bonding processes of intuitive reception and spiritual assimilation. It is also more individual and isolationist by nature.

Inquisition, The

Primarily, The Spanish Inquisition, although there were others. King Ferdinand of Spain sought to "conquer the world for God" through muscular application of Catholicism ("Convert or die," but often only after much sadistic physical torture and psychological abuse). It was particularly notorious for being a way to repress Jews, Muslims, and the occasional pagan. Part of the central process was to remove power from the Pope and place it conveniently in the hands of the super-rich (Spanish monarchy), where they could gleefully abuse poor people for fun and profit. *(Some things never change.)* It was especially useful for enslaving the native populations of North and South America. Historically, it lasted from the early 1400s until the early 1800s (CE).

Insinuating card

An aspecting card that carries an overt negative connotation towards the target card (the card it *aspects* or *insinuates* ill-fate towards). *(See also aspecting cards)*

Journal *(See Tarot Journal)*

Kabbalah and Kabbalistic *(Also: Cabala, Kabbala, Kabala, Kabalah, Qabalah . . .)*

Hermetic magical study based in large part on the tenets of a sect of *Hebraic mysticism*. Applied to the Tarot after the Tarot caught on in popularity, or conversely it could be said that the Tarot was added to it. In any case it is really, really deep stuff that requires a dedication to study along the lines of monotheistic power adaptation. Not well-suited for polytheistic magical systems. If you are interested in studying the *magical* aspects of the Qabalah, see any of the mystery schools or organizations that focus on that particular path. We have listed a few in the appendices.

Kings

(in the Tarot): The four *Kings* of the "minor" Arcana are representational of traditional male authority figures (or just old men) possessing various personality characteristics, or engaged in certain occupations, responsibilities, or meaning to the querent or the question. They embody the "values" of each suit personified by any man (usually above the age of 30). They can also represent men astrologically, each relating to the *elemental qualities* of their suit. *Clarification cards* may help as well.

Knights

(in the Tarot): Traditionally *Knights* indicate "young men" (13-30ish), although they can also indicate females if you would like to split the genders as follows: *Swords* and *Wands* to indicate males, *Cups* and *Coins* to indicate females. Actually you could assign the suits any way you like, as long as you were consistent and the decision was psychologically firmly entrenched enough to be reliable for prognostical usage. The problem is that the Tarot never included "princesses" as a counterpart to *Knights* (although *Crowley* did so in a fashion). *Knights* indicate testosterone primarily, which (combined with the image of a horse) translates into action: things happening *NOW!* This can also easily indicate travel, movement, change, quests, adventure, *or a complete lack thereof when reversed.*

Law of Parsimony

Succinctly stated: *"Entities should not be multiplied unnecessarily."* Stated in a way the rest of us can understand it: **"If you need one hammer, don't use two."** (or) "Don't go complicatin' matters unnecessarily." The law was an admonishment (vehement reminder pretty much) to researchers to not discount the obvious, and often simplest possible solution. The process of research and analysis invites complexity. "What if" is the second-favorite question of science *(the first being "How?")*. This law was designed to draw a line in the sand at some point, to create a safety valve to avoid endless speculation on possible contributors to effect. If you have a simple cause and effect situation, "I drop the ball, and it falls to the ground," it is sorely tempting to ask whether it will bounce, or if the speed of a cross wind will affect its flight time (number of seconds it takes to reach the ground), whether the shape of the ball affects its impact velocity, and on and on, *ad nauseum.* The beauty of this law in divination is that it cuts through superstition and needless questioning of variables. "See what is there," not what *might be* "if . . ."

Laws of Attraction and Repulsion

Elements of a greater natural law (Magnetism). A subset of the natural law of Magnetism is that of psychic magnetism (e.g., attraction and repulsion). Currently this is all theory, and not officially recognized by modern scientific thought, although it is extremely popular with accepted public knowledge (*"exoterica"*). The "Law of Attraction," being only one half of the law is widely popular, while its conjoined-twin sister law (repulsion) is ignored, which is why most people who try to effect "psychic attraction" have difficulty obtaining reliable and desired results. This is *Mystery School 101* stuff, so you will have to either take the *Advanced Tarot Secrets* course or enroll in any reputable mystery school, but simply stated: **You must have filters.** If you *successfully* attract without conditions and qualifications, you will be swamped with resources and entities that overwhelm your defenses and you will be paralyzed with surrounding obstacles.

Imagine a pretty woman who is wearing a very revealing dress near a construction site at lunch time. She will "attract" attention, but not necessarily the *type* or *amount* of attention she secretly desires. She will be overwhelmed with offers and verbal abuse from too many sources to ignore or contain psychologically and her *state* will be disrupted. **Never "attract" without placing boundaries first.** For a simple version of "how to do this," see *How to Get ANY MAN to do ANYTHING You Want!*, specifically pages 7-16. The entire book is a crash-course in getting results through training your psychic muscles written in an exoteric style of hiding secrets in plain sight.

Lotus Sutra

Final teaching of the Buddha ("Sid") before entering Nirvana. Not revealed until 500 years after his exit from Terra. Said to be his ultimate teaching by some. Others ignore it (at their peril). Notable fact: Only appearance of a powerful female Buddha, and often written out in misogynistic translations.

"major" Arcana

These are the 22 cards most metaphysical *über-scholars* like to concern themselves with. In most decks they have a staged feel, as if the people are posing ("Okay everyone, smile for the camera!"). Even the active scenes (*The Tower, Judgement*) are less meaningful than they are iconic. These cards are said to be the "secrets of magic, the path to [the Judeao-Christian] 'God,' and portals to wisdom." Whether they are or not, they are fun to look at and make great jewelry pendants. The main problem with these cards in *divinatory* usage (which is what this book is all about, after all) is that they tend to be rather vague, and need *clarification cards* to specify who and what they are, or mean.

Malleus Maleficarum ("The Hammer Against Witches")

Undeniably the most evil book ever written. Far worse than the "Satanic Bible," which was a collection of essays by Anton LaVey, and somewhat a parody of the Christian Bible. <u>This book</u> was a handbook for the processes of interrogating, convicting, and disposing of **<u>alleged</u>** witches. Its purpose was to prove that witches existed, that they were almost always women (naturally), <u>and to make it impossible to defend against the accusation</u> of being a witch. Once you were accused, you were guaranteed a very short life of imprisonment and torture by fanatical priests (who were probably sexually repressed by their very religion). Currently published in two volumes, and made available on Amazon.com and other retailers.

Manifold and Mystic Law of Cause and Effect *(See Aphrodite's Book of Secrets)*

<u>Simply put</u>: The basic law of cause and effect is easy to understand and stands at the base of all measurable physical experience. Expanding this concept from the physical to the ethereal we start to see how unseen forces affect seemingly "purely physical" events. This dual existence sandwiches chaos theory, where unseen forces affect the "best-laid plans of mice and men." When working with psychic matters it is best to have a general grasp of the rudimentary laws of nature as they affect your psychic exercises and workings. We have detailed this information out, in easy-to-understand terms in our book, *Aphrodite's Book of Secrets,* and our *Advanced Tarot Secrets* course.

"minor" Arcana

These are the "peasants" of the Tarot. They count for <u>well more than</u> two-thirds of the Tarot, but they are overshadowed by the "major" Arcana because these cards represent the *daily* activities and experiences of life. Therefore, they are "indicators" (or action, intent, personality, etc.) rather than simple "concepts" that need to be assigned to some tangible actuality. **<u>Every</u> card is *special*.** Don't let anyone ever convince you that any one card is "by nature" more important than another.

Mutable/Mutable energy

Astrological reference: The three primary *qualities of energy,* using the astrological system of categorization, are: *Cardinal* (beginning, pioneering, instigating, combative, etc.), *Fixed* (maintaining, stubborn, immovable, reliable, structurally sound, solid, unchanging, etc.), and *Mutable* (liquid, flexible, ever-changing, chaotic, dissolving, releasing, transitioning, etc.). *Mutable* energy is ethereal and elastic, <u>using its unique ability *to adapt*</u> to overcome all adversities. *Mutable* energy is easily harnessed but difficult to hold. Its ability to wear down or envelop its nemesis (Cardinal and/or Fixed energies) makes it a wily foe psychically. Of the three main *qualities* it is the least understood, as it is the least observable. *Cardinal* and *Fixed* energies are akin to sword and shield, and they could battle forever, but *Mutable* energy <u>seeps in and dissolves all resistance like a solvent.</u> It rots the shield and rusts the blade, so none are truly superior. *(See also Qualities)*

Opening up a card

This is the process of using three cards to help "clarify" the meaning, intent, or impact of another (usually one of those pesky "major" Arcana cards). <u>This is done outside of, or on top of the *spread*,</u> instead of *tearing the spread down* and *casting* a whole new one, although <u>it could also indicate taking the card in question and *casting a spread* about it</u>. *(See also Clarification cards and Exercise Seven)*

Pages

(in the Tarot): Catch-all cards. Can indicate: births, babies, children or young people, messages, invitations, news, *minor* events, study and/or education, miscellaneous school fees and tuitions. Also:

character qualities in a person (or in a child). The most basic meaning is "one in training," with the emphasis on *youth* and *learning a particular skill* (as revealed by the suit of the *Page*).

Persephone

Daughter of *Demeter* (and *Zeus*). Too important a goddess to summarize here. Enroll in a mystery school.

Position *(See Card Position)*

Practice Deck *(See Study Deck)*

Qabalah

Qabalah is an esoteric and mystical tradition for certain Western magical societies such as the Golden Dawn, the O.T.O., and mystical societies such as the B.O.T.A., and the Rosicrucians. Qabalah is a "salad bar" style of blending of many of humanity's oldest attempts at understanding (and controlling) the world around us. It was added to the Tarot after centuries of evolution as a card game.

Qualities

(*cardinal, fixed,* or *mutable*) From "the mother of all sciences," astrology: If there are four *elements* in astrology, there are three *qualities*. Each *element* shows up three times in *the wheel of the year* (being "all 12 signs"). As there are four *elements,* and each *element* has to appear three times (4 x 3=12 obviously) then each *element* expresses itself; Cardinal once, Fixed once, and Mutable once. Using the element of *fire* as an example: the astrological sign of *Aries* is cardinal *fire*. That means it is **the most explosive** and commanding part of the (*element* of) *fire*. *Leo* is *fixed*, meaning it is more stable than *Aries*, but not nearly as powerful in "impact value." *Sagittarius* is **highly** *mutable*, making it squiggly, or adaptable to the surrounding terrain. Obviously this means it is nowhere near as forceful as *Aries*, nor as bright as *Leo*, but it can "burn anywhere."

Look at it this way: If *Aries* were a bomb, *Leo* would be a bonfire (large, bright, not very explosive, kinda stays in one place, but still very, very *hot*), and *Sagittarius* would be a 4th of July fireworks show. It is "up in the clouds" (like most Sag's are . . .) and all sparkly and multi-colored, but you can't light your cigarette off of it (smoking is "bad," so don't do it).

In the same sense, *Taurus* is Fixed Earth, *Virgo* is Mutable Earth, *Capricorn* is extremely Cardinal Earth. *Gemini* is Mutable Air, *Libra* is Cardinal Air, and *Aquarius* is Fixed Air. Lastly, *Cancer* (the sign, not the disease) is Cardinal Water, *Scorpio* won't tell you what it is, and *Pisces* is "squishy" Mutable Water *(which by process of deduction makes Scorpio "fixed" Water, but we didn't tell you)*.

Queens

(in the Tarot): The four *Queens* of the Tarot have the responsibility of representing almost any woman you (or your client) meet, making these some of the most important cards in the Tarot (keeping in mind that no one Tarot card is "more important" than another). Traditionally these cards can represent "any woman over 30," but really they often represent any girl over the age of around 17-21 (depending on maturity level, aspecting cards, nature of the question, and so on . . .). *Queens* can also embody the "values" of each suit personified by any woman (usually above the age of 30). They can also represent women astrologically, each relating to the *elemental* qualities of their suit.

Querent

One who nags you for a *reading* (also "client," or "friend who buys you a coffee *to thank you* for taking the time out of your day to give *them* a *reading*").

Reading

The act of divining the future or answering a question for yourself or a querent ("one who asks") or even looking into the distant past, or spying on your girlfriend while she is in Ibiza.

Reversal/Reversed cards

Any card that appears in a *spread* that is facing the exact opposite direction of what you would normally term "up." If you always lay the card so the client can see them "pointing away from them," then this would be any card that pointed "at them" (180 degrees rotated). If you *read* cards so they are "upright" when you look at them, then naturally any card that is rotated 180 degrees (upside down, but not "flipped over," showing you its backside) is *reversed*. This could also be a card that comes into the *spread* face down (usually by falling out of the deck), but those cards are almost always referred to as "face down." We make this distinction, as some *readers* will *read* "face down" cards as reversals, or as "hidden, of lesser importance, or against the grain of the traditional meaning," and it is better that you know this up front. Always remember logic supercedes superstition. If a card falls from the deck, face down, away from the table, onto your cat, it may just be an accident. Especially if the card makes no sense. *The gods do have a sense of humor.*

Rote memorization

The act of learning by repetition of dogma or established fact. *"This is what I say and, therefore, it is what you will believe and teach others."* Useful for learning things like the alphabet. Not so much for mastering magic, philosophy, or the Tarot.

Significator/Significator card

A *significator* is a card that "significates" or **represents** a person, place, or thing *(just like a noun)*. It is "what the question is about." A *significator card* could represent your client, or if you like, it could represent the person they are asking about, or the situation they are seeking advice from you on. This is entirely your decision, and it should be made to help you focus your psychic energies on a particular point of enquiry.

To choose a *significator card*, think of the primary focus of the person, place, or thing you are asking about and grab the Tarot card from your deck you feel most closely illustrates, or captures, the energies involved. Place that card, *face up*, in the center of the surface you are going to place your *spread* on. That card now becomes "a part of the tablecloth." You will place your *spread* on top of that card. While you are shuffling your deck, look at that card and mentally see the person, place, or thing you are asking about. Send your mental energies (images, emotions, word associations, etc.) of that person, place, or thing into that card. Once you feel that card resonates with your target, then start the process of asking your question, shuffling until you feel the need to stop and cut or place the cards. For example: If you want the *Queen of Coins* to represent your client in her question about a job, you place the *Queen of Coins* down before you *cast* the *spread*.

Alternately, you can use the *significator* as the first card in any *spread* you cast—if the first card normally represents the person, place, or thing you are asking about (as in the *Celtic Cross spread*). If you keep the *significator* card separate from the *reading,* the next card you place (the "first card" of your *reading*) will reveal extra information about the current state of the person, place, or thing—this will be ancillary information to help you find the exact spot from which you must progress.

Spread

Simply stated, a *spread* is simply a "map" or an organizational chart of the cards created for *reading*. A *spread* is valid only if it works for you. Try out various *spreads*, but make sure that you are properly shuffling and focusing on the question(s) at hand before you *throw the cards*. It helps (but is not 100% necessary) that you know ahead of time what each *card position* in a *spread* will mean before you *cast* it. The more you know a *spread*, the better it will work for you; but you can always try out new *spreads* and still get reliable results, as long as you focus, shuffle, and interpret properly.

Things you can do to a *spread*: The following are terms (you can use these or ignore them as you like, or even make up your own). We have included them here so that you will not be caught off guard by anyone's fancy elitist "Tarot lingo."

To put the cards on the table in order: Cast a *spread*, throw a *spread*, throw the cards, build a *spread* (you get the idea).

To pick up all of the cards and put them into the deck: Collapse the *spread*, tear down the *spread*, pull down the cards, clear the table, clear the slate and start fresh (again, you get the idea).

Study Deck

Your Tarot deck when used for study purposes, specifically a deck with easy to decipher visual stimulus. We use the term *study deck* to specifically refer to the deck you use to practice your exercises when you have removed the "major" Arcana. By starting your learning process with the "minor" Arcana, you learn the processes involved in *readings* through the exercises provided, without the distraction of the "major" Arcana. When you ADD the "major" Arcana, it becomes your "practice deck." Then you do all of the exercises again, but this time WITH the "major" Arcana cards included.

Suits

The four "tribes," or "houses," of the "minor" Arcana. Usually a variation of *Staves, Batons* or *Wands, Coins* or *Pentacles, Cups* or *Chalices (Goblets, etc.),* and *Swords.* Also: *Roses, Bells, Acorns, Leaves, Hearts,* and of course *Clubs, Spades, and Diamonds.* These represent general characteristics in a theme, or aspects of the totality of existence (think: "the four winds," where they are all winds, but they blow in different directions).

Sword of Damocles

Damocles was whining one day (as he always did) about *"how great it was to be Dionysius"* (his liege) and how *"if only . . ."* and finally Dionysius got tired of his court-idiot's constant ranting and offered him to be "king for a day" (in essence). Of course, Damocles jumped at it and sat in Dionysius's chair and feasted at his table and drank his wine in great volume until, during the course of his gluttony, he caught sight of a stout sword hanging (pointy-end down) above his head. *But the sword was hanging by a single hair.* **Damocles suddenly lost all interest** in "being king of anything" like the brown-nosing coward he was. Dionysius explained to the fool that this is what his life was like every day: that aside from all outward appearances of power and wealth, there was always a blade awaiting his back, some malcontent or Judas to "end his reign." Thus the term *"The Sword of Damocles"* has come to mean anything that is potentially imminent and "could happen." (Although it also describes the peril powerful rulers live under constantly.)

Tarot Journal

Advocated by some; self-serving, narcissistic waste of (perfectly healthy) trees that never gets read anyway to others. *Our take on it:* any scribble pad, notebook, or fancy pile of papers in an elegant binding where you keep track of your most significant *spreads* and your own thoughts on the Tarot over the years. The problem is that if you are serious enough of a student to take notes, *you will have so many notes* that you will spend all of your time writing instead of *reading*.

Water *(See Elements)*

Witching Stick *(See Dowsing)*

Yods

Tenth letter of many Semitic alphabets, including Phoenician, Aramaic, Hebrew, Syriac, and Arabic. The image (of the letter) appears in various Tarot cards by various artists who probably seek to indicate an extra level of mysticism *(you have to ask the artist or enroll in their mystery school to be certain)*. The esoteric interpretation for usage in the Tarot specifically is far too complex to delve into here so you can simply ignore them, enroll in your local *hermetic* mystery school to learn more, or see them as pretty leaves or flamelets if you like. We do not discount the addition of yods to Tarot symbology, as it has its place. **But we strongly recommend** that you do not place too much value in their meaning until you have properly studied the implications of the traditional, historical, religious, and esoteric meaning of these symbols, lest you end up dispensing bad advice.

Index

A

abusive clients, 33
acolytes, 8
adepts, xiii, 9, 11, 41
ages (royal family), 116, 146, 176, 206
Agrippa, Heinrich Cornelius, 39
Air element, 8. *See also* elements
Akashic Records, 278, 308
Albano-Waite deck, 3
alternative suit names, 7, 15, 16
anima, 142
animal lovers, 40
Antichi Tarocchi Bolognesi deck, 3
Aphrodite (goddess), 8
Aphrodite's Book of Secrets, 266, 272
arcana
    major, 237-281
    minor, 115-235
Art of War, the, 130
artistic Tarot decks, 4, 14
astrological
    houses, 85-92
    signs, 8, 86, 118, 138, 142, 144, 168, 172, 174, 194, 202, 204, 206, 228, 232, 234, 272
astrology, 85-92, 94

B

B.O.T.A. *See mystery schools*
babies, 138, 168
birds of a feather, 26
Buddha, 280
Burning Times, The 248, 309

C

captions, 95-98
cards
    abundance of,
      face cards, 84
      one suit, 83-84
      similar cards, 83-84
      trumps, 83
    amplifiers, 148
    aspecting, 27-29
    blending or combining, 34, 35, 42-63, 74
    cardinal, 118, 126, 138, 148, 158, 160, 168, 174, 178, 182, 186, 190, 196, 198, 200, 208, 212, 218, 226, 228, 234
    clarifying, 27-29, 30, 31-33, 73, 74, 84, 85
    confusing ones, 73
    cutting, 19, 292-293
    dominant, primary, or priority, 24, 28, 42-63, 73, 74
    drawing, various ways, 30, 74, 293
    expansion, 84
    fixed, 122, 124, 130, 134, 142, 144, 150, 154, 170, 180, 184, 192, 202, 204, 214, 222, 224, 230, 232
    leaping, 28, 72-73
    mutable, 120, 128, 132, 136, 140, 152, 156, 162, 164, 166, 172, 188, 194, 210, 216, 220
    opening up, 27-29, 30-33, 75, 186
    practice deck, 14, 64, 65, 66, 316, 318
    reading,
      cold, 35
      reversed, 6, 10, 72, 295
    shuffling, 19, 292-293
    significator, 81, 82, 85, 86, 87, 93, 94
    study deck, 14, 18, 19, 22, 23, 26, 41, 64, 316, 318
    telling stories with, 25, 36-39, 42-63, 74
    trumps, 83. *See also* major Arcana
    working deck, 14, 297
Case, Paul Foster, 39
chaos, 238
    star, 238
    theory, 260
Chariot, the, 140, 252, 303
Charon, 188
cheat sheets, 99-113
checklists, 12-13
Coins (or Pentacles)
    ace of, 11, 91, 207, 208
    eight of, 74, 212, 222
    five of, 11, 216
    four of, 33, 214, 262
    king of, 32, 206, 234
    knight of, 146, 230
    nine of, 40, 224
    page of, 228
    queen of, 232
    seven of, 29, 220, 242
    six of, 91, 218
    specific qualities of, 207
    ten of, 40, 91, 226, 280
    three of, 212
    two of, 31, 40, 210
    versus Pentacles, 7, 16, 207
Crowley, Aleister, 7, 39, 190, 207, 301

Crusades, the, 248, 310
Cups
   ace of, 148
   eight of, 162, 164
   five of, 31, 148, 156
   four of, 154, 162
   king of, 174
   knight of, 146, 170
   nine of, 164, 166
   page of, 168
   queen of, 172
   seven of, 160, 188
   six of, 28-29, 158
   specific qualities of, 147
   ten of, 166, 280
   three of, 89, 152
   two of, 148, 150, 166
curse of inconvenience, 120

D

Damocles, 194, 311
   Sword of, 6, 82, 318
dancing, 40, 152, 262, 280
David vs. Goliath, 186
Death, 20, 244, 264, 268, 270, 278
decks
   historical, 3
   ones to avoid, 4
   practice, 14, 64, 65, 66, 316, 318
   study, 14, 18, 19, 22, 23, 26, 41, 64, 316, 318
   working, 14, 297
   See also specific deck names
Delphi, 266
Demeter, 242, 244, 248, 272
Devil, the, 20, 246, 268, 270
dharma, 258, 260
Diablo, El, 20
Diablo, Señor, 268
directions, 7
Disks, 7
dowsing, 77
Druids/Druidic path, 7, 224, 264

E

elements, 7, 138, 142, 144, 148, 177, 178, 198, 202, 204, 206, 228, 232, 234
Emperor, the, 83, 246
Empress, the, 138, 152, 244, 246
Exactly what do you have in common, 22
exercises
   Birds of a feather, 26
   Exactly what do you two have in common anyway?, 22
   extra credit, 41-63

Face value, 15
From here to there, 23
Hey! What does THIS card mean?, 27
Looking beyond "face value," 18
Me and You, 19
One plus one equals what?, 34
One plus one plus one equals what?, 35
Something to look at, 40
The never-ending story, 36-39, 303
The process of "opening up a card," 30-33
There and back again, 24

F

Face value, 15-17, 18, 27, 88
Fehu (rune), 252
ferryman, 188,
five precepts, 266
Fool, the, 238
four cardinal virtues, 266
From here to there, 23

G

games, party, 36-39, 303
gender gap or discrepancy, 146
godhead, 272
Golden Rider deck, 3
Gummy Bear Tarot, 4

H

Hades, 188, 242, 272
Hall, Manley P., 306
Halloween Tarot, 3
Hanged Man or Hanging Man, the, 20, 262, 268
Hanson-Roberts deck, 3
Hekate, 272
Hello Kitty Tarot deck, 297
Hercules, 256
Hermit, the, 256
heroes, 146
Hey! What does THIS card mean?, 27
Hierophant, the, 248, 252
high magic, 250
High Priestess, the, 242, 244
Hill, Napoleon, 299
horned god, 268

I

Illuminati, *Don't even ask*
immovable object, 154
initiates, 11
Inquisition, the, 248

J

journal. *See Tarot journal*
Judgement, 260, 278
Jung, Carl, 268
Justice, 260

K

Kabbalistic *(also Kabalah, Kabbalah, Cabalah)*, 7, 316
karma, 258, 260
kings, 116, 146, 176, 206, 246
knights, 116, 146, 176, 206
Kronos, 208

L

Law of Cause and Effect, 83, 240, 260, 314, 315
Law of Parsimony, 69, 314
Laws of Attraction and Repulsion, 8, 11, 34, 82, 83, 188, 240, 254, 260, 262
Lévi, Eliphas, 39, 268
lies, 27, 73, 88, 216, 274
load-bearing, 248
Lombardy deck, 3
Lotus Sutra, 280, 314
Lovers, the, 8, 148, 150, 250

M

Magician, the, 11, 240, 242, 254, 280
Malleus Maleficarum, the, 248, 315
marriage, 8, 83, 148, 150, 166, 192, 250, 268
Marseilles decks, 3
Masons. *See mystery schools*
Mathers, MacGregor, 39
Matrix, the, 264
Me and you, 19-21
metropolis, 214
Moon, the, 274
Morgan-Greer Tarot, 3
mulberry trees, 4
mystery schools, 9, 15, 65, 71, 87, 237, 240, 248, 262, 266, 272, 278, 297, 298, 304-306

N

Never-ending story, the, 36-39, 303
novices, 8

O

O.T.O. *See mystery schools*
objective versus subjective, 21
Ockham's razor, 69
Original Rider-Waite deck, 3

P

P.R.S. *See mystery schools*
pages, 116, 146, 176, 206
Pentacles. *See Coins versus Pentacles*
Persephone, 242, 244, 248, 272
pomegranates, 242, 244
pregnancy and birth, 138, 152, 168, 198, 228
Prometheus, 256
proposal, 150

Q

Queen Elizabeth I, 176
queens, 116, 146, 176, 206, 244, 246
Quick and Easy Tarot, 4

R

Radiant Rider-Waite deck, 3, 7
   See also Arthur Edward Waite
really advanced exercises, 65-67
Regardie, Israel, 39
review, 64
Rider-Waite deck, 3, 7
Rosicrucians. *See mystery schools*
rote instruction, xiv. *See also rote memorization*
rote memorization, 11, 317
runes, 252

S

Salvatore Dali deck, 4
seasons, 7, 118
silk, 4, 294
   scarf, 4-5
   worms, 4
sine wave, 242
Smith, Pamela Coleman, 3, 244, 301
Something to look at, 40
soul mate, 150
speed versus accuracy, 76
spreads, 69-94
   Aces-up, 76
   astrological, 85-94
   Celtic Cross, 10, 69, 80-84, 264
   hardest ever, 71
   "How long will this take?", 78
   multiple-card, 10, 71, 75-94
   one-card, 10, 72-73
   Roundabout, 10, 87-92, 260
   "This or that", 79

three-card, 10, 74-75, 94
time, 93-94
traditional, 69
two-card, 10, 73-74
"Up or down vote", 77
"Yes or no", 76
squires, 116, 146
Star, the, 272, 276
starter decks, 3
Strength, 254
study guides, 1, 9-10, 285-287
Sun, the, 274, 276
superconscious, 272
Swords
   ace of, 6, 32, 178, 303
   eight of, 29, 64, 192
   five of, 11, 186
   four of, 184
   king of, 204
   knight of, 32, 69, 74, 170, 200, 204, 303
   nine of, 27-29, 194, 262
   page of, 198
   queen of, 176, 202, 252, 303
   seven of, 40, 132, 190
   six of, 140, 162, 188, 242
   specific qualities of, 177
   ten of, 6, 156, 196
   three of, 89, 150, 182
   two of, 180

T

Tarot
   box, 5, 294
   decks. *See specific names*
   history of, 299-301
   journal, 1, 5, 10, 41
   used decks, 4
Temperance, 266
There and back again, 24
Thoth deck, 7, 190
Torah, 242
Tower, the, 8, 73, 264, 270, 278, 303
triskaidekaphobia, 264
troglodyte, 268
Tzu, Lao, 260
Tzu, Sun, 130

U

U.S. Games, 3
Universal Waite deck, 3
unstoppable force, 200
used Tarot decks, 4

V

Venus (planet), 8

W

Waite, Arthur Edward, 3, 207, 262, 301
Wands
   ace of, 15, 118
   eight of, 132, 162
   five of, 16, 126
   four of, 16, 31, 124
   king of, 144
   knight of, 27-29, 74, 140, 170
   nine of, 31, 134
   page of, 33, 116, 138
   queen of, 142
   seven of, 16, 33, 130, 134
   six of, 16, 32, 128
   specific qualities of, 117
   ten of, 136
   three of, 122
   two of, 15, 33, 120
   versus Coins, 16
weather, 26, 182, 186, 216
West, Kipling, 3
Wheel of Fortune, 258, 260
Wicca, 7
wish card, 164, 238
witching stick, 77. *See also dowsing*
wooden box, 5, 294

X

Y

yods, 118, 148, 178, 270, 319
Yule, 264

Z

Zeus, 242, 256
zombies, 278

Notes

Notes